Well Educated

Inspiring teachers, changing lives. Successful teachers teach, and good leaders lead for the love of it. Despite difficulties, most of our schools are havens of joy and good learning. This book brings together a range of perspectives from influential school leaders and others immersed in education about what's important for children, for schools and us all – and why school leadership is fascinating and exciting as well as challenging.

Well Educated demonstrates a range of independent and lively thinking from engaging education leaders and thinkers. Contributors share their principles and experiences in providing a vision for schools to develop all young people intellectually, practically and socially. The chapters cover:

- The purpose of education
- What makes a quality curriculum
- The role of examinations and assessment
- Meeting the needs of your community

With case studies and reflective questions, this will be valuable reading for all school leaders and policy-makers who want to think beyond the reductive definitions of inspection judgements to develop schools rooted in an uplifting ethos and a love of learning.

Carolyn Roberts MBE is an experienced headteacher, published education thinker and writer, a founding fellow of the Chartered College of Teaching and Co-Director of The Professional Teaching Institute (The PTI).

Hugh Rayment-Pickard MBE is Co-Director of The PTI and was formerly Co-Founder and Chief Strategy Officer of education charity **Into** University.

Well Educated

Leading Schools with Wonder, Joy and Wisdom

Edited by Carolyn Roberts and
Hugh Rayment-Pickard

LONDON AND NEW YORK

Designed cover image: © Getty Images

First published 2026
by Routledge
4 Park Square, Milton Park, Abingdon, Oxon OX14 4RN

and by Routledge
605 Third Avenue, New York, NY 10158

Routledge is an imprint of the Taylor & Francis Group, an informa business

© 2026 selection and editorial matter, Carolyn Roberts and Hugh Rayment-Pickard; individual chapters, the contributors

The right of Carolyn Roberts and Hugh Rayment-Pickard to be identified as the authors of the editorial material, and of the authors for their individual chapters, has been asserted in accordance with sections 77 and 78 of the Copyright, Designs and Patents Act 1988.

All rights reserved. No part of this book may be reprinted or reproduced or utilised in any form or by any electronic, mechanical, or other means, now known or hereafter invented, including photocopying and recording, or in any information storage or retrieval system, without permission in writing from the publishers.

For Product Safety Concerns and Information please contact our EU representative GPSR@taylorandfrancis.com. Taylor & Francis Verlag GmbH, Kaufingerstraße 24, 80331 München, Germany.

Trademark notice: Product or corporate names may be trademarks or registered trademarks, and are used only for identification and explanation without intent to infringe.

ISBN: 978-1-032-89561-1 (hbk)
ISBN: 978-1-032-89560-4 (pbk)
ISBN: 978-1-003-54342-8 (ebk)

DOI: 10.4324/9781003543428

Typeset in Melior
by Newgen Publishing UK

Contents

A note before you begin reading   ix

List of contributors   x

Acknowledgements   xiii

Introduction   Well educated – Leading schools with wonder, joy and wisdom   1
CAROLYN ROBERTS

Section 1: What is a good education?

Section 1 Essay 1   The functionalist view of education: The role of education in supporting the economic and labour requirements of the country   15
BEN WHITE

Section 1 Essay 2   Education as self-realisation   21
HANNAH KNOWLES

Section 1 Essay 3   Are all good schools alike?   26
LEORA CRUDDAS

Section 1 Essay 4   Should schools serve individuals or communities?   36
MELANIE FERRON-EVANS

Section 1 Essay 5   Who decides what is a good education?   44
TIM OATES

Section 2: A good curriculum

Section 2 Essay 1   The best that has been thought and said: the 'knowledge-rich' school   59
JON CURTIS-BRIGNELL

Section 2 Essay 2   Education for creativity   65
SALLY BACON

Section 2 Essay 3   Building educated citizens   71
RICHARD CHATTOE

Section 2 Essay 4   Is a good school conceivable without great subject teaching?   80
OLIVER BLOND

Section 2 Essay 5   Local curriculum development   89
JOHN WILKINSON

Section 2 Essay 6   Education as transmitting knowledge, values and cultural identity   97
ERIKA PODMORE

Section 2 Essay 7   Rendering tensions productive: Finding joy and seeking wisdom in the intellectual enterprise of the curriculum   102
RICHARD KUEH

Section 2 Essay 8   What is a quality curriculum?   112
DAN WHIELDON

Section 3: Is assessment fit for purpose?

Section 3 Essay 1   Assessment and children's experience of learning   127
CLARE O'SULLIVAN

Section 3 Essay 2   The role of public examination and qualifications   133
IAN BAUCKHAM

Section 3 Essay 3	The school leader as emancipator MICHAEL ANTRAM	143
Section 3 Essay 4	Understanding, embedding and assessing complex competences such as Creative Thinking BILL LUCAS	149
Section 3 Essay 5	How do we know someone is well-educated? ANNA TRETHEWEY	162

Section 4: Who benefits from education?

Section 4 Essay 1	Creating joy: What educational success looks like RICHARD SHERIFF	173
Section 4 Essay 2	Who are schools failing? KATHERINE WALSH	178
Section 4 Essay 3	Education for families who don't see the point DANIEL TALBOT	183
Section 4 Essay 4	What is fairness in education? LOIC MENZIES	189
Section 4 Essay 5	The broader societal benefits of education NEIL RENTON	204
Section 4 Essay 6	Is it possible to be overeducated? HUGH RAYMENT-PICKARD	210

Section 5: What is an educated society?

Section 5 Essay 1	Education as a means to foster a nation with a shared culture, tradition and values DOMINIC ROBSON	223
Section 5 Essay 2	Is there an education utopia? HUGH RAYMENT-PICKARD	229

Section 5 Essay 3	A vision for a better world? CAROLYN ROBERTS	238
Section 5 Essay 4	An educated society as a community of individual talents LUCY HYAMS	248
Section 5 Essay 5	Does society still value teachers? ALISON PEACOCK	253
	Afterword MICHAEL YOUNG	263
Index		266

A note before you begin reading

Read with a pencil in your hand!

Our book is designed to encourage independent thinking and reflection on school leadership. At the beginning of each section, we pose questions upon which you might want to muse before reading further. You could return to your original jottings after reading, and your gathered thoughts might encourage your thoughtful leadership. You could use the questions in staff, leadership or governance discussions, or recruitment interviews.

Contemporary English education is loud with explicit and implicit instructions to school leaders. Sometimes it is hard to clear the space to think and reflect for yourself. Our writers were given titles for their pieces, not directions for their conclusions. You might agree or disagree, but you should think!

In your professional life

1. How and where do you think?

2. What influences your thinking?

3. What are you afraid of?

4. What does social inequality mean to your school and you?

5. Can you rise above, or are you at the mercy of circumstance?

6. Where do you find wonder, joy and wisdom?

7. How free are your good teachers to think and act?

8. How would you rank: budget, metrics, character, teaching quality, recruitment and retention, compliance, behaviour, outcomes, and happiness?

Contributors

Michael Antram
Executive Headteacher, Plymouth CAST

Sally Bacon OBE
Co-Chair of the Cultural Learning Alliance and Chair of FrameWorks UK

Sir Ian Bauckham CBE
Chief Regulator, Ofqual

Oliver Blond
Academic Director of The PTI, Educational Consultant, former Headteacher

Richard Chattoe
Principal, Leeds City Academy

Leora Cruddas CBE
Chief Executive of the Confederation of School Trusts

Jon Curtis-Brignell
Headteacher, Priory School, Lewes

Melanie Ferron-Evans
Headteacher, Ysgol Rhiwabon

Lucy Hyams
Assistant Head, Plashet School

Hannah Knowles
Principal, The Skinners' Kent Academy

Dr Richard Kueh
Chief Education Officer, The Cam Academy Trust; Visiting Fellow, Canterbury Christ Church University

Professor Bill Lucas
Director of the Centre for Real-World Learning, University of Winchester

Loic Menzies
Associate Fellow, Institute for Public Policy Research, Chief Research Officer – Centre for Education Systems, and Senior Research Associate – Jesus College (IF), Cambridge University

Clare O'Sullivan
Head of Educational Strategy, The Professional Teaching Institute (The PTI)

Tim Oates CBE
Group Director of Assessment, Research and Development at Cambridge Assessment

Professor Dame Alison Peacock DBE
CEO, The Chartered College of Teaching

Erika Podmore
Headteacher, Eltham Hill School

Dr Hugh Rayment-Pickard MBE
Co-Director, The Professional Teaching Institute (The PTI)

Neil Renton
Headteacher, Harrogate Grammar School

Carolyn Roberts MBE
Co-Director, The Professional Teaching Institute (The PTI)

Dominic Robson
Headteacher, Bishop Vesey's Grammar School

Richard Sheriff OBE
CEO of Red Kite Learning Trust and Director of Red Kite Alliance

Dr Daniel Talbot
Assistant Head, Thomas Tallis School

Anna Trethewey
Executive Director, Corporate Affairs and Strategy, AQA

Katherine Walsh
Deputy Head, Thomas Tallis School

Dan Whieldon
Principal, Leeds West Academy

Ben White
Assistant Headteacher, Maidstone Grammar School for Girls

John Wilkinson
Head of Geography, St Edward's College, Liverpool and Honorary Lecturer, University of Liverpool

Professor Michael Young
Educational Sociologist

Acknowledgements

The editors would like to thank all those who are involved with The Professional Teaching Institute (The PTI): The charity's staff team, the board of trustees and academic advisors, but above all, the teachers and the children and young people in all our schools, whose enthusiasm for teaching and learning is irrepressible. This book is dedicated to them.

The charity has an enduring debt of gratitude to HM King Charles III, who founded the organisation and its vision of a rich and deep education for every young person.

Carolyn Roberts
Hugh Rayment-Pickard
London 2025

Introduction: Well educated – Leading schools with wonder, joy and wisdom

Carolyn Roberts

What is this book?

Three times a year, I write a briefing for charity trustees describing the state of English education. It often has a gloomy tone. Crises in teacher supply and retention, school funding and the legacy of decades of focus on structural and compliance mechanisms merge with children's mental health problems, attendance and the grim prospects for future prosperity. The most upbeat school leader might reasonably stagger under this burden, but the remarkable evidence of this book is that they remain doughty, determined and thoughtful. It is in celebration of these school leaders that we present this book.

Our contributors are thinkers and educators largely associated with the work of The Professional Teaching Institute (The PTI), a charity set up by HM The King as Prince of Wales in 2005. Oliver Blond's chapter describes our history and motivations, but here, I set out our priorities so that the book may be read with these in mind.

The PTI is committed to making high-quality, rigorous and enjoyable education available to every child, regardless of background or ability. We aim to raise the profile of subjects within education and encourage schools to promote coherence and challenge within the curriculum, including providing exciting extra-curricular activities. Why? Because engaging students in a deep and meaningful relationship with subjects and their disciplines enables them to understand and make sense of the world. While The PTI works with primary and secondary schools alike, this first book is secondary-focused.

Learned and highly motivated teachers are the key to educational excellence. Teachers' subject passion and expertise are essential requirements for effective teaching, so they need support to enhance, develop, explore and share their specialist subject knowledge and best practice in subject teaching. Teachers who are excited by and up-to-date in their own learning and scholarship inspire young people to learn too.

Teachers are the heart of every school. They hold the keys to opportunity for young people. The role of the teacher in society should be taken very seriously.

An intelligent reader might assume that these are shared and standard sentiments, held about teachers by everyone involved in education. While that may be so, the focus of education this century has been on the structure and performance of schools, demonstrated by compliance with national accountability measures at the institutional and child level. Any national or local vision for education has had to be susceptible to these economics of measurement. This perfectly legitimate democratic activity, however, has consequences. Where success is described in necessarily simple terms, and opprobrium heaped upon those falling short, the individual agency of the school and the teacher is endangered. Fearful leaders cling to a template which was never designed to straitjacket.

The righteous hope that standardised calibration would create the circumstances for better education outcomes for all children may have been realised. It has not yet led, however, despite school leaders' fervent exhortations to their students, to a more just and equal society in which the fruits of education bring personal prosperity and fulfilment to all. Sadly, it is obvious that not all of our children enjoy the experience of learning in its current form, or its dominant role in childhood and adolescence.[1]

The *Well-Educated* writers are not, of course, opposed to accountability or assessment in education. Many are distinguished and influential in education policy and have led significant change and improvement in the sector. All have the authenticity of a professional. We share a concern, however, about the burden of compliance, which affects school leaders' thinking, and their fearfulness of thinking about education in less measurable terms. Perhaps our book will be an encouragement to school leaders, these principled public servants who want to use their professional and intellectual skills to do their best for children and society. Perhaps it will encourage them to use ideas such as wonder, joy and wisdom alongside the metrics and performance indicators.

A kind of history

The PTI was born at a time of difficulty in secondary education. Various attempts to measure the successful delivery of education policy by GCSE examination results have led many schools to focus on outcomes alone, using GCSE equivalent courses to boost points scores and inspection ratings. **Ian Bauckham** describes this with typical cool clarity in his chapter. Such action was sometimes justified as a necessary focus on the skills young people would need for future tech-driven success, where personal subject knowledge would be of less importance than the skill to recognise their own learning needs and find out things. When policymakers realised that this focus had led to an impoverished curriculum for many children, particularly the poorest, the pendulum swung back and the tautology of the 'knowledge-rich' school was born.

'Knowledge rich' begs the question of exactly what other kind of school might exist and is itself another potentially lethal mutation, as **Katherine Walsh** argues. When the inspectorate OFSTED formulated a simple, principled way of measuring the quality of a school's curriculum (rather than just its outcomes), schools were both ready and unready. They had spent more than a decade fine-tuning their compliance processes to maximise achievement scores as **Ben White** and **Clare O'Sullivan** describe, so they could quickly swivel to meet curriculum quality indicators of intent, implementation and impact. If knowledge is what inspectors want to see, then knowledge would be demonstrated. How to do this quickly and efficiently? With standardised texts and lesson content, and a focus on memory for the new content-heavy examinations, which would demonstrate the effective teaching of prescribed knowledge.

As The PTI has some impact on this re-centring of subject knowledge in schools, it seems churlish to carp, but circumstance always takes its toll. The frenzied retooling above could have settled into long-term curriculum strength, but three other forces skewed schooling out of true: teacher supply, school funding and the immediate and lasting effects of the pandemic. This book does not directly cover COVID, though every leader writes in the context of the altered social contract between society and schools, and every teacher works in the context of significant changes in behaviour and attendance. It is teacher supply and school funding which have a particular circular effect on education quality, and which materially affect teachers' and children's self-understanding as both scholars and learners. What any of our education hopes and dreams can do for the climate emergency is another issue which should be central. **Tim Oates** starkly challenges our thinking.

Two large problems

The workforce economics of teacher supply is also beyond the scope of this book. Suffice it to say that, for a range of reasons linked to pay and working conditions, teaching is currently an unattractive career in England across almost all subjects and phases. What does that mean, on the ground?

Where subject specialists are few, school leaders rightly seek to minimise the effect on children, especially those facing public examinations, by mandating a minimum teaching content and style. Technological developments – even as basic as the existence of PowerPoint – make shared and consistent lessons easily available. Scarce subject experts can write lessons for others to teach, or the school can subscribe to an online service. As the teacher supply crisis deepens, the workaround becomes the norm. Further, as groups of schools seek to define their quality by particular teaching methodologies, teachers become used to pre-prepared lesson content and are unused to independent or collaborative curriculum development.

What might be an efficient and principled response to terrible circumstances has far-reaching consequences for teacher development and job satisfaction.

Insufficient school funding compounds the effect. Time is money in schools, where upwards of 75% of school budgets will be spent on teachers. Limited funding means teachers must spend the maximum possible time teaching. This leaves less time for curriculum development, professional reflection, planning, preparation and assessment. The efficiency of the readymade lesson is again attractive, even necessary in this context, but the intellectual satisfaction of curriculum design and development, and the professional satisfaction of devising the most effective and engaging teaching methods, are removed from the teacher's job. Sometimes described as a workload reduction solution, this misunderstands the problem: it is not the nature of the workload, but the time in which to complete its tasks that leads to despair. This cheapening of teachers' purpose makes it less likely that lively, thinking young graduates will want to become teachers, and more likely that those who try it will leave.

In November 2024, government advisor Sir Kevan Collins described teachers as being 'enslaved', fearing for the 'long-term stability or capacity in the system', arguing that in school cultures that do not prioritise 'longer, deeper' professional thinking processes, 'people aren't fulfilled and they leave'.

> I think we've sometimes slipped into a shallow compliance culture, where you see people being told what to do down to the degree of the slide stack we're going to use in every lesson....People get really fed up. [They] have to feel they have agency, responsibility and support and training to be the best teacher [they] can be.[2]

It is unlikely that any school leader has ever set out to undermine teaching as a career. However, their principled and pragmatic responses to circumstance have, perhaps inevitably, led to a narrowing of the teaching experience in schools where budget deficits and the teacher shortage are most acute, or where compliance takes pride of place.

The 2019 *Framework for Ethical Leadership in Education* offers educators the language to think about their fundamental motivations and beliefs. If schools are where society looks after its young until they are old enough to take on the mantle of adult citizenship, what do we expect school leaders to dream of, or to care about in more practical terms, as they design their timetables and recruit their staff?

We hope that the 30 essays in this book will demonstrate visionary, meaningful and useful ways of working, offering support to school leaders and teachers who wish to think differently about their role, inspired by wonder, joy and wisdom.

Our book is in five sections. It offers a menu of longer and shorter essays from practitioners, policymakers and thinkers. All are important, and together, they make up a fascinatingly complete picture. We hope that readers find the variety of approaches readable and thought-provoking.

Section 1: What is a good education?

We have a weak understanding of the purpose of education in England, preferring practical policy to a theoretical discussion. In an attempt to boost a debate, the pieces in this first section unpick some purpose assumptions.

1. **Ben White** kicks us off with a discussion of *The functionalist view of education: The role of education in supporting the economic and labour requirements of the country*. Encouraging us to consider that 'in reality, little in schools is fixed', he encourages us to look at education's role to 'support meaningful work now and consider how to transform it into the future'. Reminding us that grades are simply 'positional goods' in the careers marketplace, he seeks to unpick the 'tacit acceptance of meritocracy', to which many of our writers allude. His magnificent painting of the hassled school leader who hasn't got time to think about larger issues is wonderfully summed up with 'working in and leading schools is demanding enough without the burden of existential futility'. Nonetheless, think we must.

2. **Hannah Knowles'** snapshot of *Education as self-realisation: personal development, personal formation and character development* makes us think about another purpose of schooling, the development of individual character. This important topic, to which we return, forces us to look at 'part of education we cannot see, we can't measure'.

3. Answering the question: *Are all good schools alike?* **Leora Cruddas** reflects on national-level leadership. While education is a good in itself, it relies on an understanding of its purpose. Introducing Professor Deng's work, she investigates schools' roles in developing autonomous and responsible individuals who may become free and independent adults, and the contribution of academic disciplines thereto. 'Schools are where society is created. They must be places in which everyone is treated with dignity, places which create relational community, build prosocial norms, where a love of knowledge and the joy of learning is experienced, places that nurture self-efficacy and agency, where children, adults and their families feel a sense of belonging.'

4. **Melanie Ferron-Evans** picks up this theme in *Should schools serve individuals or communities?* Taking the reader from Nelson Mandela's tiny cell to the red Welsh bricks of Ruabon, she asks 'difficult questions about our communication and relationship with our families and stakeholders'. Describing long years of trying to improve family and community engagement, she asks, 'Do our children feel they are part of a community that cares about them?'

5. **Tim Oates** takes our thinking global in *Who decides what is a good education?* Is it local or national? School and profession-based, or political? What happens when forces are misaligned, and 'an overloaded curriculum erodes the space

for "curriculum making?"' Is a good education measurable? By outcomes, by job-readiness, by quality of subsequent life? With a fascinating comparison of English and German routes, he challenges us to examine whether a good education can be said to exist in an unequal society, on an endangered planet.

Section 2: A good curriculum

We move from our discussion of purpose to practical school and subject leadership. This section combines leaders' actions to realise curriculum principles, with some specific pieces: Sally Bacon on creativity, Richard Chattoe on devising and maintaining a school's 'DNA' and John Wilkinson on principled subject-level development.

6. First, **Jon Curtis-Brignell** discusses building a school curriculum inspired by the hugely influential Michael F D Young and Gert Biesta, important to several of our writers. His very useful description of powerful knowledge, domains of purpose and authenticity, has practical repercussions for our young if we enable them to engage with the subject in ways that give them entry to its uses beyond the classroom and in later life. 'A "good" curriculum, then, needs to be one which ensures children are thinking critically, engaged in creativity and the development of original ideas and action'.

7. **Sally Bacon**'s *Education for creativity* follows with a specific look at the national economic and personal value of the arts, comparing these disciplines with those where testing factual knowledge is simpler. 'During the 2010s, subjects seen as unambiguous – or obviously "right or wrong" – edged out subjects which aim to elicit young people's ideas, originality and opinions, and hone creative and practical skills through exploration and experimentation. But when faced with candidates with the same level of qualifications, employers will often look for these so-called soft skills'.

8. **Richard Chattoe** also talks about intertwined learning and personal development in *Building up educated citizens*. Developing Citizenship as a curriculum department has enabled a formerly troubled school to redevelop by centring shared, explicit values. All successful school leaders will recognise his eureka moment one Tuesday at 0230, which changed the school's direction. His observation that 'some school leaders may be drawn towards and see external metrics as a key indicator of a school's success' is a clear challenge to think otherwise.

9. **Oliver Blond** asks, *Is a good school conceivable without great subject teaching?* He describes subjects as 'the heart of a good school'. His analysis of the 'spark, that moment of recognition, that sense of wonder or sudden enlightenment, is often about your connection to an idea, a body of knowledge, and a way of thinking that can become a lifelong passion'. Teachers enable people to best serve their unique purpose in the world, so subject teachers themselves need leaders' support in order to embrace and deepen their own sense of purpose.

10. **John Wilkinson**, in turn, gives further detail in his *Local curriculum development* example, focusing on the development of a geography curriculum in North Liverpool. Setting out to develop a challenging, innovative and encouraging curriculum with hugely popular subject-based activities beyond the curriculum, enriching teachers' subject knowledge and linking with universities, his 'St Edward's geographers think globally and act locally, future-proofing the global village with forward thinking, outward-facing values, the result of intellectual and emotional investment in local curriculum development'.

11. **Erika Podmore's** piece on *Education as transmitting knowledge, values and cultural identity* speaks to us from 30 years of Inner London experience. Her clear explanation of quality curriculum development by individual teachers and teams alert to changing circumstances demonstrates the power of intellectual reflection on local and global issues. The teachers she describes are fired by a mission to enable students to understand themselves in their world and use the discipline of history to envisage better. It is 'filled with optimism'.

12. **Richard Kueh's** *Rendering tensions productive: on curriculum construction, leadership and professionalism* asks us to consider 'joy and wisdom: joy through love of subject and wisdom through discerning judgement'. He covers four 'high-level challenges' about curriculum, progression, pedagogy and assessment and concludes that the curriculum designer is 'someone trusted with a great – but not impossible – task. The task is not dissimilar to that of a curator, who acts as an intermediary – acquiring, caring and developing artefacts of content – ultimately for the benefit and enrichment of others'. How do we listen to the symbolic effect of past curricula? Which idols do we tear down?

13. **Dan Whieldon** tackles the question, *'What is a quality curriculum?'* in a semi-autobiographical way, taking us memorably from his own schooldays through the years of subjects' subjection to the assessor and the National Curriculum to curriculum development as essential to the improvement of a challenging school. He describes children's opportunities opened up by teachers enabled to collaborate and to put together a quality, modern curriculum: 'a foundation for rebellious learning' which is dynamic and interactive but built upon sturdy foundations of 'knowledge and intellectual depth'.

Section 3: Is the assessment fit for purpose?

14. This huge area of discussion is ably launched at all levels by **Clare O'Sullivan**'s *Assessment and children's experience of learning*. Taking us from the learner's plaintive: 'Is it on the test?' Through the unsustainable war boards and interventions, she makes us face the question: 'What happens if we prioritise

monitoring and checking over learning opportunities?' Aiming for subject-specific 'assessment to promote deep learning and critical thinking', she assesses the extent public accountability has warped the way curriculum, assessment and monitoring work together in school.

15. **Ian Bauckham's** *The role of public examination and qualifications* brings his distinguished experience as school and trust leader, and as Chief Regulator at Ofqual. Referring to Professor Rob Coe and Dr Steve Munby, he makes a vital case for trustworthy qualifications, explaining the decisions and trade-offs needed at national level to support them. His eloquent description of teachers' misuse of qualifications' assessment structure in the classroom should give pause for thought to any leader encouraging teachers to focus purely on assessment techniques and rehearsal rather than good teaching.

16. **Michael Antram** uses stories from his school in *The school leader as emancipator,* making us confront what happens when 'quality outcomes are prioritised over the formation of the individual' and offering an overdue observation about an increasing focus on the brain, causing us to lose sight of the young person. Asking what sort of leader can free teachers to be creative practitioners, he exhorts a duty to be 'emancipatory and prophetic', cultivating the growth of the young towards adulthood, as 'education's gift to the future'. What is to be gained if results go up, but people go down?

17. In helping us to understand *embedding and assessing complex competencies such as creative thinking, collaboration and communication*, **Bill Lucas** challenges school leaders to tackle the mindset of 'if it's not going to be assessed, it cannot be a priority in an overcrowded curriculum'. Looking at creative thinking across the curriculum and across the world, Professor Lucas offers a definition of what it means for a human being to be well-educated in these times, reaching 'beyond the simple, often simplistic, binary approach to what matters in schools'.

18. **Anna Trethewey's** authoritative piece on the challenges and opportunities of the public examination system tackles *How do we know someone is well educated? What do national standards do for children and society? How do we know if it has worked?* From the purpose of a public education system to issues with AI, she requires us to think about the lessons of the past and present for the future. How does an assessment system 'create students that embody what it means', to be well-educated?

Section 4: Who benefits from education?

19. **Richard Sheriff** begins our discussion with *What educational success looks like?* Drawing on Aristotle, Estelle Morris, and 'Fundamental British Values', he balances ideas of economic prosperity, civic society and personal fulfilment

with a lovely description of joyfulness in school. Crucially, discussing Ofsted, he asks if its Framework has done away with the need 'for this generation of school leaders to even consider the notion of what educational success looks like. The state has decided, and our job is to implement that view'.

20. **Katherine Walsh** asks *Who is education failing?* from the context of a very large, inclusive London comprehensive. Concerned that 'we make assumptions about what they should want out of life without asking or advising' young people, she discusses conforming, creativity, behaviour, SEND and the effects of exams. She describes the value of a young person's journey in the classroom, and of their demand for increasing personalisation to reflect their passions, stifled by financial resources which 'increasingly dictate a universal approach to classroom teaching'.

21. **Daniel Talbot**'s *Education for families who don't see the point* tackles he effectiveness of Arnold's best-that-has-been-thought-and-said. Why do some students move effortlessly through the system while others don't, and kick against it? He observes that 'parents and their communities are held responsible for cycles of underachievement, obfuscating the socio-economic and political root causes. What story one sees as the best that's thought and said is, in fact, little more than a 'cultural arbitrary'. How can we engage all parents and students without seeing some as 'a deficit to be remedied'?

22. **Loic Menzies** therefore takes us onto *What is fairness in education?* Usefully reminding all readers that 'meritocracy' was coined as a dystopian, not utopian, concept, he discusses the determinism of a popular understanding of deserts, capabilities, talents and potential. Bringing Sen and Rawls into a captivating discussion of what a fair system should look like, and the limitations of any single system to eradicate inequality, he makes six points which any school's staff could usefully discuss before reminding us of the pressing issue: making education fair is a struggle we're losing.

23. *The broader societal benefits of education,* on the other hand, are discussed in **Neil Renton**'s essay, in which he looks at classic sociological theory and the long-term impact of current policies in schools, 'the focal socialisation agency'. Seeing education as 'a transformative tool for addressing existential risks and ensuring the long-term well-being of humanity'. With an interesting funding proposal, he demands that we integrate 'long-termist principles into educational planning to magnify the societal benefits of education far beyond the present moment'.

24. **Hugh Rayment-Pickard**, however, asks *Is it possible to be overeducated?* If, as Dewey said, 'education is life itself' is it possible to have too much? Already a trope in popular culture, he calmly sets out the reasonable wish of ordinary non-graduate citizens to be taken seriously and the supposed problem of too

many graduates. He concludes with a warning that 'overeducation is a concept that should be treated with maximum suspicion' and that we should not assume that education itself is without powerful enemies.

Section 5: What is an educated society?

25. **Dominic Robson** begins our thinking with *Education as a means to foster a nation with a shared culture, tradition and values,* reflecting on his leadership of an ancient grammar school. Giving a very useful description of the relationship between modern education and national identity, he covers education policy, social unrest and the value of inclusivity – including a captivating adaptation of the so-called Fundamental British Values. 'Honouring tradition while embracing inclusivity ensures that each generation upholds the values that bind societies'.

26. **Hugh Rayment-Pickard** returns with a final question: *Is there an education Utopia?* Taking us through Harold Wilson, Tony Blair, Greta Thunberg, Petrarch, More, Bacon, Diderot, Marx, Illich and Kant, he looks at the impact of the idea of the future on educators. How can humans build their own brilliant future, free from ignorance and oppression? Is it enough to emulate Renaissance thinkers, looking at the past while trying to incorporate current developments into a total system of knowledge? As Friere says, we 'can't respect the teacher who doesn't dream of a certain kind of society': the Utopian dream is critical to educational thought.

27. **Carolyn Roberts** builds on this in *A vision for a better world,* trying to plot a course through twentieth and twenty-first-century education policymakers' ideas of what might constitute a better society. Noting that the 1926 Code warned that 'the balance of the curriculum should not be interfered with by examination requirements', she takes us through the thinking behind the 1944 Act, the 1965 circular on comprehensive education and its detractors, the development of the National Curriculum and Ofsted. 'The lingering perverse incentives of a well-meaning accountability system seem to have led to a focus on performativity in place of thoughtful, considered expertise evaluated in the long term'.

28. **Lucy Hyams** writes on *An educated society as a community of individual talents.* She discusses the concept of the broad and balanced curriculum, specifically focusing on the importance of the curriculum as a 'window or a mirror', the importance of decolonising and unpicking 'what or who is othered or absent within existing curriculum content'. If Piaget is right that the 'principal goal of education is to create people who are capable of doing new things, not simply repeating what other generations have done', we need to make sure that learners encounter self-discovery as well as collective growth.

29. **Alison Peacock** begins her piece on *Does society still value teachers?* by asking how much teachers really value themselves. Using the considerable knowledge base of the Chartered College of Teaching, she discusses the cognitive, ethical and legal-social domains of teacher professionalism, and the importance of the College to teachers' self-understanding. Noting the 'exemplary practice' she sees on hundreds of school visits, she recognises the critical social role of teachers with 'the intellectual capacity to hold theoretical and practical knowledge about their pupils but do so with an ethical and altruistic stance'.

Conclusion

Our society, like our education system, is complex and contested.

Schools have adapted to the belief that social inequity may be addressed by simple outcome measures in education. Because these are so important, there must be a single focus on what it takes to reach them: what kind of schools, what kind of teachers, what kind of teaching. Our book, however, challenges leaders and policymakers to conceptualise strong schools as built on strong curriculum foundations. While understanding both the importance of results and their apparent impotence to transform society, we encourage leaders to move away from the rhetoric of measurement and struggle to think about wonder, joy and wisdom, so that children are happier and teachers stay.

Michael Young's afterword, however, challenges this. What of the deep social inequalities in our communities? What of the dissociation and alienation which fuelled the 2024 riots? Is it enough to talk about the importance of specialist subject teachers? Are we fiddling while rearranging the deckchairs?

This generation of school leaders cannot solve the social problems in which they serve, but they can solve some of the educational problems with which they battle. They can't pay teachers more, but they can help them to love teaching and stick with it for decades. They can't resolve the social conditions of their students, but they can open their eyes to a better way of ordering the world. School leaders are daily exercised and – for the huge majority – entirely committed to social justice, but they have few levers to pull.

The world our writers inhabit is contradictory. We wanted an educational world where knowledge and learning are central, but inadequate measurement and funding have shrunk it to the very thing Michael quotes. Subject knowledge may have become little more than memorisation of facts. The opportunity for new thinking, by pupils or teachers, is squeezed by a shortage of teachers, money and vision. In the hope of improving education, we have adapted ourselves to the perfect conditions for discouraging independent thought.

The best teaching and learning roots itself in a child's self-understanding. It brokers a relationship with knowledge and enables them to envisage different ways of living and their own place in the world. Structure and social context notwithstanding, all children deserve an engaging, compelling education from skilled, learned and happy teachers. Because this can't be taken for granted, it is where we begin, building up education from first principles.

Notes

1 *The Good Childhood Report 2024*, The Children's Society, www.childrenssociety.org.uk, August 2024.
2 Dyson J, '"I've never seen teachers more enslaved" says school standards tsar: Sir Kevan Collins warns of a "narrow compliance culture" in some schools', *Schools Week*, 7 November 2024.

SECTION I
What is a good education?

This section expects you to think about the purpose of education in England: what schools are *for*. Our ultra-scrutinised professional lives are filled with discussions of the 'how?' of schools, but not the 'why?'. Spend a little time thinking about your answer to the big questions. What *are* schools for? What do we think we are doing?

Think

1. What is a good education, to you? Did you have one?
2. Do you experience 'existential futility' (Essay 1)?
3. Should education have a defined social function? What?
4. In education, what can't we see or measure? Does it matter?
5. What does it mean to be an autonomous and responsible individual?
6. What do children and young people need to be autonomous and responsible?
7. How does your curriculum build up these powers?
8. Should schools serve individuals or communities?

Section I
Essay 1

The functionalist view of education: The role of education in supporting the economic and labour requirements of the country

Ben White

What's the point of learning this?

A wet Thursday afternoon in November, the class settles down to a written task when the question comes, genuinely quizzical but laced with more than a hint of frustration:

'What's the point of learning this?'

Do we address it head-on or try to sidestep? Fortunately, in this A-level Sociology lesson, we can segue into the Functionalist view of education. As developed by Durkheim and later Parsons, this perspective sees schools as institutions that build social cohesion, impart core values, and allocate roles based on merit. Schools socialise young people and prepare them for future employment, teaching crucial skills and ensuring that, in theory, all students have equal opportunity to succeed. The function of schools is to contribute to society by helping prepare students for future employment, by teaching foundational skills and knowledge. They also provide crucial opportunities for socialisation, teaching young people how to relate to, communicate and work with a diverse community. This is all provided free of charge, theoretically offering all students equal opportunity.[1]

It does feel that those of us working in schools are expected to provide these vital functions, and more, to the young people in our care. More recently, this has expanded to include

- promoting British values
- imparting powerful knowledge
- making sure that people leave knowing enough about pensions, technology, healthy living and more, in order to thrive in the modern world
- providing childcare so that both parents can work (as illustrated by the challenges of school lockdowns in response to COVID-19)
- supporting mental health
- tackling socio-economic inequality

At their best, schools are places rich in opportunity, and they offer a genuine life-enhancing community. Does this theory match reality?

The scale and scope of schools' current roles certainly stretch their capacity. Sustaining a healthy school environment is a challenging task. It helps those of us working in schools to know that what we are doing is vitally important. However, that same core belief can sometimes get in the way of clear thinking and action. In A-level Sociology, students learn that employing a single lens can simultaneously clarify and limit our understanding of society. This applies to the Functionalist view, which emphasises schools' positive role in a healthy society, aiding policy clarity and empowering school leaders to see their impact. This view also reinforces the idea that schools are fixed, rational institutions with clear, achievable functions, potentially overlooking their complexity and fluidity.

In reality, little about schools is fixed. Their processes, systems, and daily routines – what complexity theorists call 'procedural regularities' – have evolved as schools adapt to changes in technology, society and politics. For instance, summer holidays were extended to support the harvest, and GCSEs emerged as exit qualifications when most students left school at 16. Today, students are grouped by age and follow a fixed curriculum from ages 5 to 18. Previously, students progressed independently through courses based on ability, with teacher and peer support, allowing for more tailored learning but sacrificing a standardised curriculum progression.[2]

Messiness and the danger of a single perspective

Schools are not entirely functional. Naive solutions devised and implemented with the benefit of a single frame of reference are unlikely to work. This is easier to see with hindsight. Most of us working in schools will be able to identify multiple 'big things' that we worked hard on in different educational eras, which we have eventually come to see as misguided. Many experienced school leaders can now look back on historic processes relating to data use and analysis, which were in vogue under a previous Ofsted framework. The reasonable assertion that schools should help students to make progress in their learning led to the less reasonable expectation that this should translate into steady, linear progress for each individual student. This, in turn, led to a range of statistically illiterate and time-consuming processes which the Department for Education itself explicitly warned against.[3]

American Economist Brian Caplan critiques modern schooling as often inefficient and costly. He claims that in post-primary education, once students have mastered the essential skills of numeracy and basic literacy, much of what they 'learn' is arbitrary. He also argues that most people forget much of what they learn, even if they pass the qualifications. Grades, in his view, serve more as 'positional goods', signalling relative ability and work ethic to future employers. Caplan illustrates this with his course example: if his students had half the time to complete their assessments, it would still serve the same purpose – differentiating students by their ability and disposition towards academic work.[4] According to this view, if no students study on Thursday afternoons, GCSEs and A-Levels would still function in exactly the same way. The 'powerful knowledge' we value may not be as essential as we believe, as most students forget specifics and do fine in later life regardless. Once you start to look for it, this inherent contingency is present in much of what we take for granted within our schools. However, looking too closely or too long may not be healthy. Dwelling on complexity can be bewildering rather than empowering.

I can't think about that now Ben. I've got to complete data tracking for year 10.

I vividly remember this response to my attempt to point out the statistical illiteracy of our school intervention programme several years ago. With Ofsted looming and students apparently coasting, the work still needed doing. Stopping to mine the depths of this particular procedural regularity was both time-consuming and discombobulating. At the time, I thought that the senior leader's response was absurd and incomprehensible. I may even have labelled it as stupid. It was not. It was highly functional in the more personal sense of the word.

The function of a functionalist view

Our Thursday afternoon question is actually an existential question for the teacher as well as the student. They will want to find a satisfactory answer, not just to help get this student back to work, but to quell any concerns that they might be onto something. Mary Kennedy has written of the persistent problems that teachers, regardless of context, will encounter. Her fifth persistent problem, which she suggests all teachers encounter, is 'finding a way [of working] that is consistent with their own personalities and personal needs'.[5] This hints at the personal function of schools for those of us who work within them.

Humans are creatures who want to find meaning and purpose in their life course and decisions.[6] Teachers are humans who have chosen to find meaning (as well as a salary, of course!) by working within our complex and inherently compromised school system. Leaders are generally teachers who have managed this for long enough to move into positions which involve managing other teachers as well as teaching directly. To remain within teaching and leading, we need to find a way of working with which we can cope, both logistically and existentially.

From this perspective, the teacher asking what to say to the student querying the point of their Thursday afternoon lesson is asking for themselves too. If Caplan is 'right', then everyone in that room – teacher included – is arguably wasting their time. The senior leader, who perhaps spent a late night preparing tracking spreadsheets, is perhaps making a similar response when they patiently explained to me – before rushing off to tackle whatever drama had recently erupted with 'that student' in Year 10 – that they could not think about the implications of statistical illiteracy right now. Working in and leading schools is demanding enough without the added burden of existential futility!

There is a right and a wrong time to contemplate the complexity and compromise built into our school system. Those of us prone to introspection may err by employing this lens in the wrong moments. Sometimes, a simple response is best. However, as leaders in a complex system, there are moments when we need to step back and think the unthinkable. Otherwise, irrational processes, like the statistically illiterate data tasks mentioned above, simply continue *ad infinitum*. Sometimes, schools are not 'functional' for specific young people. If we leave the system as it is, are there students for whom the 'point' of a particular Thursday afternoon lesson is hard to define?

A colleague of mine has taught Chemistry exceptionally well in a range of schools over the past twenty years. In selective academic A-level environments, prior academic success, hard work and good teaching allow students to realise their ambitions. Schools function very well for them. Other groups of students may not fit so neatly into our current school system. This same teacher has also spoken of classes with students so far behind academically that they are very unlikely to pass the qualifications that they must take. In this case, hard work and progress can happen, but the public examinations are likely to be demoralising.

In *A Good Life,* authors Rees and Newmark assert that tacit acceptance of the principle of meritocracy in our school system has distorted how we support young people with learning disabilities. They write of 'an outdated medical and deficit model, where to receive additional support in schools and throughout life, people with disability and their families have to demonstrate failure, regularly and repeatedly'.[7] This approach is, of course, compounded by an SEN system that lacks the funding and capacity to provide students with the support that they require to make the most of their time in school. We only reach this insight by stepping back and questioning the lens most commonly used to evaluate our schools.

The far side of complexity

Schools are complex, contested and at times unusual, even irrational, places. Their inherent complexity is not going away. Nor are the complex social problems which they are expected to contribute to dealing with. Simplistic solutions and strategies which ignore this complexity are unhelpful. So, too, is merely dwelling on the complexity. We need simple, hopeful strategies informed by a sophisticated understanding of the system.

I think it helps to recognise that this messiness, the inevitable irrationality of school processes and practices, is not a problem to be neatly solved. We can make changes, some of which will be positive, in particular areas. We cannot change the inherent complexity of the system of mass schooling, which we are part of. Learning to live with and work within this is one of the challenges of school leadership.

Ignoring complexity is not helpful, but neither is fixating on it. Leaders need to step back periodically to question established practices. This fosters adaptability and humility. Our reflection may lead to no change if the best option is the current compromise, or it may inspire big changes, even in processes once seen as essential.

However, we must be cautious. Schools serve vital personal functions for students and staff alike. Humans are more motivated and resilient when they feel their work is meaningful and manageable. As leaders, we should help staff engage meaningfully with their roles and navigate challenges thoughtfully. Excessive questioning and deconstruction without a practical focus, however, serve little purpose. We need to both support meaningful work now and consider how to transform this very same work in the future.

What is the point of learning this?

What does the student need to hear? They probably need to know that what they are doing has value. That their effort is important and will eventually lead to success. They deserve to have an enthusiastic teacher ambitious for all of their students to achieve. One who can foster a sense of hope.

> *Hope is the thing with feathers-*
> *That perches in the soul-*
> *And sings the tune without the words-*
> *And never stops- at all-*
> *Emily Dickinson*[8]

Notes

1. Giddens A and Sutton P, *Sociology,* (9th edition), Polity Press, 2021.
2. Allen R, Evans M and White B, *The Next Big Thing in School Improvement,* John Catt, 2021.
3. Allen R, *Making Data Work. Report of the Teacher Workload Advisory Group,* Department for Education, 2018.
4. Caplan B, *The Case against Education: Why the Education System is a Waste of Time and Money,* Princeton University Press, 2019.
5. Kennedy M, 'Parsing the practice of teaching', *Journal of Teacher Education,* 67/1, 2015, p 13.
6. Frankl V, *Man's Search for Meaning,* Rider, 2004.
7. Newmark B and Rees T, *A good life: towards greater dignity for people with learning disability,* The Confederation of Schools Trusts and Ambition Institute, 2022, p 5.
8. Dickinson E, *Poems* [Second Series], Eds Higginson TW and Todd ML, University Press, 1891.

Section 1
Essay 2

Education as self-realisation

Hannah Knowles

To understand the complexities of this age-old discourse regarding the purpose of education, I am going to start where all headteachers normally do, with an assembly: An assembly, I find particularly effective when encouraging students to think about the importance of looking not just at what is being shown to you, but more importantly, what is not. This particular assembly uses the work of Abraham Wald, a mathematician who worked as part of the statistical research group in the US Military during the Second World War. Wald was tasked with working out where the bomber planes, used at the time, needed better reinforcement, considering armour was too heavy to be placed all around the aircraft.[1] Commanders of the US Military studied endless planes returning to base after being hit, believing that it was clear that the areas with the most bullet holes were indeed the parts of the plane that required such reinforcement. Wald disagreed. Wald argued that the Commanders were looking at the data incorrectly. They were excluding the data that was, in fact, the most important and, as such, were about to make significant errors resulting in little or no impact, with the same number of fatalities likely to occur. Wald argued that the US Military should be placing the armour on the areas of the planes that did not have bullet holes. Why? What was missing in the data set for these Commanders were the other planes. Those that did not return. Quite simply, Wald argued, it was the areas without the bullet holes on the returning planes which told the story about why the others did not. If a plane were hit in these areas, all those within it could not survive and subsequently not return to base. Wald, one of the invisible heroes of the Second World War, was celebrated for saving several lives through what became known as 'survivor bias'.

I use this story to highlight to students that it is clear through examples such as Wald, that to have impact and to make sure you are having impact in the right areas, this often means taking the time to ask the difficult questions and to look beyond what we might expect in the first instance to be the correct and only answer.

With this in mind, are we confident as educators that we are having an impact in the right areas? That is the purpose of our role, our profession and the experiences and subsequent successes of students are rooted in not only what we see, but also what we might not see. Do we have the confidence to argue that education should be as much about students gaining the skills and attributes that no accountability systems can measure, as well as providing young people with a currency to move on to their next stage of life after education? Perhaps the starting point is, what are we here to do? Who are we serving, and how should we do this?

Some may argue that schools in today's society are redundant. John Taylor Gatto suggests that anything learned in school could be learned on your own,[2] which is an interesting concept. On reflection, this could be true. If a young person has a way of accessing information and if they are engaged, have all the necessary resources they require and the support they need, then a school itself may no longer be needed. It is hard to imagine society without schools, though. They are not simply just a place where knowledge is sought and gained; they serve a purpose that is much greater. Dame Rachel de Souza, The Children's Commissioner, explains: 'There are a few common and uniting themes amongst children, and one is education. Every time I speak to children, they tell me how important school is to them... It's the place where children make their first friends, learn about the world, and discover their talents'.[3] It is also a place where young people are exposed to different people, different views and this, in turn, provides better members of society.[4] The purpose of a school is one which divides academics, parents, students and teachers alike. Key questions surrounding how we should measure and value the impact we have, alongside what exactly schools should prioritise in terms of learning.

One of my favourite thoughts I share with our new Year 7 parents, when we meet them for the first time, is that we have their child for roughly 273 weeks of their secondary education, 273 weeks in which we are trying to support them to prepare for, on average, a further 3,276 weeks of life. A mere 8.3% of their time.

So, with such a small percentage of a young person's life, it is imperative that we utilise the power of the classroom to ensure that a young person feels ready to take on the challenges that life throws at them. And within this 8.3%, we as educators and school leaders have a choice. We can choose what we value, we can choose what opportunities we present to our young people, and fundamentally, we choose our own definitions of education. This, in turn, shapes the definition of education for the young people who experience each of our educational settings.

That is, for many of us, one of the parts of leadership that excites and motivates us. The thought that we have the opportunity to shape the educational experience of all the young people in our care. Though, and with a nod towards a second assembly, with great power comes great responsibility.

And it is a responsibility. As a school leader, there is a responsibility to decide to what extent the culture of your school and the learning within it are based on character education. For some, it is a crucial part of the school context, and for others, it is not deemed necessary. There is no intended judgement here, or suggestion about the right answer, (as school leaders must make endless and daily decisions about what is right for their contexts) but as a Principal of an IB (International Baccalaureate) World School, where the IB attributes of learning and the IB learner profiles are taken as seriously as the knowledge students are learning in their different subjects, there is a real sense of purpose in ensuring that students recognise the value of character and its importance for their future lives.[5]

The attributes of learning that an IB learner works towards such as communication or research skills, or of the IB learner profiles, being Open Minded, Caring, a Risk-Taker and Reflector to name just a few, sit alongside and are very similar to that named in the Education Endowment Foundation's 'Improving Social and Emotional Learning in Primary Schools'.[6] These, in turn, can be seen within the government's Character Education Frameworks of the past few years.[7] There is, therefore, a strong narrative that defining education as self-realisation, personal development and character development for a young person matters and has a clear place in the classroom. Character development has the potential to not only focus on the individual but also on our communities. It is not just the 'who I am' but 'who we are' that should become a pivotal part of education. The Jubilee Centre for Character and Virtues, in its 2015 report, discuss the link between the importance of character attributes in our young people and the potential solutions these might bring to the wider challenges facing society.[8]

Perhaps then, character education is needed now more than ever before.

Within education, we are acutely aware of the deterioration in young people's mental health, the increase in young people's addiction to phones and social media[9] and worries about a decrease in children's communication skills. So, it would seem even more important at such a time to ensure that character education is a fundamental right of every young person who passes across the threshold into our settings. Although the debate about the extent to which character education is needed has been around for years, (sitting somewhere between the mixed ability versus setting and the Ebacc debate), what is becoming more transparent when working with the young people of today's society is that the children we are educating now, need more from us than ever before, if they are to make wise decisions in an increasingly complex context.[10]

Society has changed; as educators, so should we.

We are at a potential sea change within the education sector with regard to what should be education's next priority. As I write, the Curriculum and Assessment

Review led by Professor Becky Francis, alongside the change in political leadership, is providing the sector with a moment of reflection. Where do we head now for 2025 and beyond, and what is and what will be important for the young people we serve as we help them navigate this version of their society?

So, as a leader faced with such change, I will finish with my own reflection.

It is no surprise to me that the majority of secondary school teachers came into our profession to make a difference to children.[11] It is not unrealistic to suggest that if we look back to our own schooling, the reasons we probably came into teaching might have been an excellent lesson on algebra, the distinctive lesson on volcanoes or the fascinating science lesson on osmosis.

It might be this, yes.

Though, if I might suggest, I do not think it is.

It is the character education provided within school life that brings us to reading this chapter or working in schools themselves. It was the teacher who went out of their way to encourage a passion or interest. It was the lesson you struggled with until something clicked, and the subsequent feeling of pride and success followed you for days, sparking a sense of resilience. It was that school trip, where you did not think you could do the extreme sport activity, but you did, sparking that sense of courage. It was the feeling of speaking another language, in another country, travelling abroad for the first time, sparking a sense of risk-taking. It was helping in the charity event, supporting a younger student in a time of need; it was the moment of experiencing support and returning it in abundance to those around you, sparking kindness and compassion.

The power of the classroom lies in…

…the character education you received, without sitting in a lesson to receive it.

…the personal development you gained, without picking up a textbook, to learn it.

…the personal formation of views, opinions, thoughts and feelings, without the need for pen or paper, to remember them.

This is it. The part of education that we cannot see, we cannot measure. The part of education that will not appear in any accountability measure. Ever. The part that tells us intrinsically as educators that what we do matters; that over time, working daily with our young people that we have an impact on all the right areas.

The Wald effect, if you will.

Notes

1 Beckett J, 'Statistician Abraham Wald's Counterintuitive Insight Saved Lives', warhistoryonline.com, 2021.
2 Gatto J, *Dumbing us Down: The Hidden Curriculum of Compulsory Schooling*, New Society Publishers, 2005.
3 De Souza R, 'The Big Ambition: Children's views on school', The Children's Commissioner's Blog, www.childrenscommissioner.gov.uk, April 2024.
4 Postman N, *The End of Education*, Vintage Books, 1995.

5 'Our mission - International Baccalaureate®', ibo.org, 2024.
6 Van Poortvliet M, Clarke A and Gross J, *Improving social and emotional learning in primary schools: Guidance report*, Education Endowment Foundation, 2019.
7 *Character Education Framework: Non-statutory guidance to schools on character education and development for pupils*, Department for Education, 2019.
8 Arthur J et al, *Character Education in UK Schools: Research Report*, Jubilee Centre for Character and Virtues, University of Birmingham, 2015.
9 Hoyle B, 'The Silicon Valley insider who says turn off your phone', *The Times Magazine*, 4 January 2020.
10 Gross J and Robinson L, 'Character – caught or taught?', *Insight*, Special Issue, Chartered College of Teaching, November 2020.
11 '4 Reasons People Become Teachers', teachertapp.co.uk, 2019.

Section 1
Essay 3

Are all good schools alike?
Leora Cruddas

Introduction

Good schools are not all alike. There is no one model of a good school; however, I do think good schools have some things in common. In this chapter, I will try to address the kinds of things that good schools may have in common. I offer these thoughts in the spirit of both curiosity and humility. I doubt all good schools will have all of these features, and schools may give priority to different aspects of culture and practice.

I would like to begin with a short analysis of the purpose of schooling. I will start by saying that I believe that education is a good in itself. It does, of course, serve other purposes. But these purposes are secondary to the fact of education as a public good.

Professor Zongyi Deng is right when he says that education is centrally concerned with the formation of individuals through the cultivation of human powers predicated on the contribution of knowledge, and that is vital to preparing students for the current and future world.[1]

I believe a good school articulates a powerful vision of education and, in the context of that vision, both the children and adults flourish. Achieving and flourishing are not unrelated things – they are fundamentally connected.

In a recent paper I have authored with the Church of England and the Catholic Education Service, we have described human flourishing as a collective vision for our education system. We believe our political leaders, schools and school leaders have a foundational question in common: how do children and young people, and those who educate them in our schools, flourish?

We believe flourishing is both the optimal continuing development of children's potential (the substance of education) and living well as a human being. In our joint paper, we propose that this is a core purpose that is enacted in the dignity with which everyone is treated, the hope with which each is instilled, the relational community in which each is located and the practical wisdom with which each is taught.

We jointly believe that this is a vision centred on serving the common good, relentlessly prioritising the most vulnerable in every classroom, corridor, school and community. It is a vision that not only enables academic excellence but also makes long-lasting life-enhancing contributions to the flourishing of society through mutuality and solidarity, the pursuit of peace, the pursuit of social justice and prioritisation of the environment.

In asserting the need for a vision of education, which is centrally concerned with human flourishing and the cultivation of human powers in today's and future contexts, Deng asks three powerful questions:

- 'What does it mean to be an autonomous and responsible individual who is actively participating in and interacting with the current and future world characterised by transnational economies, an ever-increasing rate of information exchange and mobility, rapid developments of new technologies, uncertainty, climate change, human-induced environmental disasters, and wars, among others?'
- 'What intellectual, emotional, moral, social, cross-cultural, and technological powers would he or she need to develop to become free and independent individual and to face the challenges of the world?'
- 'How and in what ways would academic disciplines and specialised fields contribute to the development of such powers?'[2]

These are important considerations about schooling and its social purposes. School leaders are, in my view, public leaders, and must be able to articulate the purpose of the school they lead within this wider social and global context.

These questions can be answered in different ways. In considering these questions, we should also be alive to the significant evidence base and literature we now have on effective schooling.

In the rest of this chapter, I will attempt to consider what a good school might look like through four different perspectives: for the children it educates, for the adults it employs, for the parents and families, and for the community it serves. I offer these thoughts as a reflection rather than a blueprint.

What a good school might look like for children

A sense of belonging and feeling included

I have written elsewhere[3] about the importance of belonging. Owen Eastwood, author of *Belonging, The Ancient Code of Togetherness*, writes: 'To feel a sense of belonging is to feel accepted, to feel seen and to feel included by a group of people, believing that we fit in, trusting we will be protected by them. To not feel belonging is to experience the precarious and insecure sense of an outsider'.[4]

There are some worrying trends in terms of our children and young people feeling like they belong in our schools. The PISA 2022 report for England[5] found that pupils in England reported a significantly lower average level of satisfaction with their lives, and fewer reported that they feel they belong at school than their peers across the OECD. These data are supported by other reports, like the Children's Society *Good Childhood Report*,[6] which shows trends in children's wellbeing. The Children's Society research seeks to understand how young people feel about different aspects of their lives. 10 per cent of the children aged 10 to 17 who completed the household survey in May and June 2023 had low wellbeing, and almost a third were unhappy with at least one specific area of their lives.

According to Coe, Kime and Singleton, 'School belonging is a construct that has been the subject of a significant body of research, originating in the humanistic psychology of Maslow and Rogers'.[7] They cite a widely-used definition, from Goodenow and Grady: 'the extent to which students feel personally accepted, respected, included, and supported by others in the school social environment'.[8]

The current crisis of school attendance is perhaps an expression that some of our children do not feel that they belong in our schools. We cannot educate our children if they are not in school, so we need to do more to make sure each and every one of our children feels that they belong. This is especially true for some of our more vulnerable children, those with special educational needs and disabilities; those who live in poverty, are in the care system; children who are deemed to be young offenders and those at risk of offending; children experiencing mental ill health; children living with acute health needs; unaccompanied asylum-seeking children and those fleeing violence; children living in families where there is domestic violence, drugs or unsafe homes; and those experiencing trauma.

A truly inclusive school is one where all our children feel they belong and are included.

A positive and safe environment

Children cannot flourish in environments that are unsafe, where pupil behaviour is disruptive or dangerous. A good school has safe and secure routines and expectations of behaviour that are well understood by adults and children.

This includes not just the behaviour policy of the school and how it is implemented, but also student peer culture and behavioural norms. The *School Environment and Leadership: Evidence Review*[9] offers the following reflections about the importance of peer culture and behavioural norms:

- Shared beliefs among students about the value of school and education;
- Norms and expectations about behaviour around the school and in classrooms; and
- Pro-social values and behaviours: cooperation, respect, inclusion.

So, arguably, a good school focuses not just on its behaviour policy but on supporting the pro-social norms of cooperation and harmony, respect and a sense of community between and among both children and adults in a school.

A knowledge-rich curriculum that cultivates human capacity and joy

Finally, what is taught is vital. I am a strong advocate of Michael Young's powerful knowledge.[10] I believe that knowledge is both powerful and joyous. The end it serves is the development of human capacity. Deng writes:

> 'Inextricably intertwined with the teaching of knowledge is another equally important purpose of education—the formation of individuals through the cultivation of human powers—that is vital to preparing students for the current and future world. The recognition of this important purpose calls for an understanding of what students should become and what powers they need to develop in the 21st century and beyond. It too calls for a recognition that specialized and disciplinary knowledge is not something taught for its own end but a powerful resource/vehicle for developing human powers.'[11]

Children need to feel that what they are taught is meaningful, that they are contributing to the human endeavour and that they are connected to what they are learning. There is much research on the importance of self-efficacy in learning, in classrooms where pupils are motivated to achieve a high standard, where responsive action is taken when they are not reaching the standard, and a curriculum and approach based on the principle that every pupil will master key ideas.[12]

So, our children need to feel that they belong in our schools; they should not just be safe but learn prosocial norms, have good relationships with peers and teachers, and have a sense of their own agency, feel connected to what they are learning, and enjoy being at school.

What a good school might look like for adults

As Lynn Swaner and Andy Wolf say, 'where there are few flourishing adults, there will be few flourishing children'.[13] So it is perhaps as important to pay attention to the flourishing of adults in our schools as the flourishing of children.

Data from the Education Support Teacher Wellbeing Index (2023), corroborated more recently by The Working Lives of Teachers (2024), tells us that 78% of all education staff report being stressed, and this rises to 89% of all leaders and 95% of headteachers. And 36% of teachers report experiencing burnout.[14]

So, there is a problem for us to solve here. This is a duty of care we must exercise as a principle in its own right – the ethics of being a good employer. But it is also important because of the recruitment and retention crisis we face.

The Education Endowment Foundation reviewed the evidence base on school leadership, culture, climate and structure for staff retention.[15] They find that there are three interrelated leadership approaches and associated practices highlighted in the report:

- Prioritising professional development;
- Building relational trust; and
- Improving working conditions.

Prioritising professional development

The Education Endowment Foundation's rapid evidence[16] review finds that there are some practices that contribute positively, in particular to teacher retention:

- Providing constructive feedback to support teachers in innovating and working collaboratively to address specific challenges they may be facing.
- Giving teachers opportunities – and removing any barriers – to accessing professional development opportunities.
- Cultivating leadership potential by supporting early career teachers to innovate in their practice or take part in mentoring opportunities.

I have written previously that professional development is most effective in a school culture in which teachers feel supported, valued and trusted and where leaders have thought carefully about how to protect the time needed to engage in professional development.[17]

Building relational trust

People do not want to work for leaders or organisations they do not trust. The authors of the Education Endowment Foundation's rapid evidence review[18] suggest that leaders should:

- Demonstrate individualised consideration;
- treat people with respect;

- consider teacher [or staff] voice; and
- promote collegiality.

What is striking about this is that it is not rocket science. Building relational trust in our organisations is core to the way in which we enact culture and make our schools places where adults can flourish.

Improving working conditions

I have written elsewhere[19] that I do not think that workload should be viewed on its own, but rather as part of a wider set of conditions in our schools and trusts – we should not be focused only on the *transactional* nature of workload reduction. We should also be building *relational* cultures.

The Education Endowment Foundation defines working conditions in schools as 'a variety of physical, organisational, sociological, political, cultural, psychological, and educational features of teachers' jobs'.[20] Synthesising the findings of these relevant studies allowed the Education Endowment Foundation to identify and categorise a range of leadership practices associated with the approach of improving working conditions. These include:

- supporting teacher professional autonomy;
- promoting collegiality in schools;
- developing an equitable support and recognition system;
- establishing an effective communication structure; and
- supporting teachers with student disciplinary matters.

We should also not underestimate the influence of headteachers on their schools, as recent research from the Education Policy Institute[21] has shown. The headteacher controls, to a large extent, the climate and working conditions within each school. In a good school, the adults would have a strong sense of their own agency, good collegial relationships with other adults and feel recognised and trusted.

One of the most important points here is perhaps the last bullet point – supporting teachers with pupil behaviour. We know that poor pupil behaviour is an important factor in teacher wellbeing. So there is a direct read-across from what a good school feels like for children to what a good school feels like for adults. As I wrote in the section above, a good school focuses not just on its behaviour policy but on supporting the pro-social norms of cooperation and harmony, respect and a sense of community between and among both children and adults in a school.

What a good school might look like for parents and families

Elsewhere, I analyse the decline of trust and confidence in public institutions.[22] I cite the report, *Democracy in Dark Times*, in which professors James Hunter, Carl Bowman and Kyle Puetz describe a slowly evolving crisis of credibility for American institutions.[23] The UK has long prided itself on the strength of its institutions, but the World Values Survey[24], one of the largest academic social surveys in the world, shows that the British public is not as convinced as they once were, and we are now more negative than many other countries.

The fracturing of the social contract can be seen in the critical fall in school attendance, an increase in poor behaviour and an exponential rise in parental complaints. Lemov *et al* argue that 'schools can no longer count on receiving the goodwill and trust of the parents they serve'. They go on to say that 'Like the nations they are part of, schools are institutions that rely on a social contract to do their work'.[25]

So we must turn our attention to rebuilding the social contract.

A secure social contract

Because things are difficult right now, it is hard to write that a good school is one where there is a high level of trust between the school and its parent and families. In many cases, schools will be in the process of rebuilding that trust and confidence. It is very hard work to rebuild the social contract, but it is only through establishing a secure social contract that I think we can flourish together.

Doing what we have always done in schools to build parental and wider public trust and confidence is unlikely to remain a good option. We have to think differently, 'do' differently. Lemov *et al* propose that we need to be much more purposeful and deliberative in building connection and belonging. There are many ways to do this in our schools and our trusts. Working with parents and the wider public in a collaborative way, directing our shared attention at resolving social problems and achieving shared goals or purpose, is a way to rebuild trust and confidence, to rebuild the social contract.

Building relational trust with the parents and families

Building relational trust is a key way in which we rebuild the social contract.

In a wonderful blog, 'The Case for Strengthening Family-School Coherence', Verity Howorth, Director of Training at The Reach Foundation, writes that 'we should stop thinking that relationship building is a magical gift that only a certain few possess' (Howorth, 2024).[26] She talks about the 15-year interaction with the education system that families experience. She writes:

'What is consistent throughout though, is that they [families] will always require a relationship, because all people do. We agree with Professor Robert Waldinger, in the 80-year-long Harvard Study of Adult Development:

> To say that human beings require warm relationships is no touchy-feely idea. It is a hard fact. We need nutrition, we need exercise, we need purpose and we need each other.

Our job, as school, trust and community leaders, is to acknowledge the immense privilege we have in holding these relationships, to humbly give up any idea we might have of ourselves as saviours, and to crack on with working together in our shared village.'[27]

This is not an additional thing or a nice-to-have. The Education Endowment Fund finds that for a relatively small investment, positive parental engagement can add an average of four months' additional progress. For the Education Endowment Foundation, 'family engagement means teachers and schools involving parents in supporting their children's academic learning'.

So, a school that is 'good' for parents and families may be one where they feel a sense of connection, where the social contract of trust and confidence feels secure, and where they experience strong relationships and positive engagement with the school.

What a good school might look like in its community

A good school is anchored in its community. It is not perceived in its community to be a distant, somewhat remote or detached thing. And it also has a deep sense of being accountable to the community it serves.

Accountability to those we serve

The highest form of accountability is the individual's professional accountability for the quality of her or his own work and to the people whom the profession serves.

I reflected in *New Domains of Educational Leadership* that: 'Rather than accountability being perceived as something that is only externally imposed by the government, we could shift it in the direction of governance boards being ever-more explicit and eloquent about their vision, their "theory of change" and their measures that will evidence success. The measures will need to include the government's performance measures but need not be constrained by them'.[28]

I would like to note here the importance of strong governance of a good school. Governance in our school system in England takes different forms depending on the type of school, but I do not believe a school can be a good school without strong governance and without a strong belief that we are accountable to the communities we serve.

Seeing our communities as an asset

It is perhaps easy to talk about some of the impacts of endemic poverty and disadvantage in the communities we serve. And we should not underestimate the impact of poverty on the life chances of children. We must also insist that the government uses the big levers of state to reduce child poverty. But we should also not lose sight of the strengths and assets in our communities. I think a good school helps to identify and build strength in communities.

In a lovely blog, 'Bacon sandwiches and academic excellence: an unlikely alliance', Victoria Hirst, Director of Communities at The Reach Foundation, reflects on the desire to develop really strong school-community partnerships to strengthen families' wraparound support and improve their outcomes in school. She makes the case that this is not new work:

> There are many examples of schools working with wider partners—be it public, private or third sector organisations—to alleviate some of the pressure on schools and families, and increase their capacity right from birth (and, in some cases, pregnancy). And there have been many advocates for the development of comprehensive place-based cradle to career models, with schools playing an integral role.[29]

The Reach Foundation's Cradle to Career Partnership is codifying the ways in which schools can build collective capacity by working directly with their communities.

Concluding thoughts

In this chapter, I have not tried to argue that good schools are not all alike. I have tried instead to reflect on the things that good schools may have in common through an exploration of what this might look like for children, adults, parents and families and communities.

I would like to return in these concluding thoughts to the concept of human flourishing as a collective vision for our education system. Schools are where society is created. They must be places in which everyone is treated with dignity, places which create relational community, build prosocial norms, where a love of knowledge and the joy of learning is experienced, places that nurture self-efficacy and agency, where children, adults and their families feel a sense of belonging. This is not an academic exercise, but rather a practical wisdom.

Notes

1 Deng Z, 'Powerful knowledge, educational potential and knowledge-rich curriculum: pushing the boundaries', *Journal of Curriculum Studies*, 2022, 54:5, 2022, pp 599–617.

2 Deng Z, 'Powerful knowledge, educational potential and knowledge-rich curriculum: pushing the boundaries', *Journal of Curriculum Studies*, 2022, 54:5, 2022, p 612.
3 Cruddas L, *New Domains of Educational Leadership*, John Catt, 2025.
4 Eastwood O, *Belonging: The Ancient Code of Togetherness*, Quercus, 2021, p 22.
5 Ingram J et al, *PISA 2022:National Report for England*, Department for Education, 2023.
6 *The Good Childhood Report 2023*, The Children's Society, 2023.
7 Coe R, Kime S and Singleton D, *A model for school environment and leadership (School environment and leadership: Evidence review)*, Evidence Based Education, 2022, p 29.
8 Goodenow C and Grady K, 'The relationship of school belonging and friends' values to academic motivation among urban adolescent students', *The Journal of Experimental Education*, 62,1, 1993, p 80.
9 Coe R, Kime S and Singleton D, *A model for school environment and leadership (School environment and leadership: Evidence review)*, Evidence Based Education, 2022, p 31.
10 Young M and Lambert D with Roberts C and Roberts M, *Knowledge and the Future School: Curriculum and Social Justice*, Bloomsbury, 2014.
11 Deng Z, 'Powerful knowledge, educational potential and knowledge-rich curriculum: pushing the boundaries', Journal of Curriculum Studies, 2022, 54:5, 2022, p 612.
12 Coe R, Kime S and Singleton D, *A model for school environment and leadership (School environment and leadership: Evidence review)*, Evidence Based Education, 2022, p 41.
13 Swaner L and Wolfe A, *Flourishing Together: A Christian Vision for Students, Educators, and Schools*, William B Eerdmans Publishing, 2021.
14 *Teacher Wellbeing Index 2023*, Education Support, 2023.
15 Nguyen D, Huat See B, Brown C and Kokotsak D, *Reviewing the evidence base on school leadership, culture, climate and structure for teacher retention*, EEF, 2023.
16 Nguyen D, Huat See B, Brown C and Kokotsak D, *Reviewing the evidence base on school leadership, culture, climate and structure for teacher retention*, EEF, 2023.
17 Cruddas L, *New Domains of Educational Leadership*, John Catt, 2025.
18 Nguyen D, Huat See B, Brown C and Kokotsak D, *Reviewing the evidence base on school leadership, culture, climate and structure for teacher retention*, EEF, 2023.
19 Cruddas L, *New Domains of Educational Leadership*, John Catt, 2025.
20 Nguyen D, Huat See B, Brown C and Kokotsak D, *Reviewing the evidence base on school leadership, culture, climate and structure for teacher retention*, EEF, 2023.
21 Zucollo J, Cardem Dias J, Jimenez E and Braakmann N, *The influence of headteachers on their schools*, EPI, 2023.
22 Cruddas L, *New Domains of Educational Leadership*, John Catt, 2025.
23 Davison Hunter J, Desportes Bowman C and Puetz K, *Democracy in Dark Times*, Institute for Advanced Studies in Culture, 2020,
24 Duffy B, *How the UK lost confidence in its institutions*, www.uk-values.org, 2024.
25 Lemov D, Lewis H, Williams D and Frazier D, *Reconnect: Building School Culture for Meaning, Purpose and Belonging*, Jossey Bass, 2023, p xxi.
26 Howorth V, 'The case for strengthening family-school coherence', The Reach Foundation, 2024.
27 Cited in Howorth V, 'The case for strengthening family-school coherence', The Reach Foundation, 2024.
28 Cruddas L, *New Domains of Educational Leadership*, John Catt, 2025.
29 Hirst V, 'Bacon sandwiches and academic excellence: an unlikely alliance', The Reach Foundation, 2024.

Section 1
Essay 4

Should schools serve individuals or communities?

Melanie Ferron-Evans

It is valuable for individuals to reflect on personal history every so often to remind themselves of experiences and personal stories that have shaped their fundamental beliefs and principles, and the contributions they make to our communities as a result.

It is a sign of my age that, as a young child, I clearly remember being able to list my name, village, county, country and telephone number by rote; in case, my mum said, I got lost! Almost six decades later, this can still be recited, never to be forgotten. On reflection, I belonged to a small village community, and this is all I knew. The knowledge of communities and the wider world grew slowly and surely alongside me. It appeared to make some sense as I moved into early adulthood, without the use of technology or a sense of the global complexities of the vast world community we all now inhabit in these fractured times. It is an important reflection and comparison to draw on in the 2020s, where young children do not recite their sense of place and belonging, finding themselves propelled at lightning speed, into a big world at a small age, reliant on families and/or schools to make sense of it all.

Five decades in education, and the young child referred to above often feels lost, for good, challenging reasons. Different school communities have meant teaching in Wales, England, a village, town and city, Japan, a township in South Africa, and for the last decade, leading a school as headteacher. In all of these places and roles, a sense of community has been at the heart of the many schools experienced, but in such vastly complex ways. Learning has taken place in shacks and shanty towns with the same sense of purpose, awe and wonderment as a brand-new build in a UK city or town. Place, in terms of the concrete buildings or constructs where we learn, is less important than the power of teaching and learning itself.

A trip to Robben Island in 2005 and Nelson Mandela's 6x6 cell illustrated this power to me. Mandela inspired prisoners to use their innate knowledge and skills, creating a university of life born out of years of oppression and incarceration. A tour of the island takes visitors to a rock quarry where the political prisoners were put to work, day after day, year after year, in unsafe conditions. In the quarry, there is a cave. It was used by prisoners, from the most educated to those who could not read or write, gathered there under Mandela's leadership to learn from each other. The cave's mantra, 'each one, teach one', epitomises the power of serving individuals amidst intense suffering. This provided an education to those deprived of formal learning in their past, producing future leaders in medicine, law and other inspirational roles post-apartheid. It is interesting to note that these life stories are shared with visitors by ex-prisoners themselves, adding an extra layer of true understanding to this unimaginable experience.

In 1995, Mandela returned to the quarry following his release, alongside other former prisoners, as part of the remembrance of the past. Mandela placed a stone in the middle of the quarry. Each former prisoner followed his example until a pyramid of rocks formed a memorial of their time together on the island. This still stands today. Where is Mandela's stone? In the middle, at the bottom – a metaphor for transformational leadership rooted in a belief that the future will be better. Leadership which inspires wonder, joy and wisdom in the midst of desperation and oppression. 'Each one, teach one' and the cairn symbolise, powerfully, the importance of serving the individual and community as the two are intrinsically linked and survive anywhere humans will survive.

Some may disagree with the phrase 'to serve'. It can appear old-fashioned, linked to images of subservience and inequitable hierarchies. We are less likely to disagree with the need for excellent, enthusiastic, inspiring teachers. The very definition of such excellence involves hard work, dedication and belief in each child's achievements and overall success. This, it can be argued, is service. Such teachers are dedicated to meeting the needs of the students in their care. This idea of service can be misconstrued by some and devalued. It can appear demeaning rather than a powerful commitment to empowering the next generation to be lifelong learners. The Oxford Dictionary provides a straightforward description of the verb 'to serve': 'The action of helping or doing work for someone'. This notion is one we could emphasise with pride when speaking about the teaching profession. It is a privilege to teach and lead in our schools, whatever challenges we face, and the language we use to describe our vocation has the power to inspire others into the profession. George Bernard Shaw's famous comments about the purpose of life resonate with the purpose of teaching.

> This is the true joy in life, being used for a purpose recognised by yourself as a mighty one. Being a force of nature instead of a feverish, selfish little clod of ailments and grievances, complaining that the world will not devote itself to making you happy.[1]
>
> I am of the opinion that my life belongs to the whole community and as long as I live, it is my privilege to do for it what I can. I want to be thoroughly used up when I die, for the harder I work, the more I live. I rejoice in life for its own sake. Life is no brief candle to me. It is a sort of splendid torch which I have got hold of for the moment and I want to make it burn as brightly as possible before handing it on to future generations.[2]

A teacher's role is to find the 'splendid torch', feeling proud that it is a noble profession. It is a profession that serves our children, our community and wider world, making a real difference. Teachers and those who work in schools need to be reminded of this constantly to lift spirits and self-belief in current times, where some appear not to care about the profession, which inherently serves others. School Leadership can make a huge contribution to the belief in the teaching profession and the way individuals transform individuals in school communities across the UK and beyond.

Just defining 'community' in the world of academia highlights the range of different understandings there are when it comes to grouping people together and what this means.[3] This is highlighted by Ted Bradshaw, who observes that a community can be a group of people with diverse characteristics, linked by social ties and a sense of place.[4] Yet, in stark contrast, it can be groups of people who share common interests or a sense of identity which transcends place. For the sake of this discussion, with a focus on schools, the former definition appears the most useful.

The question around whether schools serve individuals or the community is perhaps the wrong one if we accept that it must be both. Instead, it is more important to ask with some urgency: how do we serve individuals in the community, especially in the current era? Not since the Second World War has education or worldwide communities experienced such a seismic shift as that posed by the COVID pandemic. In a time of enforced isolation for individuals and families, exacerbating social inequalities, the power of schools and the power of individuals within the school community entered a new way of serving. A new community language was born through rules and regulations beyond the school remit: Bubbles, testing, hand sanitiser, safe distances, remote learning, you-are-on-mute, Google Classroom, face masks and keep-your-distance. It took educational leadership to make sense of this foreign world for families and learners of all ages in our local communities. It took educationalists to make sense of this with no blueprint or exemplar materials, or textbooks. Interestingly, in a time of broken, fractured connections and isolation, schoolteachers demonstrated the power of schools to reconnect and reinvent ways of teaching and learning. This included embracing technology, innovation and a commitment to helping the community way beyond the classroom. Schools made

PPE, they delivered provisions, they found new, effective ways to communicate, and they cared for the children of key workers to ensure that essential services could still be provided in our local communities.

Technology connected us all, and those most in need were still able to access school sites. Looking back, this time seems to inhabit a different world as schools return to 'normal'. The connotations of this world are not helpful, as there is no return but a new educational landscape to navigate. Whilst COVID itself both connected and disconnected community members, it contributed to the growing mental health crisis in our younger generation in the UK, and it can be suggested exacerbated underlying vulnerabilities and fractured family situations already present. This growing crisis, with other sources of help through the NHS, Children's services and social care less available, places a greater strain on schools and the urgent need to ensure that we address wellbeing as well as learning. As a result, there is a growing expectation that schools and the world of education will continue to provide services for individuals and the community which are different from pre-COVID times. Jonathan Beal, in his research work, summarises the effects of this isolation in three areas: a widening attainment gap, learning loss and heightened emotional and social needs. For these reasons, he argues for more collaborative networks within communities to establish more holistic support for our children.[5]

How do we continue to adapt quickly and effectively with such conflicting demands on finite and underfunded resources? Whatever the challenge, schools have to be underpinned by firm foundations which link to the local community, its past, present and future. Whatever the level of change and challenge, we need to have teaching and learning at the heart of all we do, underpinned by core values.

During a recent staff training session in our school, Mark Burns reminded our staff of the power of the past and what he called 'cathedral-building'. He presented a picture of a stonemason chipping away at a huge stone for a cathedral he would never see through to completion.[6]

As educators, one of our core purposes is to make a positive difference to the lives of the individuals we teach; just like Liverpool Anglican Cathedral, started by stone masons in 1904 and finished 74 years later. It was built across two World Wars and through the economic decline of Liverpool. Like the stonemason, we are able to see the outcome of individual successes, but rarely. There is a huge joy to be found in the student we meet in later years in their line of work and the comments on how we contributed personally, or as a whole school, to their success. The rare letter or card sent, the visit back to school or the chance encounter is a 'cathedral moment'.

The challenge is that we cannot always see the finished product. We often make the most difference to those who are the hardest to teach and may never see them again. We have to believe in them and the difference we have made, and imagine their success. This belief is part of the joy of teaching.

In the toughest of times, core values and fundamental beliefs are the bedrock of a school and community. The example of the cathedral resonates in our school, situated in a small Welsh village in North Wales. At the heart of the village community, in its not-too-distant history, was the Ruabon Red Brick industry.

Henry Dennis, a famous industrialist in Wrexham in the late nineteenth century, founded a company in 1878 that would become Dennis Ruabon Tiles Ltd. Dennis was born in Bodmin, Cornwall, studied civil engineering and travelled to Wales to supervise the construction of a tramway at the Llangollen slate quarry. He spent some time in Spain at a lead mine and later returned to Wales after amassing a considerable personal fortune. Dennis became managing director of the Hafod Colliery and, by 1878, had established the Hafod Brickworks. The business flourished at a time when demand for red bricks and terracotta was high. By 1893, a new factory was established, and it became known as the 'Red Works'.

Workers in the factory produced massive amounts of terracotta, earning the village of Ruabon the nickname Terracottapolis. An individual brought fame to the small village of Ruabon through the distinctive red bricks from that area. Each red brick formed the popular resource, used to build schools, hospitals, universities, law courts, public houses and other key buildings in cities across the UK. Most notably of all, they helped, piece by piece, to build the Pier Head Building in Cardiff Bay as well as the Liverpool University Victoria Building, housing the world of governance and learning.[7]

Many years after 1893, I became personally involved in a moment of awe and wonder linked to the Ruabon Red Brick. I was on holiday with my family in Europe. We were walking on the beach following a storm, and one of my young sons found half a red brick embossed with half the letters of the village school where I taught. Whilst they were not as involved in my own sense of wonderment surrounding this find, it led to some very thought-provoking discussions about how the brick found its way so far from home and lots of opportunities for future assemblies and the promotion of awe and wonder in our school.

The Red Brick is a solid link between the individual and the local community. It promotes pride in history. It is used in innovative ways in our curriculum, enriching local knowledge and skills through the past, and preparing students for the future. It is a constant extended metaphor used to emphasise our culture and ethos, building success on firm foundations.

Every school and community has a story to tell which transcends time and can sustain us in times of challenge. 'Effective implementation of culturally relevant education which requires significant levels of cultural competence and understanding, is positively associated with increases in academic and effective outcomes across content areas'.[8]

Such community stories unite a school and anchor it in its local community. This forms a dual partnership where school and community complement and benefit from each other. Teachers and school staff, knowing their local stories and demography, build understanding and trust amongst stakeholders and contribute to student success. New teachers need to be encouraged to know the history of the local community they serve and the demographic makeup, particularly important in areas where there is a diverse intake, to ensure efficacy is based on understanding of the individual and the area where they live.

Ruabon Red Brick may work for our school at this moment in leadership, through the symbolism of something historic, solidly rooted in local pride. A community story has to be practical, however, rooted in the present reality and challenges, which we need to understand. A change in demographics can impact the socio-economic makeup, and knowing the individual needs of the students and staff in the school community. This can be found, in part, through group data and test analysis, but more importantly, through the time it takes to know the stories of individuals as well as those of the collective community. This is a particular challenge now as we navigate our way through an educational era, post-pandemic.

'The COVID-19 Pandemic may be a thing of the past, but its impact in schools is not' by Tim Oates presents a research-rich picture of the impact the pandemic is now having on each cohort passing through our schools, 'in waves'.[9] This is posing different challenges across the primary and secondary sectors, including literacy and numeracy levels, difficulties in reading at secondary entry, and arrested language development and lack of toilet training at primary. This is why there is no 'return to normal' but the need to lead through the ongoing challenges in an informed and effective way, depending on different contexts.

The response required depends on us ensuring that our learners are, in fact, ready to learn, academically, socially and emotionally. In the current climate, with increased anxiety and mental health concerns for our children, the demands on services beyond teaching in the classroom are so great, against a backdrop of significant budget cuts.

It also poses difficult questions about the purpose of education at this moment in history. As each cohort works through our schools, the teaching profession will need to be resilient, patient, innovative and part of a compassionate community where teachers are attuned and generous in the time given to individuals. It will require kind, resolute, innovative leadership to provide solutions to the current problems. The teachers who connected so well with distance learning during the pandemic are the same professionals who will be required to reconnect learners in the classroom and beyond. Time is showing that being 'back at school' is not necessarily being 'ready to learn' for so many complex reasons, some of which are still emerging. Support will be needed for staff and students at the primary and secondary levels and in university studies. This is not a quick fix and will take a decade at least to work through, with possible far-reaching consequences for teaching and learning and the purpose of education.

A good education for every individual cannot rest on the functionalist view, where schools prepare learners to meet the demands of the labour market. Instead, we must educate our children so they have opportunities and choices, regardless of background or ability.

In the current climate, we will need to continue to rely on our core values and teaching and learning strategies that continue to serve us well, but we will also have to adapt and align educational support programmes alongside specialist support for individual wellbeing. Far from distracting from the core purpose of teaching and learning, this will ensure that our children are able to progress as we remove barriers to learning, many of which are currently COVID-related. This will take time, appropriately funded resources and effectively targeted interventions.

This brings us back to the question: Should schools serve individuals or communities? A school by itself cannot fulfil the learning potential of our children without renewing and revitalising connections with family and community. We will have to ask some difficult questions about our communication and relationship with our families and stakeholders. How do we improve family and community engagement? Do our children feel they are part of a community that cares about them? Are they building trust or suspicion? Are they hearing inspiring, hopeful stories which add to their self-worth and sense of belonging? Is the balance right between looking after their general wellbeing and their learning? Are they developing transferable real-life skills alongside subject knowledge and engagement in learning for learning's sake?

Today, as we work in difficult circumstances and amidst global conflict and instability, the need to create a future generation that can adapt to a rapidly changing landscape is a moral, social and economic imperative for leadership in our schools. This is emphasised in Eleanor Roosevelt's last important work, *Tomorrow is Now*. Her book was written at a time of great world danger and uncertainty, just like now. Inspirationally, it was written as she was dying, yet she felt compelled to share something of real importance with the world. In her words, 'We face the future fortified only with the lessons we have learned from the past. It is today that we must create the world of the future. Spinoza, I think, pointed out that we ourselves can make experience valuable when, by imagination and reason, we turn it into foresight. It is that foresight we must acquire. In a very real sense, tomorrow is now'.[10]

Our 'now' depends on our belief in the profession and our ability to drive the difference we make, knowing that we will make a significant difference to the lives of young people in our local communities and, thus, collectively, the wider world.

Notes

1 Shaw GB, 'Epistle Dedicatory to Arthur Bingham Walkley', *Man and Superman: A Comedy and a Philosophy*, 1903.
2 Shaw GB, 'Art and Public Money', a speech given at The Municipal Technical College and School of Art, Brighton (1907) quoted in Henderson A, *George Bernard Shaw: His Life and His Works*, 1911.

3 Link H, McNall T, Sayre A, Schmidt R and Swa, R, 'The definition of Community: A Student Perspective', *Partnerships: A journal of Service Learning & Civic Engagement*, Volume 2, Autumn 2011.
4 Bradshaw T, 'The Post-Place Community: Contributions to the debate about the Definition of Community', *Journal of the Community Development Society*, Volume 39, Issue 1, 2008.
5 Beal J, *The Importance of Community and Collaboration in Education after Covid-19*, The Tony Little Centre for Research and Innovation in Learning, June 2020.
6 Burns M and Griffiths A, *The Learning Imperative*, Crown House Publishing, 2018.
7 *Terracottapolic: Local History*, Ty Pawb Publication/Exhibition, May 2022.
8 Aranson B and Laughter J, 'The Theory and Practice of Culturally Relevant Education: A synthesis of Research Across Content Areas', *Review of Educational Research*, Volume 86, Issue 1, 2016.
9 Oates T, *The Covid-19 pandemic may be a thing of the past – its impact in schools is not*, ASCL, September 2024.
10 Roosevelt E, *Tomorrow is Now: It is Today That we Must Create the World of the Future*, Penguin Classics, 2013. Michaelis D, *Eleanor. A biography of Eleanor Roosevelt*, Simon & Schuster, 2020.

Section 1 Essay 5

Who decides what is a good education?

Tim Oates

At exactly the time of writing, England is in the midst of a government review of the National Curriculum and national qualifications. During such times, the answer to 'who decides what is a good education?' tends to focus on who is leading the review, such as the three crucial reviews of curriculum and qualifications by Sir Ron Dearing in the 1990s, and the voices, evidence, political pressures and 'assumptions of the Zeitgeist' which they take into account in making their recommendations. In those reviews, Ron Dearing was regarded as a master of reconciliation and negotiation of the beartraps of competing views of 'good education'.[1]

When the National Curriculum was reviewed in 2010, over 2,000 submissions were received in the statutory consultation on the Secretary of State's proposed changes. In late 2024, over 7,000 responses were received during the 'national conversation' on 'what's working well and what could work better in the curriculum'. Interestingly, both of these figures pale into insignificance in the light of the 103,000 received by the national qualifications regulator, OFQUAL, during the suspension of national examinations during the COVID-19 pandemic. The National Curriculum and national qualifications are seen as the policy instruments which dominate the school curriculum. Add accountability measures, national inspection and a national funding formula to that list, and the picture of state control of what constitutes 'good education' seems pretty absolute. 'Who decides?' appears to be located in state control, with the development of these instruments punctuated by periodic national consultations. Ask AI who controls education in England – that seems a contemporary thing to do – and unequivocally the answer comes back: 'The Department for Education...is the government department that controls education in England...[and] the Secretary of State is responsible for the Department for Education (DfE)'s work'.[2] It is true that, in England, in law, the Secretary of State for Education does indeed determine the content of the National Curriculum by proposing to parliament, following statutory consultation, any changes to the National Curriculum. Simple. But actually, too simple. And very ahistorical in its perspective.

RA Butler's 1944 Education Act set up an interesting balance of power between central and local government. National measures such as a raised school leaving age, the implementation of Spens' proposal for the tripartite system of technical, grammar and secondary modern schools provided a common structure, whilst over 100 local authorities would determine precise arrangements regarding curriculum, with their plans approved by the Secretary of State.[3] With this, 'who decides' was designed to allow a measure of commonality, but with local representation regarding precise focus and details of the curriculum. Inspection continued, as it had done since its inception in 1839, to focus on children's acquisition of fundamentals of the '3Rs'. The 1944 Act was explicitly focused on raising standards and reducing inequalities. As Andy Green's international comparisons highlight,[4] this reflected rising state engagement with a diverse education system previously dominated by highly varied church and local interests. When England implemented its first National Curriculum, few nations had national curricula – France, Finland and Sweden notably had a history of national curricula. As of 2024, almost all nations possess one.

Standards and equity. These are not only at the heart of the 1944 Act and the public funding of schools and compulsory education, but remain central to all later changes and reforms, right to the present. While the aims may have remained remarkably constant, there have been sharp disagreements (for example, The Black Papers and The Great Debate[5]) about the means of achieving them, including comprehensive versus selective education, vocational versus academic focus, competence-based approaches versus knowledge-rich models, exam reform and so on. But the consensus on aims (equity and attainment) persists, and is important. The immense variation in structural forms of education in England (size of schools, selective/comprehensive, age of school transfers, availability of places in special schools, etc, academy status, etc.) suggests high levels of localised determination of 'good education'.

But fluidity in this diversity is interesting – relaxation of some factors, tightening of others, then further pendulum swings. No national curriculum until 1988; National Curriculum and national assessment required of all state schools; then relaxation for schools moving to academy status; then, in 2024, a proposed reversal: all schools other than independent to be required once again to follow the National Curriculum.

The development of the National Curriculum in 1988 marked a watershed in 'who decides what a good education is' – a shift from local determination within Local Education Authorities (LEAs) to state determination – its implementation accompanied by fundamental yet under-recognised changes in the patterns of funding of schools; all reducing the power of LEAs in respect of educational provision. These changes were major step changes in 'who decides'. But this was not a sudden cliff-edge of change; the previous decades had been punctuated by escalating restriction through national 'guidance circulars', school inspection and qualifications reform, with concerns about variation in the quality of schooling and inequality of outcomes being present in official records and public statements regarding policy intent and practical actions.

Post-2010, we saw a relaxation of some elements of restriction – an emphasis on 'school autonomy'; the formation of 'free schools' and academies – but tightening of other central policy instruments such as accountability measures, inspection, national assessment and qualifications, teachers' standards, and high-fidelity teaching initiatives in maths (Maths Mastery) and literacy (phonics-based reading schemes).

One interesting aspect of forms of restriction is 'relative loading' of the curriculum – the emphasis on some subjects versus others. This is prone to very different 'signalling and restriction' in different national settings. In the putatively 'high school autonomy' nations of Finland and Estonia, it has historically been the case that the amount of contact time which should be spent on each subject is stipulated as a formal requirement of the national curriculum. In England, this is specifically excluded by law – the Secretary of State cannot state or require specific time allocations. Time on the subject is highly defining of what standards can be attained. It is intrinsically tied to models and assumptions of 'good education'. In England, the relative loading – the relative importance – of subjects is heavily determined by labelling subjects in different ways, e.g. 'core' and 'foundation' subjects; the amount of material in each programme of study; whether they are tested; how they appear in national performance targets and other accountability measures such as inspection; special funding to subjects and schools; and the general messaging about relative importance.

The 2010 review of the National Curriculum also strongly emphasised the distinction between the National Curriculum – a parsimonious listing of desired outcomes – and the school curriculum, the reality of what is taught minute by minute in the classroom.[6] This is Lawrence Stenhouse's 'curriculum-making at the level of the school'[7] where the listed outcomes of a national curriculum or a national qualification are built into a set of motivating and engaging learning activities, optimised by teachers for specific groups of young people. This is a vital process in 'who decides what makes a good education'. An overloaded curriculum erodes the space for 'curriculum making'[8] as well as precipitating local decisions about what to teach or drop. When this happens in a system, the power of a national curriculum in providing 'entitlement' is sharply eroded, and the aims of national education policy are compromised. 'Who decides' is shifted.

In England, the dominance of national qualifications in determining the shape of education is notable – GCSE specifications dominate discourse and practice at Key Stage 4 – they have greater potency than the National Curriculum, not least by being the focus of attainment across all classes of schools – both those formally required to deliver the National Curriculum, and those who are not. Who decides the content of these has changed almost unnoticed; previously, the content decisions were controlled by agencies such as the School Curriculum and Assessment Authority (SCAA) and Qualifications and Curriculum Authority (QCA), but with the dissolution of the QCA in 2010, these powers transferred to the Secretary of State.

But while a lot of movement in the locus of control over the past century has been towards the centre, relaxations have occurred in key elements, and 'increased school autonomy' has featured in policy. The commitment to 'school autonomy' is very much focused on 'academisation' and formation of free schools – the proposal: 'unleashing innovation' (in order to improve equity and attainment). On academies:

> One of the key elements of continuity with the Labour administration was retention and expansion of the Academy Programme, originally formulated by Andrew Adonis to effect rapid transformation of poor-performing State schools – crucially taking those schools out of Local Authority control, running them through direct contract.
>
> A difficult judgement here is whether the Academy Programme was simply expanded, or appropriated and fundamentally changed – the same form but fundamentally differing in character. Originally it focussed on very low performing schools, it appeared as a limited and constrained initiative. It remains ambiguous as to whether massive expansion was actually contrary to the Adonis model, or whether massive expansion already was latent in the policy.
>
> The expansion of the Academy Programme represented continuity with Labour policy but also had deep continuity with 'unfinished business' associated with Conservative thinking prior to and around the very first National Curriculum in 1988, particularly the propositions of Stuart Sexton.[9]

If the 1944 Act established control of 'good education' at the Local Authority level, in the mechanisms of local government, and more recent restrictions have consolidated State control and unlocked elements of 'school autonomy', then individual and family control is located principally in two places: school governance and school choice.

With free schools, parental and community engagement were given a new opportunity for expression, through the formation of new schools; in 2023, 650 were in place. Since launch, 55 free schools, studio schools and University Technology Colleges were closed or re-brokered.[10] No public data exists on the number of refused applications – an interesting aspect of state criteria regarding the quality of education versus the impetus from communities.

Outside of direct involvement of decision-making and governance of schools, parental choice and young persons' personal choice has been invoked as a motor of quality improvement – a public policy measure requiring variation in schooling (genuine' choice), excess school places, signalling of quality, understanding of choice and quality by those choosing, and sensitivity on the part of school governors, managers and teachers to what improves quality in schooling. The latest analysis of the role of school choice as the principal means of enhancing both specific and national quality of education has been seriously questioned in Sweden[11], a nation which placed this mechanism at the heart of its system and experienced a serious decline in outcomes.

What choices can exist in a local community? A quick look at Brighton (East Sussex) shows an interesting local economy of academy and non-academy schools, Steiner provision, a Buddhist school, Montessori provision, independent schools, schools with sixth forms, sixth form colleges and Further Education (FE) colleges. And many, many private tutors delivering evening and weekend support. And of course, some of the 66,000 children are being homeschooled in England, up from 28,000 in 2019.[12]

The issue of 'every school a good school' has appeared and re-appeared over time in policy commitments, invoking issues of 'what variation allows choice and what variation constitutes inequalities of quality?', while issues of supply of places, catchment areas and attaining 'first choice' has dominated local communities – from inner city to sparsely-schooled rural areas.[13] Whilst over 80% of secondary applicants achieve their preferred school,[14] the complexity of local variations in choice is joined by the fact that the ability to exercise choice is constrained by knowledge, financial resources and social capital.

The persistence of these debates and the annual crescendo of local media comment makes it clear, even when major features of the system have not been relaxed – national curriculum, assessment, qualifications, accountability – there remain preferences amongst parents and young people for what they perceive as distinctive features of specific schools. They are making choices about what they consider to be 'good education'. School choice, subject choice at 14 and 16, a choice of vocational or academic balance in provision—all decisions about what is best for a specific child, even within a constrained and restricted offer. And then there is 'opting out' and activating homeschooling. And supplementing contact time with additional tutoring.

The pendulum swings of restriction and relaxation affect so many aspects of education – the 'control factors'. On the curriculum, in 1954, Hannah Arendt's brilliant paper 'The Crisis in Education'[15] suggested that any curriculum should restrict itself only to that which enables young people to be capable, critical creators of new, progressive social and economic arrangements. In the early 2000s, the Cambridge Primary Review suggested a balance of 60-40 in nationally-determined versus locally-determined content.[16] These ideas informed the 2010 review of curriculum, its principles carefully balancing precision, over-specification and overload. On qualifications, the number of available subjects has, in turn, swollen and contracted, and choice further constrained by accountability measures. But the data at A level tells a story of huge choice – there are no formal restrictions, only operational ones and issues of expectations, on how many subjects can be taken and in what combination. Even the most common combination of maths, chemistry and biology is taken by less than 6% of candidates, and over 20,000 combinations appear in national statistics.[17]

'Who decides…' has deep complexity; national discourse contains calls of 'government responsibility', 'government meddling', 'rights', 'entitlements', 'freedoms', 'choice', 'postcode lotteries'. Agency is exercised by parents, teachers, young people and school managers on a continuing basis, within a balance of central and local restrictions, subject to almost constant movement. Meanwhile, as data suggests pupil mental health and well-being is declining, and residual COVID effects manifest with terrible persistence, the definition of 'good education' itself is tangibly shifting.

If we focus on the individual benefits of education and push benefit to society and the economy into the background but not out of the picture entirely, then we have a wealth of evidence from the big cohort studies in England – the 1958 National Child Development Study (NCDS), the 1970 British Cohort Study (BCS) and the 2000 Millenium Cohort Study. Each of these has followed around 19,000 people throughout their lives, from birth. If 'good education' leads to a 'good life', then these studies give us excellent insight into health, wealth, avoidance of criminality, lifelong learning and personal wellbeing and development. What these studies show, through their successive sweeps of questions and scrutiny, is that basic education is very good for you. They show that the fundamentals of literacy and numeracy are essential, and that the higher the level of education beyond these essentials, the greater the chances are that a person engages in further education and training. Education leads to more education, and higher skills and knowledge lead to better professional progression and higher income. The studies have not been restricted to tracing the relationship between formal educational outcomes (e.g. level of qualification) to life outcomes, but also have looked at dispositions, such as concepts of personal agency. Currently being emphasised by the Organisation for Economic Co-operation and Development (OECD) as a 'general good' of education, a higher sense of personal agency is linked to better life outcomes. That is the overall picture – and it's a consistent one from all of the successive cohort studies. Of course, this general trend may not be present in all the individual life stories which are included in these studies, but this is indeed the overall reality. So if we view health, stable relationships, avoidance of criminality, financial return as 'good things' then this does give us a picture of 'good education': high levels of basic education – literacy, numeracy, science – are an essential foundation for all, and higher levels of learning beyond this tends to lead to a virtuous circle of more and more learning and more and more progression.

This seems to answer the question 'Who decides what is a good education?' in an objective way; it is independent of any individual or group stating '...this is (what we believe is) good education...' It uses utility – good life outcomes – as a determinant of what we should include in a national curriculum, in the experience of the school curriculum, and national qualifications.

But there are some fractures in this seemingly straightforward and empirically-driven approach.

The first is evident the moment we switch our attention from how people are progressing to whether education is meeting the needs of society and the economy.

On society: one of the most important aspects of modern society is inequality. Amongst many adverse issues, high and increasing inequality drives child poverty, poor social cohesion and heightened social tension. Education remains one key means of breaking the relationship between deprivation and poor life outcomes, so the trend in the relationship between social background and educational attainment is an important thing to watch. A 'good education' can rightly be seen as one which reduces the impact of social background on attainment. The four-year Programme for International Student Assessment (PISA) survey gives us some important insights. Pre-COVID, there was a stark contrast between France and England. France has been going in the wrong direction.[18] There, despite policy efforts to increase attainment and reduce inequality, it is possible that factors external to the education system (social fragmentation linked to housing segregation, patterns of economic development) have impacted educational outcomes, and this inequality in outcomes feeds further social inequality. In England, prior to COVID, the impact of family background on attainment weakened from 2000 onwards, at the time that successive governments, Labour, Coalition and Conservative, put in place well-evidenced, high-fidelity focused programmes for raising standards in foundational literacy and mathematics. But, as is so often the case in the large and complex society we have in England, the fact that the impact of social background on attainment is decreasing does not mean that overall educational inequality is decreasing. The first can go down (a good thing) at the same time that the second can increase (a bad thing). And that does appear to be the case in the post-2000 decades in England. Various nations are looking at England's PISA performance and are rightly examining the features of policy which are associated with an overall rise in performance in maths and an improvement in England's international rank position in literacy. Good things have indeed happened, and a revised national curriculum, reformed national qualifications, refined accountability arrangements, and high support programmes in maths and literacy all have played their part. But even prior to COVID, the figures for within-school and between-school variation showed that the system remained one with entrenched inequalities. As I outlined at the outset of this chapter, having a national curriculum, national assessment, and national qualifications does not mean strictly comparable and coherent implementation in every school and every classroom.

If a 'good education' is one which delivers individual benefit in a specific economic context – the advanced economy of Europe, or England, located in a dynamic global economy, then one perspective on 'good education' is that it meets the needs of economic production and activity. 'Who decides' then becomes a question of 'what skills and knowledge does the economy need?' – again, invoking the idea of objective forces driving the content and focus of education. This suggests that the constant refrain – heard in UK education debates since the 1970s – that education should be linked to labour market needs. The latest expression of this comes from the aims of the 2024 National Curriculum Review: '…it will seek to deliver…a curriculum that ensures children and young people leave compulsory education ready for life and ready for work'.[19]

Whilst this notion of 'work ready' seems self-evident and driven by objective forces (the pragmatic needs of the economy), even a quick glance at the shape of vocational education and training in a range of nations shows that it is laden with human judgement – it is full of hidden values and implicit assumptions. Those assumptions are thrown into sharp relief when we look at nations with highly developed vocational routes.

In Germany, the system traditionally possessed an academic route and a vocational route, the Dual System of apprenticeship, into which over 60% of young people progressed at the age of 16. Since the 1990s, participation in the academic route has increased, but it remains lower than in many other comparable nations, at around 28%.

In Germany, there is no notion that young people are immediately 'work ready' when leaving compulsory schooling. It is true that Germany has seen a rise in Higher Education participation due to shifting social aspirations, and it is true that the apprenticeship route is under stress from economic retrenchment and employer requests to make that route more focused on the needs of specific employers. But participation patterns and underlying values around 'good education' are starkly different in Germany. Over 50% of 15 to 18-year-olds in Germany move into the vocational route, with over 30% of those enrolled in the Dual System of apprenticeship, compared with 6% participation in England. There is high employer engagement: 98% contrasting with 41% in England. Employers in Germany do *not* expect young people to be 'work ready', they expect to contribute to the initial vocational education and training of young people. Again, in contrast to England, both the college-based route and the apprenticeship route in Germany focus on wide occupational competence, not narrow job-specific training.[20]

There are two key issues in 'who decides' in the German vocational system. Firstly, the vocational system: both the state college system and the apprenticeship system are dominated by standards which are the result of discussions between the state, employers and 'social partners' – unions. This balancing of interests, which this partnership represents, is seen as essential. Young people are protected against any tendencies to make vocational education and training narrow and instrumental. Skill supply and links to the needs of the economy are safeguarded.

The interests of the state in ensuring a well-trained labour force enjoying full participation in current and future economic activity are ensured. Secondly, it is an established assumption that employers should take substantial responsibility for initial vocational training and make a significant financial and practical contribution. Given the traditions, culture and long-established arrangements in Germany, the idea that young people should leave compulsory education 'work ready' would be regarded by German employers as a very odd idea indeed.

In England, the vocational route continues to be dominated by voluntarism. The rhetoric of 'work ready' has been reinforced by long-standing calls from employer organisations such as the Confederation of British Industry (CBI). Apprenticeship has grown at the higher and degree level, but starts have declined – 30% overall, with level 3 starts declining by 25% and level 2 by 60%. It is vital to note that apprenticeship in England did not enter its period of growth as a result of a wave of high employer commitment breaking out of the dominant culture of voluntarism and expectations of 'work ready from school' – it came through the illiberal imposition of a levy by an economically liberal series of governments. And this is all too telling: 3.3 billion GBP of unused apprenticeship levy has been returned to the Treasury,[21] even at a time when over 50% of UK enterprises report skills shortages, and successive surveys show that all employers feel that current shortages could impose a limit on their growth. Of huge significance, the green skills gap currently lies at 50% – 200,000 of the 400,000 required.[22]

If a 'good education' is one in which there is a high linkage between the needs of the economy and the curriculum – its opportunities and routes—then things are not looking good in England. Arrangements do not have the same balance of interests and responsibilities as we see in countries like Germany, Switzerland and Austria. Looking at the last 50 years of policy on vocational education and training in England, we seem to aspire to the quality of European nations yet embody the economic instrumentalism of the USA – where regulation is almost exclusively linked to local 'licence to practise' rather than driving employer-state partnerships and broad-based training – and where differences in education are wrapped up with serious social inequality.[23]

Any reflections on 'good education' must consider initial vocational education and training – a crucial bridge between school and work. And the scrutiny of systems with high quality in their initial Vocation Education and Training (VET) shows that 'who decides' is based on long traditions of social partnership and joint development by key interests.

But the last 30 years in England have also seen the dominance of the idea that participation in Higher Education (HE) is a key bridge into the labour market. The new arrangements for university fees introduced in 1998 were accompanied by wide messaging about returns to degrees, while later messaging emphasised that higher personal borrowing for higher education – genuine investment by individuals and families – would cause migration towards subjects and courses with high labour market saliency. Rather than 'a degree, any degree', later policy and messaging focused on the returns to a degree. A 'good education' again is signalled as one which enables students to recoup their investment, repay their loans and gain financial return and occupational progression. In analysis and discussion, it is frequently forgotten that well over 50% of courses in Higher Education have a direct labour market link – medicine, law, surveying, engineering, accountancy, computer science, and that many academic disciplines – maths, physics and chemistry – have a high labour market premium. Many occupationally related degrees are externally accredited by professional bodies – they indeed determine directly what makes 'good education' in their sectors. Much of Higher Education is very much a 'vocational route' even in the context of some highly academic subjects. But it is clear from unforgiving data that the Higher Education option in England has not realised the 'perfect market matching' which the policy rhetoric of recent decades has emphasised. Broadly, it is good news that the labour market return, to a degree, has remained present. This is true in general, and, of course, there is variation across individuals and across subjects, and across the type of Higher Educational institution. It is unsurprising that medicine, dentistry, maths and economics have the highest returns. What is salutary is that around 30% of graduates have negative total returns – the combined returns to them as individuals and to the state.[24] Recent OECD analysis across a range of nations has shown that England now ranks at the top of 31 advanced economies in respect of overqualification, moving from 30% in 2012 to 37% in 2022, holding qualifications which exceed the requirements of their jobs.[25]

This gives us rather mixed messages about 'good education'. If a criterion of 'satisfied with the experience' is used, Higher Education in England seems to hold up well. Recent surveys suggest high and recovering levels of satisfaction following the decline during COVID-19 disruption, with 85% 'happy with teaching'.[26] However, the news on overqualification is adverse. Is this simply indicative of a moribund labour market and poor economic growth following the shocks of COVID-19, war and conflict and other negative externalities? Regrettably, this does not provide a complete explanation of what we are seeing. If an economy has high levels of overqualification and no skills shortages, then education may well be oversupplying necessary skills. But if an economy has high levels of overqualification and rising levels of structural skills shortages, then either 'good education' (in terms of education of high economic utility) is not being supplied, or there is poor utilisation of skills by employers and/or poor signalling and mobility on the part of qualified people. And skills shortages indeed are rising in England, even as economic growth stalls. In 2022, around 30% of vacancies were skills shortage vacancies, and the number of skills shortage vacancies increased to 531,000 in 2022 – double the figure in 2017, and growing most sharply in medium and large employers.[27]

This adds up to a system in which choices matter. The degree which you do, or the vocational programme in which you will enrol, is determined by your choices and attainment in exams at 16 and 18. And national policy has relied on those choices as a motor of 'good education' – students will make rational choices, which will be driven by a sense of economic utility and return to education. An 'invisible hand', powered by choice, will drive the system towards perfect arrangements. But the problem is this: that is not what we are seeing.

So much for economic utility as a perfect deciding force in what makes 'good education'. And there is another thing to consider: Martin Wolf's upbeat analysis of advanced global capitalism, with all the benefits of material prosperity and improving health outcomes, with its sting in the tail – no one is looking after the environment to the degree required. Speaking in 2002, Martin Wolf did not know we would exceed the dangerous level of 1.5 degrees of warming in 2024, but he predicted the absence of governance and action, which would give rise to it.[28]

And the question about 'good education' that this gives rise to? If 'good education' is measured in terms of an economic criterion of financial return and prosperity within a specific form of economic production and technological development…what would need to change in that education if that very form of economic organisation, its attendant social organisation and consumer expectations and trajectory of technological development all need to change radically in order to protect the biosphere – the very thing on which human existence depends?

When the National Curriculum for England was revised in 2010–13, climate change was heavily contested. The science was uncertain, yet certainly complex. Action to mitigate climate change was even more uncertain. In the light of this, a reasoned decision was made during the review – young children needed proximity to nature – to explore the natural world in their locality – and they needed to acquire an understanding of the fundamentals of the sciences and geography in primary and early secondary, moving onto the specific issues of climate and mitigation in later and upper secondary education.

'Who decides what is a good education?' is a good question. 'Is what we are deciding is a 'good education' adding up to what human society needs?' is yet another.

Notes

1 Pyke N, 'Dearing's "treacle" works its wonders', *Times Education Supplement*, 5 April 1996.
2 Google AI Overview accessed 12 January 2025.
3 Mandler P, 'Educating the nation 1: schools', *Transactions of the Royal Historical Society*, Sixth Series Vol 25, Cambridge University Press, 2023, pp 1–26.
4 Green A, *Education and state formation*, Second edition, Palgrave Macmillan, 2013.
5 The 'Black Papers' were a series of articles on British education, published from 1969 to 1977 in *The Critical Quarterly*. 'The Great Debate' about the nature and purpose of public education began in 1976 with a speech by Prime Minister James Callaghan at Ruskin College, Oxford and ended officially in 1977.

6 Oates T, 'Could do better: using international comparisons to refine the National Curriculum in England', in 'Reviewing the National Curriculum 5-19 Two decades on', *The Curriculum Journal*, Vol 22, 2, 2011, pp 121–150.
7 Humes W, 'Stenhouse in Scotland and England: context and culture in curriculum development', *The Curriculum Journal*, Vol 35, 4, 2024.
8 *Survey of adult skills 2023 England (United Kingdom)*, Organisation for Economic Co-operation and Development, 2024.
9 Oates T, *Preparing for power: policy making around the school curriculum from 2010*, Institute for Government, 2024.
10 Whittaker F, 'Fact check: How many free schools have actually closed?', *Schools Week* 15 December 2018.
11 Oates T, Mouthaan M, Fitzsimons S and Beedle F, *Changing texts – an international review of research on textbooks and related materials*, Cambridge University Press & Assessment, 2021.
12 Hattenstone A, 'More families being "forced" into home education', BBC News, 14 November 2024.
13 Burgess S, Briggs A, McConnell B and Slater H, *School choice in England: background facts*, Working Paper No. 06/159, The Centre for Market and Public Organisation (CMPO), University of Bristol, 2006.
14 '2024 Curriculum and assessment review', www.gov.uk/government/groups/curriculum-and-assessment-review.
15 Arendt H, 'The Crisis in Education' (1954) in Arendt H, *Between Past and Future. Six Exercises in Political Thought*, Penguin, 1961.
16 'Towards a new primary curriculum', a report from *The Cambridge Primary Review Part 2: The future*, University of Cambridge, 2009.
17 Rodeiro C and Sutch T, *Popularity of A Level subjects among UK university students*, Statistical Report Series 52, Cambridge Assessment, 2013.
18 Doyle AM, 'Twenty years on – what can PISA tell us about educational inequality in England and France?', *Compare: A journal of comparative and international education*, Vol 53, 4, 2023, pp 603–617.
19 '2024 Curriculum and assessment review', www.gov.uk/government/groups/curriculum-and-assessment-review.
20 Clarke L and Winch C, 'A European skills framework? – but what are the skills? Anglo-saxon versus German concepts', *Journal of education and work*, Vol 19, 3, 2006, pp 225–269.
21 Camden B, 'DfE records £96m apprenticeship underspend in 2022-23', *FE Week*, 26 September 2023.
22 'Skills shortages in the UK: what that means for your organisation', The Access Group, www.theaccessgroup.com, 2025.
23 *What is driving wealth inequality in the United States of America?* ILO Working Paper 105, International Labour Office, 2024.
24 Britton J, Deardon L, Van der Erve L and Waltmann B, *The impact of undergraduate degrees on lifetime earnings*, Institute for Fiscal Studies, 2020.
25 *Survey of adult skills 2023 England (United Kingdom)*, Organisation for Economic Co-operation and Development, 2024.
26 'Higher Education in numbers', Universities UK, www.universitiesuk.ac.uk, January 2025.
27 *Skills shortages in the UK economy*, Edge Foundation, 2024.
28 Wade R, *Globalisation, poverty and income distribution: does the liberal argument hold?* Reserve Bank of Australia, 2002.

SECTION 2
A good curriculum

This section is about the role of the curriculum in schools. What do we teach, and why? Who instructs our choices? What is 'the best that has been thought and said'? Our writers range widely, from broad questions and high-level decisions to some very specific exemplar pieces on particular curricular areas, schools and topics.

Think

1. What decisions have you made about the curriculum? Why?
2. Are original ideas and actions important? Who to? Why?
3. How lived are your school's values?
4. How do you support your teachers to ignite passions in young people?
5. Where have you seen the best curriculum?
6. How do you trust your teachers to design curricula and teaching?
7. Who is a quality curriculum thinker in your school? Who needs help?
8. How does your curriculum respond to external, local and global forces?

Section 2
Essay 1

The best that has been thought and said: The 'knowledge-rich' school

Jon Curtis-Brignell

Here at Priory School in Lewes, East Sussex, our aim is to be the leading inclusive and creative state secondary school in the region, a school in which all children acquire powerful knowledge, feel a strong sense of social connection and belonging, and become ethically aware citizens who are ready to confidently take their place in the world. Based on the principles of educational philosopher Professor Gert Biesta, education at Priory School is oriented towards three domains of purpose: 'knowing', 'belonging' and 'becoming', through which we support students to strive for academic success, contribute positively to the school community and embrace personal growth. Biesta writes about the purpose of education being:

- *Qualification*: powerful knowledge which prepares children for the future, whether that be work, citizenship or further study
- *Socialisation*: children will become part of society or culture by learning knowledge, values and norms that make up that society
- *Subjectification*: children will develop their sense of individuality through learning knowledge, so that they can make sense of themselves, others and their place in the world.[1]

While Biesta's first domain is known as 'qualification', for him, education should reach far beyond what he terms the current dominant 'culture of measurement', and ought to be oriented instead towards the 'good' rather than measurement, accountability and efficiency. But what is a 'good' curriculum in this sense, and who decides? An answer no doubt familiar to readers of this book is what Professor Michael Young in *Knowledge and the Future School: Curriculum and Social Justice* calls 'powerful knowledge', according to which concept the purpose of education 'is to enable all students to acquire knowledge that takes them beyond their experience. It is knowledge that many will not have access to at home, among their friends, or in the communities in which they live. As such, access to this knowledge is the right of all pupils as future citizens'. However, enormously influential as it is, as Young himself has suggested,[2] the concept is not without its problems, specifically:

- *The ambiguous meaning of power*
- *The incompleteness of the model of powerful knowledge as a curriculum principle*
- *The neglect of the interdependence of curriculum and pedagogy*

In this chapter, I want to argue for three curriculum principles which, if adhered to and enacted, can help to address and overcome these problems and provide genuine access to a 'knowledge-rich' curriculum for all. These are:

- Deep and rich knowledge, which empowers all children as future citizens
- The distinctive value of individual subject disciplines
- Enrichment and enhancement which challenge children beyond their previous experiences

Knowledge is powerful 'if it predicts, if it explains, if it enables you to envisage alternatives'[3], and so children need to learn concepts and knowledge to move beyond their current contexts to become active citizens in employment and society. But if powerful knowledge enables children to make their own choices and lays the foundation for challenging thinking that could change the world, then the question of 'what' knowledge to select within a curriculum becomes fundamental. While widely cited, Matthew Arnold's phrase, 'the best which has been thought and said in the world' is itself rightly contested. For a school to describe its own curriculum as 'knowledge-rich' is, in the absence of further methodology, rather to beg the question, as Young tells us: 'powerful knowledge is not a tool that can tell you what knowledge to include in your classes or how to structure them – that is your responsibility as members of the teaching profession'.[4] While powerful knowledge, then, is not a curriculum principle in precise enough terms to tell us what to teach, what it does do is to lay down the gauntlet to us to decide, as teachers, what children need to know in order to make sense of themselves, others and their place in the world, and how we approach this with them in the classroom in order that they build a relationship with this knowledge that enables them to develop subjectivity.

As Biesta says, 'education always comes to the student as an act of power, even if it is well-intended and even if what is at the heart of this intention is interest in the student's freedom, in his or her existence as subject in and with the world'.[5] If we try starting with genuine student empowerment as a founding principle, this may offer us additional guidance in respect of what constitutes genuinely deep and rich knowledge: 'Our hope is that, at some point, students may turn back to us and tell us that what we tried to give them was actually quite helpful, meaningful, even if, initially, it was difficult to receive'. To further build student empowerment, depth and richness in the curriculum also come from offering the space and time for teachers to explore knowledge in detail with students, to enact, apply and bring ideas to life rather than reducing knowledge to inert lists of decontextualised facts to be memorised. The 'richness' in those schools which are truly 'knowledge-rich' lies in recognising the interdependence of curriculum and pedagogy. And the key, of course, to bringing rich knowledge to life is in embracing the distinctive value of individual subject disciplines.

Powerful knowledge is specialised, and so a rich array of academic subjects must be the foundation of any school curriculum. These subject disciplines are living and breathing communities composed of the academics, teachers and students we induct as novices into these 'communities of specialists'.[6] These specialisms involve so much more than the substantive knowledge stipulated in a curriculum's programme of study, involving as they do not only the essential concepts, knowledge, skills and principles of each subject, but also the disciplinary knowledge comprising each subject's 'distinctive pursuit of truth',[7] as well as the distinct and unique signature pedagogies used to make the curriculum within each community.

A key component of disciplinary pedagogy is authenticity: as Barbara Bleiman puts it, 'really engaging with the subject in ways that are valid and legitimate in terms of the wider practices that we know to constitute it beyond the classroom'.[8] It is our responsibility as teachers to induct our students as novices into the real, authentic disciplines we represent, rather than a narrow, spurious and impoverished version of the subject as set out in an examination specification. A great anecdote illustrating the importance of this is told by trainer and consultant James Durran, who tells of a student, in response to the question, 'What is English?' answering: 'Analysing texts'; when asked about the purpose of analysing these texts, they responded: 'To prepare for assessments'.[9] If this seems an extreme example, consider the student experience in many Key Stage 4 lessons: in children's eyes, are they truly learning about the subject discipline itself, or are they, for example, learning how to answer 6 or 12-mark questions using practice papers? To combat this, we need to offer students a clear rationale or even a manifesto for what our subjects mean to us. Why do students *need* to study English? Why has the specific content been selected? How are English lessons delivered at *this* school?

To take one example, The Association for Science Education (ASE) identifies not just the importance of Scientific Knowledge in the planning of a curriculum – the 'big ideas' – which represent a convenient way of clarifying which are the most important concepts in science amongst the detail of the national curriculum and GCSE specifications, but also the importance of Scientific Attitudes and Capabilities as well. 'Scientific capabilities' describe the knowledge of how to gather and use scientific evidence. This is not just the 'working scientifically' identified in the National Curriculum, but also subject-specific literacy and numeracy skills. Disciplinary knowledge within science is diverse, technical and challenging, and the value of scientific conventions learnt early in scientific studies may only become apparent later. Finally, 'Scientific attitudes' promote the kind of scholarly approach that is essential to success in all the sciences (for our Science team at Priory, these are Curiosity, Collaboration, Creativity, Thoroughness, Studiousness and Honesty). Each of these Attitudes is exemplified by the biography of an inspiring scientist, displayed prominently in the department. At Key Stage 3, in each topic, these attitudes are linked to particular tasks, and students' accomplishments are recognised through the award of a badge-like sticker. The development of studious habits is also supported by a regular structure of review and revision before the end of topic assessments.

As well as being clear about our own rationales for our subjects – what our subjects are like, *for us* – we need to focus on the student experience as well. What are our subjects *like*, for them? We need to ensure that our curriculum offers enrichment and enhancement, which challenges students beyond their previous experiences (Young's 'envisaging alternatives'). While I will certainly steer deftly away from any use of that problematic and much-maligned term 'cultural capital' (in either its Ofsted or Bourdieu definitions), cultural learning as defined by The Cultural Learning Alliance is an active engagement with the creation of our arts and heritage and encompasses an individual's understanding of themselves, their material culture and the world around them. A 'good' curriculum, then, needs to be one which ensures children are thinking critically, engaged in creativity and the development of original ideas and action. 'Good' cultural learning takes place across all subjects, which means a strong offering within those subjects traditionally associated with arts and culture, as well as an offering across science, the humanities and technology that involves both learning through culture and learning about culture.

However, I do want to dwell for a moment on the importance of a 'good' curriculum of those subjects traditionally associated with arts and culture. As Tambling and Bacon put it:

> The arts are an essential tool in building a humane society. They are a building block for social cohesion; they are important for understanding our collective

histories, and for promoting inclusion, and enabling agency within a diverse society. They underpin our cultures and the economy, and are important for personal development, health and wellbeing. They provide memorable experiences and a creative outlet which enables children to explore and express their emotions and their identities, and can help in supporting children who are struggling with their wellbeing. They can enable young people to collaborate and flourish as individuals in their schools, communities and the wider world, as well as in their future careers.[10]

And yet, despite all that we know about the value of arts subjects for children and young people, there is currently a lack of value ascribed to the arts and culture within the state education system in England. In recent years, owing to the previous government's focus on STEM subjects and the narrowing focus of various accountability measures, including the introduction of the English Baccalaureate, we have witnessed the systemic downgrading and exclusion of arts subjects and experiences, with many schools now neglecting to prioritise creative and cultural learning within the curriculum. The prioritisation of EBacc subjects in secondary accountability measures has meant a reduction in the level of arts subjects, teachers and resources available, and, therefore, declining take up of arts subjects at GCSE and A Level: since 2015, GCSE Arts entries have fallen by 35% and entries for Arts subjects at A Level have fallen by 16%.[11] Why is there not as much concern about ever-declining numbers of boys studying English literature and dance as there is (quite rightly) desire for more girls to study maths and physics? The cost-of-living crisis has also led to acute funding pressures for schools, meaning that access to arts, culture and creativity is not equitable, with the arts more highly valued in independent schools. The effects of this are hardest felt by children from low-income families, where parents have less scope to find and pay for access to cultural enrichment opportunities; disadvantaged students are therefore, far less likely, in most schools, to be able to develop a rich understanding of themselves, their material culture and the world around them. I would argue that this sets an imperative for school leaders to make our schools and curricula not just knowledge-rich, but arts, culture and creativity-rich, with a coherent rationale and vision for all subject areas, equal status for arts subjects with other subject areas within a broad and balanced curriculum, and an access entitlement built on inclusion and equality.

A knowledge-rich school, then, is one in which all students have an entitlement to powerful knowledge which will unlock their understanding of themselves, their material culture and the world around them. A curriculum is powerful when it embraces the distinctive value of individual subject disciplines, enrichment and enhancement, which challenge children beyond their previous experiences, and deep and rich knowledge, which empowers all children as future citizens.

Notes

1. Biesta G, 'Good education in an age of measurement: on the need to reconnect with the question of purpose in education', *Educational Assessment, Evaluation and Accountability* (formerly: *Journal of Personnel Evaluation in Education*) 21, pp 33–46, 2009.
2. Young M, 'From Powerful Knowledge to the Powers of Knowledge', in Sealy C (ed), *The Researched Guide to the Curriculum*, John Catt Educational, 2020.
3. Young M and Lambert D, *Knowledge and the future school: curriculum and social justice*, Bloomsbury, 2014.
4. Young M, 'From Powerful Knowledge to the Powers of Knowledge', in Sealy C (ed), *The Researched Guide to the Curriculum*, John Catt Educational, 2020.
5. Biesta G, 'Risking ourselves in education: Qualification, socialization, and subjectification revisited', *Educational Theory*, 70:1, 2020, pp 89–104.
6. Young M, 'From Powerful Knowledge to the Powers of Knowledge', in Sealy C (ed), *The Researched Guide to the Curriculum*, John Catt Educational, 2020.
7. Counsell C, 'Taking curriculum seriously', *Impact - Issue 4: Designing a Curriculum*, Autumn 2018.
8. Bleiman B, *What Matters in English Teaching: Collected Blogs and Other Writing*, London: English and Media Centre, 2020.
9. Durran J, 'In this school, English is about…', James Durran's Blog, 2017. https://jamesdurran.blog/2017/07/31/in-this-school-english-is-about/
10. Tambling P and Bacon S, *The Arts in Schools: Foundations for the Future*, A New Direction and Calouste Gulbenkian Foundation, 2023.
11. *GCSE and A-Level Arts Entries and Grades 2023*, Cultural Learning Alliance, 2023.

Section 2 Essay 2

Education for creativity

Sally Bacon

How should we educate for creativity? Creativity, or creative thinking, is not unique to the arts. As is asserted in *The Arts in Schools: Foundations for the Future* report, there is a question of whether the arts are always creative or have a special role in creative learning.[1] There is general agreement that the terms creativity and the arts are *not* interchangeable and are two separate things. Creativity is an approach to learning that can also be applied in the real world. It is not a subject in itself and is not particular to the arts. Nor is all arts education creative per se. Many aspects of the arts require things other than creativity: for example, the practice and rehearsal for a play or orchestral performance are often repetitive and restricted in the extent of improvisation or interpretation. Creativity and creative learning approaches are important, but this is distinct from learning through expressive arts subjects such as art and design, dance, drama and music. However, expressive arts subjects are the biggest engine we have in schools for driving creativity as a capability for learners, which is why it is a problem if there is not a national entitlement to an arts-rich education, and if we lose sight of the fact that an arts-rich curriculum is vital in fuelling education for creativity.

Governments since the 1970s have increasingly focused on the link between education and the economy, so it is strange that from 2010, there was an education policy focus on knowledge transfer in England, and what could be easily tested came to be seen as synonymous with 'what worked'. Employers, when surveyed, tend to look for different things in new recruits and graduate applicants, and routinely cite attributes such as resilience, communication, leadership, adaptability, problem-solving, creativity and teamwork: qualities beyond grades in public examinations.

In 2019, the Durham Commission reported that according to 'The Economic Graph (a digital representation of the global economy based on 590 million LinkedIn members, 50 thousand skills, 30 million companies, 20 million open jobs, and 84 thousand schools), creativity is the second most desirable competency in an employee'.[2]

Compared with testing knowledge of facts, these creative skills are difficult to measure and are often developed through group work, special projects, or challenges that are not defined by a particular subject area. During the 2010s, subjects seen as unambiguous – or obviously 'right or wrong' – edged out subjects which aim to elicit young people's ideas, originality and opinions, and hone creative and practical skills through exploration and experimentation. But when faced with candidates with the same level of qualifications, employers will often look for these so-called soft skills.

When considering arts subjects and education for creativity, there is also an important point around failure. Failing – involving exploration, messiness, mistakes – is a vital part of pedagogy in arts subjects, as it is in science. *The Arts in Schools* report consultation roundtables with school leaders and teachers revealed that fear of failure had filtered down to students and their need for the right answer or approach to get them marks was blocking their creativity.

Uniformity of arts work to meet assessment expectations is not always helpful for creativity or for any capability developed through studying expressive arts subjects. Considering how we educate for creativity begs a question about how achievement and progression should be assessed. Expressive arts subjects require an assessment and progression system that is relevant and proportionate. Written assessment does not always effectively take originality into account. Arts subjects require different kinds of measurement, including the use of digital learner profiles and achievements beyond exams. This would allow for inputs across artistry, community, creativity, critical thinking and collaboration.

Good arts teaching almost always involves creative thinking, but also skills development, sharing and exchange, and understanding the artistic work of others. The professional arts are ever-changing, contestable and rarely lead to a clear set of answers. Rather than solving questions or closing down discussion, they often generate more discussion and debate. The skill of the arts teacher is less about passing on knowledge, and more about drawing out ideas and helping young people to express them in particular forms of arts practice: from dance to drama; from music to art-making, and much more. When young people commit to their own arts practice in their chosen medium, they are better placed to respond to the work of other artists, past and present.

Expressive arts teachers and school leaders navigate the complex path of value, and whose culture we are including and excluding, and how to teach in a way that accords value to young people's efforts: 'If we want to promote independent critical and creative thinking, we shall be working against ourselves if we try to achieve these things by methods of teaching which stifle initiative and promote the acceptance of some authoritarian fiat of a body of elders or establishment'.[3] In educator consultations for *The Arts in Schools* report, creativity and creative learning approaches were described as immensely valuable. School leaders and teachers stressed the important role of the arts in collaborative learning – so much of what happens in schools is about individual achievement, whereas in workplaces we often work in teams, and in fostering problem-solving, imagination and originality.

All expressive arts subjects are important for developing creativity and creative skills. However, one of the problems in describing the value of arts subjects in fostering creativity in schools is that there has not been an evidenced value narrative which describes this in ways that are helpful in building a shared language for educators and policymakers. The Cultural Learning Alliance has now developed this shared language in the form of a Capabilities Framework, which sets out the particular affordances of studying arts subjects in terms of their personal benefit for the learner and the resulting societal benefit.[4] The Framework is of value for making the case for an arts-rich education, but also as a self-improvement tool for schools, and a new lens to apply to arts pedagogy and provision.

The Framework describes a series of capabilities, one of which is creativity, and it is helpful to look at the full Framework to see where creativity resides within it. The capabilities are expressed through three pillars that represent the kinds of capabilities/qualities that expressive arts subjects and experiences provide; these, in turn, encompass seven capabilities that have personal benefits for the child, which then lead to societal benefits: agency, wellbeing, communication, empathy, collaboration, creativity and interpretation. These three pillars and seven capabilities (as they relate to personal benefits only) can be summarised as:

BEING AND BECOMING: Agency | Wellbeing

1. *Agency* – confidence | identity | autonomy

2. *Wellbeing* – self-worth | resilience | pleasure

RELATING: Communication | Empathy | Collaboration

3. *Communication* – self-expression (including oracy) | listening skills | relationship building

4. *Empathy* – compassion | understanding and appreciation of difference | open-mindedness

5. *Collaboration* – co-operation | participation | connectedness

COGNITION AND CRITICAL THINKING: Creativity | Interpretation

6. *Creativity* – imagination | curiosity | originality

7. *Interpretation* – independent critical thinking | reflective judgement | meaning making

Within the full Capabilities Framework, each capability has a more detailed specification. Creativity can be more fully described as encompassing:

- **Imagination:** creative thinking, invention, divergent thinking

- **Curiosity:** problem-solving, ingenuity, experimentation, ideation, risk-taking, agility, inquisitiveness

- **Originality:** innovation, novelty, testing and trialling.

There is a wealth of evidence behind each capability.[5] There is no hierarchy of value, and all seven are interconnected: creative self-expression can develop agency and benefit wellbeing; communication and collaboration are vital for the creative process. All provide important skills for life and employment. Expressive arts subjects offer opportunities for different kinds of learning experiences which provide students with a range of skills and capabilities to benefit them in their further or higher education, in their future employment and their own independent pursuits in later life.[6] Within a coherent vision for a broad and balanced curriculum that makes explicit the distinct value of the arts, across all key stages and in all schools, adopting a collective term to describe the arts – expressive arts – is helpful. Having a clearly defined curriculum area gives clarity to their role, in line with other subject areas. And film and digital media would be an important addition to art and design, dance, drama and music, as in the Curriculum for Wales, given the dominance of both in young people's lives.[7]

If a creativity capability is developed in schools, then creative and innovative problem-solvers enter the workplace and wider society, and become cultural makers, cultural consumers, innovators, and entrepreneurs. The personal benefits of an arts-rich education become societal benefits – the two are closely linked. One additional benefit of this capability is that it allows young people to use their voices for positive arts-based activism in creative and productive ways. UNESCO makes the same point in the report of its International Commission on the Futures of Education: 'Curricula that invite creative expression through the arts have tremendous future-shaping potential. Artmaking provides new languages and means through which to make sense of the world, engage in cultural critique, and take political action'.[8]

A system built on knowledge acquisition alone cannot be fit for purpose when employers are seeking a broader skills-based approach.[9] There is employer demand for the capabilities that we know are developed through arts subjects, and it would be helpful to have these mapped onto core and future-facing purposes for schooling. Young people require a rounded and ambitious set of purposes for their education, which are reflective of the world in which they live and will work, and which prepare them for healthy and fulfilling lives. If we want capable, enterprising, creative contributors, ready to play a full part in life and work, then we need a national entitlement to an arts-rich education to enable every child to achieve and to thrive.[10]

If there is a weekly entitlement of a minimum number of curriculum hours for expressive arts teaching throughout a child's education, then it becomes easier to teach for all the capabilities set out in the new Capabilities Framework, and for all children to benefit from the positive and evidence-based impact afforded by an arts-rich education, as happens in the independent sector where arts subjects are highly valued. If these subjects are pushed outside of the formal structure of the school day, into an extracurricular space, or provided intermittently through a carousel model, it becomes harder to deliver the learning, personal and social development made possible by these disciplines. Extracurricular arts provision is not a substitute for curriculum arts provision, but is valuable for children and young people to extend their in-school arts and creative engagement to a deeper level, or to pursue interests and recreation beyond their qualifications choices.

Expressive arts subjects play an important role in addressing the social and emotional health of children and young people and in enabling them to become creative human beings. An expressive arts curriculum can teach us who we are now and who we might become. If children in primary school have opportunities to explore the widest range of arts activities, it is possible for them as young people to explore and benefit from the arts subjects for which they have developed an affinity, and which can enable them to flourish and thrive as creative contributors to society. Arts subjects are a vital component of a modern curriculum for the future, and they have an evidence-based impact on outcomes, making young people happier and healthier and equipping them for life and work. In doing so, they become a powerful way to drive our creative economy. We should not forget that the unique affordances of expressive arts subjects are the rocket fuel for creativity, in schools and beyond.

Notes

1 Tambling P and Bacon S, *The Arts in Schools: Foundations for the Future*, A New Direction and Calouste Gulbenkian Foundation, 2023.
2 'Creative competencies and employment skills', *Durham Commission on Creativity and Education*, Arts Council England and Durham University, 2019, p 35.
3 Tambling P and Bacon S, in the work cited. A quote from a school leader participant in 'The Arts in Schools' consultation roundtables.
4 Cultural Learning Alliance. www.culturallearningalliance.org.uk/evidence/#capabilities.
5 See Cultural Learning Alliance evidence work: www.culturallearningalliance.org.uk/evidence/.
Also see, for example: Deasy R, Catterall JS, Hetland L and Winner E, *Critical links: Learning in the arts and student academic and social development*. Arts Education Partnership, 2002; Hetland L, Winner E, Veenema S and Sheridan K, *Studio Thinking 2: The Real Benefits of Arts Education*. Teachers College Press, 2013; Thomson PO, Coles R, Hallewell M and Keene J, *A critical review of the Creative Partnerships archive: how was cultural value understood, researched and evidenced?* CCE, 2014; Halverso, E, and

Sawyer K, 'Learning in and through the arts', *Journal of the Learning Sciences*, 31(1), 2022, pp 1–13. Bowen D and Kisida B, 'Investigating the causal effects of arts education', *Journal of Policy Analysis and Management* 42(3), 2023, pp 624–647.

6 *Fostering Students' Creativity and Critical Thinking*, OECD, 2019. 'These are the top 10 job skills of tomorrow – and how long it takes to learn them', The Jobs Reset Summit, World Economic Forum, October 2020.

7 'Expressive Arts', Curriculum for Wales: www.hwb.gov.wales/curriculum-for-wales/expressive-arts/.

8 *Reimagining our futures together: A new social contract*, Report from The International Commission on the Futures of Education, UNESCO, 2021, p 73.

9 '70% of Employers Say Creative Thinking is Most In-demand Skill in 2024', Forbes, 28 January 2024.

10 'Four Purposes', Curriculum for Wales, https://hwb.gov.wales/curriculum-for-wales/designing-your-curriculum/developing-a-vision-for-curriculum-design/

Section 2
Essay 3

Building educated citizens

Richard Chattoe

Introduction

In considering how to begin this article and the best way to sum up the influence and impact a values-driven school culture can have on building young people into educated citizens, I concluded that hearing the voice and reflections of one such young person was both an appropriate and important starting point.

Serena is a Year 11 student who has attended Leeds City Academy (LCA) since Year 7. She has provided her personal reflections about the Academy and the role and importance of our In Partnership Values.

> The Leeds City Academy community is truly unique, embodying values that uplift our school experience and have profoundly enriched my life. As a student, I was and remain drawn by its inspiring leadership and guiding principles. Through our In Partnership Values, we cultivate unity, respect, and an unbreakable sense of belonging. Leeds City Academy instills lasting values in both students and staff, nurturing confidence, integrity, and a spirit of citizenship essential for a life of purpose and impact. Of all the values, respect has had the most profound impact on me and those around me. It has taught me the importance of valuing other people's perspectives and treating everyone with dignity. Respect isn't just about politeness—it's about genuinely understanding and honouring differences, which has strengthened my relationships and allowed me to grow as an individual. At Leeds City Academy, I've seen respect create stronger bonds within our diverse

community, building bridges where there might have been barriers. It's this value that inspires me daily and drives the positive change I aim to bring into every part of my life.

Reading Serena's reflections makes me feel immensely proud and privileged to be able to lead, shape, and cultivate an environment where she feels such a strong sense of belonging, support, and empowerment.

Through this article, I hope to share a small number of ideas, practical steps, and considerations in building a culture, curriculum, and opportunities where young people have every chance to develop into educated and empowered citizens.

Origins and the important 'Why?' question

I think it is first important to explain the origins and experiences that have shaped my philosophy and vision, as I believe these have helped conceptualise, introduce and embed this at Leeds City Academy. There cannot be any shortcut or superficial approach to making this mission work. This approach and philosophy must be believed, authentic and cherished if it is to lead to sustainable influence and impact.

Firstly, I have had the absolute privilege to be the Principal of Leeds City Academy for last six years. Prior to this, I was a senior leader across three very different inner-city schools, each with unique and differing social and community contexts. This important apprenticeship to my later senior leadership role was twenty-five years, initially as a Teacher and later Director of PE and Sport, roles I absolutely loved, cherished, and which helped shape me as the leader I am and the educational philosophy I hold.

Secondly, in my opinion, as with many practical curriculum subjects, enrichment activities and interests outside of school, PE and sport have the amazing ability to shape young people, their behaviours, and indeed their value set. I am a good example of this, with my many years participating in various sports and enjoying a fulfilling career playing semi-professional football. The highs and lows, unique scenarios, personalities and characters met along the way help shape your attitude, outlook, and understanding of the impact of collegiate effort, camaraderie and a sense of place, worth, responsibility, and duty to 'family'.

Thirdly, it is my belief that my close and extended family has influenced and shaped my behaviours, providing strong positive role models. My later responsibilities as a husband and father are also enormous factors in my philosophy, vision and rationale for what we have developed and embedded at Leeds City Academy. An example to illustrate this is when I welcome new staff or address parents at Consultation and Open Evenings. I provide a simple anecdote of attending my three daughters' parents' evenings through their formative primary to sixth form years, explaining that I always asked two sets of questions, in a specific order, much to my daughters' shock and embarrassment. The first set of questions always focused on whether my daughters were polite, respectful, considerate, could build and retain friendships and displayed resilience and resourcefulness when things were challenging. I would often ask the teacher to provide an example, and once I was happy and satisfied, I felt that I could say thanks and move to the next appointment, as I knew that if each of my three daughters possessed, displayed and developed these values, the rest, including academic success, would follow. Clearly, as an embarrassing father, I always then asked about their progress and what support my wife and I could provide in their subjects, but this was always a secondary consideration.

The above is true of Leeds City Academy. While we are absolutely committed to developing and shaping young people, we have also completed a tremendous amount of excellent work in redefining and restructuring the curriculum, so it is ambitious, relevant and secures increasingly impressive outcomes for students. Providing a high-quality environment and climate where young people can thrive through both highly effective Personal Development opportunities supported through and by a curriculum that is ambitious and implemented with skill and increasing finesse is essential. The combination of these two strands is affectionately referred to as Leeds City Academy's double helix or DNA.

Initial steps

When I secured the role of Principal at Leeds City Academy in April 2019, I reflected on many things, one of which was assessing the school's unique context and history. At the time, Leeds City Academy was a small secondary school of just over 600 students (the academy now boasts 1,040 students), was placed and remains in the lowest decile for deprivation, had endured a problematic history characterised by students' low attendance, poor academic progress and attainment outcomes, had a very poor reputation locally, had a limited identity and very inconsistent standards, systems and leadership.

However, despite its clear challenges, there was something quite unique and special about the school. I believed its significant cultural diversity, with over 50 different first languages at the time, was the unique selling point and something that I would focus on, build from, and celebrate. As I pondered my first thirty days leading the school, I considered what I could do and how I could shape this multicultural school with vastly different educational reference points, cultural perspectives, life experiences, and motivations into a single entity or family. At approximately 2:30 am on a Tuesday morning, only two weeks into my role, the idea of developing and shaping a 'values'-centred school was formed.

Vision and values

Any successful leader will reference the importance of having and articulating a mission or vision, but also the absolute need for clarity, simplicity, and connectivity across the organisation in order to secure this mission or vision. The process of connectivity has been particularly important in establishing this work at Leeds City Academy. Essentially, I believed that I needed to establish a common language and framework that could become the backbone of the school, the way we operated, interacted, made decisions and behaved. After much consultation with leaders, teachers, wider staff, parents and most critically our students, we decided to establish a set of six values felt to be important in creating a sense of collective mission, understanding and sense of family. We decided on establishing the mission of 'working In Partnership to secure the aspirations and ambitions of all our young people' and the introduction of the values of Caring, Respect, Tolerance, Professionalism, Aspiration and Resilience that would help drive and shape this mission.

This, in itself, was nothing new, groundbreaking or particularly impressive. Indeed, I have worked in and visited schools where similar values exist and are often illustrated on a wall in reception or the main school hall and are shared on the school website, prospectus or letterhead. However, to help influence and shape our young people, I felt that our work needed to go far beyond this, and we worked with determination to introduce, promote and ensure the mission and In Partnership Values became a common language across every school day.

Alignment, high profile and evolution

A critical decision and significant step in embedding the six values was to align them to the school's established positive behaviour system. This was not a particularly difficult process, but providing clear explanations, examples and how both the positive and negative impact of applying the six In Partnership Values could affect students and people was crucial. Everyone understanding why the values were important was essential in this process, and this took time, patience and tenacity.

To support this, we modelled interactions to both formally reward and challenge behaviours that displayed, neglected or omitted the values and included all six values in various literature, including the student planner, letterheads, student badges, certificates, student reports, parents' evening feedback, computer screensavers and numerous wall and visual displays around the school. Consequently, the values became high profile, woven into all elements of school life, and became an absolute must in everything we did. Students now receive daily recognition for displaying the expected behaviours and values, whilst students who consistently exemplify and demonstrate our In Partnership Values are now recognised, celebrated and rewarded at our end-of-term award assemblies.

However, we also did not insist that every conversation needed to reference or include an In Partnership Value, as we wanted this to become a natural evolving process rather than a forced or required expectation, as I have experienced in some schools. It needed to be embraced and have a chance to grow rather than be an expected process or compliance exercise; it needed to be authentic.

Stefan-Adrian, a Year 11 student who has attended Leeds City Academy from Year 7 and a dynamic and proactive member of the Leeds City Academy Student Parliament, summarises his thoughts about how the In Partnership Values have become essential and significant in shaping him and his peers: 'Across Leeds City Academy, the six In Partnership Values have been implemented as a foundation in our daily lives. This foundation has created a routine which is beneficial to our conduct in and outside of the academy. The foundation of these six values has helped me and many others to achieve our best, it has created challenges through which we have persevered, and mostly it has created a family and a strong sense of community and togetherness'.

Curriculum

As we began to introduce the values across the school, we also felt that to truly embed them, we needed to review the intent and implementation of our curriculum so that students could develop an understanding of how the values influenced their learning behaviours in the classroom. We wanted these behaviours to be seen, evidenced and impact the content of the curriculum both within each subject and more broadly across subjects, securing both width and breadth of understanding and connection.

At the start of this process, I was fortunate that an established and amazing teacher of Citizenship held the precise philosophy and vision I had. Therefore, due to the importance that citizenship would play as a curriculum subject, across the wider curriculum and daily life of the school, I decided to promote this member of staff into an Assistant Principal position with the key responsibility for Academy-wide Personal Development, placing citizenship at the heart of and as a high-profile feature of the school, a decision fundamental to both our early and prolonged success.

In addition, and equally critical, was working with key leaders and colleagues to review, refine, and adapt the curriculum so that all students studied a discrete weekly Citizenship-based curriculum lesson, entitled 'DNA'. This curriculum was designed and shaped very skilfully so that it ensured Leeds City Academy students not only covered statutory topics and content, but also subject content that enriched and deepened their knowledge and understanding of the world, with our six In Partnership Values carefully woven within, across, and beyond the curriculum so there was always a meaningful application and exemplification to the everyday school scenarios, interactions, and relationships they experienced.

This work can be illustrated by Kelly Allchin, Assistant Principal, Personal Development, and Ayla Malik, Director of Personal Development: '"DNA" might be an unusual word for a secondary school subject, but for us, it completely contextualises everything that we are aiming to achieve through the curriculum. At Leeds City Academy, we view DNA as the very essence of what should run through every student to ensure they are happy, safe, and responsible citizens both now during their time at school and beyond as they become young adults. The topics they explore within DNA will enable them to understand and appreciate diversity, develop critical thinking, and explore their rights and responsibilities. DNA incorporates PSHE, citizenship, and careers education via umbrella topics, ensuring students can both consider these topics as a whole, whilst also ensuring breadth and depth within each separate discipline'.

Dynamic and responsive

Due to the context of both our school and the local community we serve, we are frequently faced with having to dynamically respond to sudden or emerging events, influences and trends. As a result, our DNA curriculum has become ever-evolving and is, therefore, shaped and designed in response to our students' experiences and context. To ensure we can rapidly respond and adapt the curriculum and learning experiences for our students, opportunities to gather masses of student data regarding their health, personal experiences, concerns, aspirations and more are intentionally mapped across the curriculum. Our DNA team then forensically explores and uses this data to shape and amend the curriculum.

Through the DNA curriculum and wider whole-school citizenship activities, we teach students that their contributions are valid, important, and that their voices can and should be heard. In educational terms, the vast majority of our students are classed as disadvantaged, but our curriculum sees things differently. Their unique, global experiences allow us to teach an emotionally mature curriculum in which all students can benefit. When exploring topics such as media responses to immigration, the impact of international law, and global human rights abuses, our students have lived these experiences, and it is our job to unpack these experiences and frame them within a wider citizenship education.

We know that there is ample research suggesting political apathy can occur from Year 7 onwards, and we have therefore curated a curriculum that is ambitious, current, and exciting. Students learn about the role of government, how laws are made, and the concept of democracy. They debate current affairs and are encouraged to be critical thinkers when learning about issues taking place locally, nationally, and internationally. As a result, Citizenship Studies is a popular GCSE choice, with students at LCA performing very well compared to national results.

Law and Politics, two subjects that are covered in depth during DNA, continue to grow in popularity, and increasing numbers of students successfully enrol on to Post-16 courses. This is something we are immensely proud of, as we believe our students can and should be directly involved in the constitution of this country, bringing their own personal journeys to the table and contributing a diverse perspective. We encourage our students to aspire to be more, do more, and contribute more to shaping the future.

Enrichment beyond the curriculum

While the clear introduction, refinement, and maturation of the DNA curriculum have been central to our success, we also introduced and rapidly increased the range of enrichment activities, educational trips, and programmes for students across this period so that they could explore new opportunities, develop their knowledge and skills, and enjoy opportunities beyond the curriculum. Over time, the number of regular activities within our Peak Performance programme has increased from just four when I started as Principal in April 2019 to sixty-four as of December 2024, with the range of activities providing a wealth of opportunities, including sport, performing arts, technology, leadership and science.

Each week, in addition to supporting and enriching our form time programme, all students also attend either an assembly or an academic lecture, which are used to reference, emphasise, and explore one or more of the In Partnership Values. The academic lecture programme is also aimed at providing students with the experience and development of Cornell note-taking skills, required to be successful at Post-16 and University. The academic lecture also provides staff and students with the opportunity to present advanced topics and concepts, interests, or the skills and attributes of famous people, events and traditions whilst linking to and exploring the In Partnership Values and the fundamental elements that characterise becoming an aspirational High Performing Learner.

Additionally, the emergence of our Sector Experience & Employability Days (SEED) has been developed in partnership with well-established and, in some cases, internationally recognised organisations. It has been designed in partnership by the academy, colleges, universities and employers to inspire and provide students with an insight into the world of work in a chosen employment or industry sector. Each SEED day comprises a range of workshops, hands-on activities, and visits to employers in the Leeds City Region, including ASDA, KPMG, Exa Networks, Northern Ballet, and Mills & Reeve solicitors. The range of employers, activities and project-based learning has become key for increasing student engagement, and our students are in turn able to display our academy values, including resilience, tolerance, and professionalism.

Finally, our three annual Culture Conference Days provide a wonderful opportunity to embrace and celebrate the cultural diversity that exists at Leeds City Academy, with students and staff participating in externally led conferences and immersing in explorative learning that is closely linked to our In Partnership Values. Across these days, students and staff proudly wear and celebrate the traditional clothes and garments that represent their country of origin, culture and faith.

Impact – seen and unseen

As a Principal, and through my competitive streak, no doubt born and ingrained through my PE and sporting life, I have never really chased external results, validation, awards or accolades. While these external benchmarks and frameworks provide important structure and support key decision-making processes, I have always placed great faith and trust in my moral compass, as this is often the best marker of 'what is right' and 'what is best' for young people. However, I appreciate that some leaders might be drawn towards and see external metrics as a key indicator of a school's success.

While my philosophy places personal development as a high priority at Leeds City Academy, I equally remain committed to raising academic and vocational outcomes for our young people and place significant importance on the school overseeing an improving trend of results. However, I believe that for sustained success and impact, these two things can and must co-exist.

In August 2024, Leeds City Academy secured the best academic results in its history, achieving a very pleasing Progress 8 score of +0.42 and significant improvements in both Attainment and Basic measures. Attendance continues to improve and is very close to the national average, while incidents and data relating to poor behaviour and attitudes, such as suspensions, continue to rapidly fall.

Leeds City Academy was awarded the Association for Citizenship Teaching School of the Year in 2024, with the Spiritual, Moral, Social, and Cultural (SMSC) verification remarking, 'The shared values permeate all aspects of the Academy to create an excellent culture, which enables students and staff to achieve and flourish so effectively. The DNA curriculum is carefully and thoughtfully planned and yet is also adapted to local needs and to meet the statutory components of relationships and sex, and health education. It is also prepared to be reactive to local, national, and global issues. This is further supported and triangulated through assemblies and the Culture Conferences, to which the students contribute and respond so very positively. We were particularly impressed by the various opportunities across the school to demonstrate and develop active citizenship skills which have in turn fostered a citizenship climate'.

Leeds City Academy has also achieved the Young Citizens SMSC gold status quality mark and is recognised as a 'beacon school of excellence' within this area. It was also selected as the host school for the 2022 UK Parliament Week launch video due to our engagement with Parliament UK and identified as a UK Ambassador School for Parliament Education at the gold level. In 2023, Leeds City Academy also achieved School of Sanctuary status for the positive work undertaken to ensure students seeking asylum or with refugee status are fully supported.

Serena, a Year 11 student, beautifully summarises this by saying, 'At Leeds City Academy, our values aren't just words – they make a real difference. Over time, I've seen how they have transformed the school into a supportive and inclusive environment where every individual feels valued. For instance, the emphasis on tolerance and care has fostered a culture of acceptance and kindness, making it easier for students from all backgrounds to thrive. Similarly, the focus on aspiration has encouraged both students and staff to aim higher, leading to noticeable improvements in attitudes, achievements, and school morale. These values have also influenced my behaviour and outlook beyond school. At home, I find myself practising greater patience and respect with my family, listening more intently, and resolving conflicts with understanding. Resilience, in particular, has helped me navigate challenges with a positive mindset, both inside and outside of school, ensuring I approach life's hurdles with determination rather than defeat'.

Tameika, a Year 11 student who has faced significant personal challenges and tragedy in recent years but who remains an immensely strong, passionate, and aspirational young woman, remarks, 'Growing up, I've always been inspired to make change within disadvantaged communities, and seeing corruption firsthand in countries like Ethiopia really inspired me. Throughout Key Stage 3, the DNA curriculum showed me what challenges you might face living in any community. I chose to study citizenship to learn more about not only my own rights, but also the rights that many people around the world still lack today'.

Rola, the parent of Serena, a Year 11 student, explains how Leeds City Academy has supported her daughter since Year 7: 'The core of achieving career goals lies in how your character is shaped by your values, morals, knowledge, skills, and judgment. The most successful individuals embrace values such as professionalism, care, respect, aspiration, resilience, and tolerance. I was pleased to hear my daughter learned these values at school, and I have consistently found students to be well-presented and who exhibit excellent behaviour. This reflects the school's commitment to instilling positive values in its students, ultimately shaping them into responsible and decent young citizens. The school has played a vital role in preparing my daughter to be a responsible and engaged citizen and has provided the support, values, and commitment that align closely with what we believe is essential for any person to become a better version of themselves. Values improve how we live'.

Closing thoughts

While there are clearly tangible and quantifiable outcomes to our work, as Principal I reflect more on the idea of the 'sum of the parts' and that in shaping and embedding this work, you may never see the impact due to the fact that shaping, influencing and supporting young students into adulthood is often difficult or potentially impossible to measure or quantify, as it ranges from the very subtle to extremely profound.

What is sure is that students at Leeds City Academy attend a school that places great value on the critical role of values, behaviours, and responsibility at its core. These add value in supporting students to develop behaviours that will help support, influence, and shape their current and future lives for the better. We remain absolutely committed to this.

Section 2
Essay 4

Is a good school conceivable without great subject teaching?

Oliver Blond

Think of the times that you were inspired by a teacher at school, and how that impacted you, and the development of your interests and confidence. Such moments can be immeasurably important as they cannot only change your understanding, but they can also change your life.

And the nature of that spark, that moment of recognition, that sense of wonder or sudden enlightenment, is often about your connection to an idea, a body of knowledge, and a way of thinking that can become a lifelong passion.

Developing our understanding and feeling that we can grasp something that was once beyond us is deeply empowering; building and connecting knowledge so that we can move to more complex and challenging material develops our independence and confidence. Neurologically, it changes the pathways in our brains and makes new ones, and it can do the same with our aspirations and ambitions.

If we turn to teachers, one of the key agents in this transmission of ideas, we hear people talk about being motivated by a passion for their subjects, a love of communicating about them, and a belief that learning about them can make a difference to others' lives and futures.

Great subject teaching is about the process by which specialist teachers focus on teaching powerful knowledge (systematic, specialised, uncommon, creative, transformative) that enables and empowers young people to develop their own passions, to think critically and profoundly, to understand the world they live in, to apply themselves to challenges, to shape their interests and make positive decisions.

A good school is a multi-faceted and complex organisation. In its primary role as the social mechanism through which all young people are inducted into adult life, it must be broad and holistic in its aims, and dedicate itself to several purposes, including the educational, physical, social, moral, spiritual, personal and environmental. A good school must enable its young people to thrive in school and beyond school. It must develop their knowledge, skills and understanding, and help them to live healthy and fulfilling lives. And for a good school to be effective, it must also ensure that its teachers and support staff can thrive, enjoy and play their part in making a difference.

A 'good' school

To conceive of a good school without great subject teaching, firstly, seems simply unnecessary. Of course, great teaching must be a key part of a good school, because great teaching is essential for young people to thrive, advance and develop their understanding. Without it, we lose so much, not only by limiting the impact of teachers and reducing their motivation, but also in the loss of the key transformative and empowering aspect of education.

The importance of great subject teaching does not reduce the importance of all the other elements that are vital to a good school, but in a good school, while all parts are valued, there is often a clear sense of what the primary purpose is, and which elements best serve that purpose.

A school's success and purpose will have different elements. There will be a social and visionary aspect, which is about the overall purpose of society and our role in it, to which schools actively contribute. There will be the key agents of change that schools believe are vital to serving this overall purpose. There will be several supportive elements of school life whose purpose is to ensure pupils can access and make the most of their learning. And there will be a set of organisational functions and rules which are seen to best serve the overall purpose of the school.

Put simply, this version of a good school will have a strong social and moral vision, a dedication to teaching and learning, a commitment to the health, safety and wellbeing of its community, and a positive and shared culture. In this simplification, teaching and learning are the key agents of change. Without this core element, there is no means by which healthy, engaged young people can develop and support themselves in contributing to the wider society's vision.

While this is all, to a degree, self-evident, it is worth digging a little deeper to consider why this question needs to be asked in the first place. If it seems unarguable that great subject teaching is a foundational part of a good school, why is this discussion needed? To answer that, I want to go back to the foundation of the Professional Teaching Institute (The PTI), an organisation that has dedicated itself to the promotion of subject teaching and which has, over its 20-year history, developed a deep understanding of the nature and importance of putting 'powerful knowledge' at the centre of teaching and learning.

The challenges of 'learnacy'

The PTI was founded at a time when the primacy of subject teaching was under significant threat. In the 1990s, for a variety of reasons, including technological advances, shifts in employment markets and a focus on economic outcomes, there was a strong focus on learning and skills rather than acquiring subject-specific knowledge.

The key idea was that learning could be taught as a skill in itself, so that schools could create people who could learn how to learn and, therefore, adapt easily to a world in which change was becoming central to all industries. It was seen as the best way to prepare young people for a future which couldn't be predicted.

This approach prioritised a person's economic futures over a holistic view of a fulfilled life and a successful society. In addition, the rhetoric of this movement tended to reduce the teaching of specialist subject knowledge to 'rote learning'. A false polarisation was set up between learning as a distinct discipline which could be applied to any and all situations, and subject knowledge, which was caricatured as a form of recall.

While there was much to be gained through a consideration of skills and concepts that could make people more effective learners, detaching these from any particular and specialised knowledge, and the mastery of specific concepts, bodies of knowledge and ideas was, in time, seen to be damaging and debilitating for teachers and students. The key criticisms of 'learnacy' were that it could lead to a loss of subject rigour, prevent deeper learning and would leave young people without key knowledge, both scientific and cultural, that could result in a less fair and equitable society.

This approach to education, at least in its more populist form, seemed not to recognise that specific specialist knowledge is required for the development of critical thinking, problem-solving and creativity. It did not consider the way that skills are very subject-specific, nor acknowledge that committing knowledge to memory enables the brain to take on more difficult challenges.

Criticisms of this approach centred on the shallow, transactional nature of skills-based learning and the view that skills cannot be simply transferred across disciplines. In addition, there was a serious concern that young people were being denied access to a rich body of cultural knowledge, which not only prevented access to participation in many aspects of social life but could further disadvantage children who did not have independent access to such knowledge or resources.

While the key criticisms of loss of breadth and depth are important, teachers who attended PTI courses reported that teaching with a focus on skills rather than subject knowledge was more difficult and could be dull. It was the subject matter itself that could spark and engage and inspire, not the skills that these ideas developed. A scheme of work and assessment that prioritised skills could lead to uninspiring lessons, and the lack of intellectual progress or curiosity could demotivate teachers and pupils.

One of the core ideas of 'learnacy' was based on the belief that we should bend education to the needs of the future workforce, but it was argued that focusing on transferable skills could lead to a loss of knowledge that would impact on the country's global competitiveness and reputation, and also on all those careers that are based on deep and specialised knowledge.

The focus on learning and skills led to a better understanding of the importance of subject knowledge, and the centrality of great subject teaching not only to schools, but to the quality of the workforce, cultural richness, global competitiveness, intellectual curiosity, and the motivation of students and teachers.

The return of knowledge

The particular debates about skills versus knowledge that raged when the PTI was founded reduced somewhat throughout the early 2000s, as the arguments for a focus on skills did not stand up to scrutiny. As educational thinking tends to move as a pendulum, it was no surprise that the response to 'leaning to learn' culture was a renewed emphasis on knowledge and a 'knowledge-rich curriculum', with British policy-makers turning to educationalists like ED Hirsch for their inspiration, and renewing the call for 'cultural literacy', 'the best that has been thought and said', and the importance of a core body of knowledge at the heart of education.

National Curriculum reforms focused on clearly delineated subject knowledge that, it was argued, would empower students, aid social mobility and provide the foundation for academic success. Associated with this shift was a focus on rigour, which was a reaction to the perceived lack of rigour of the skills-based educational model.

While there were certainly positives in this focus on subjects and powerful, transformative knowledge, there were also difficulties. Focusing on knowledge and identifying which concepts and content should be taught in school could be seen to deskill teachers and provide so much material that teachers and pupils are overwhelmed. In addition, if knowledge is approached in such a centrally controlled manner, there is a danger of a return to rote-style learning, and a loss of critical thinking, creativity and genuine understanding.

The importance of teachers

While policymakers and theorists argued between skills and knowledge, and the educational landscape moved first one way, then the other, the importance of the teacher's role and engagement was not given due consideration. Teachers, with both approaches, became instrumental to the educational values and systems decided far away from their classrooms.

While it may be difficult to argue that the current crisis in teacher recruitment and retention is directly related to successive policy decisions which have reduced professional judgement, teacher autonomy and decision-making, it is certainly an important factor. As has been argued earlier, teachers are passionate subject specialists and need an environment which allows them to develop and share this passion. Both educational models outlined have, in different ways, narrowed educational choice and reduced the capacity and reach of teachers.

So, while questions about the teaching of subject knowledge continue and focus on any number of different issues (such as content selection, depth versus breadth, assessment and accountability), they fail to focus on the centrality and importance of the teacher to great subject teaching, and that is key to the future of the profession.

Great subject teaching

While today, it seems clear that a good school depends on great subject teaching, there are very different views about what great teaching consists of, and how it is sustained and achieved. One of the first cohorts of teachers who attended a PTI subject residential course remarked on the fact that she had taught for 30 years, and never had any professional development which developed her subject knowledge, and re-inspired her in her love of the subject, which she felt was detrimental to what she was trying to achieve as a teacher.

Many teachers who have been associated with the PTI over the last 20 years are of the view that a good school depends on high-quality, teacher-led education and teachers who are encouraged, empowered and engaged. It is the quality, passion, engagement and skills of the teacher that are central to pupil development and success. This depends on teachers being inspired, encouraged and challenged, not only to do their best for their pupils, but within their own knowledge base and in their pedagogy. It is vital for great subject teachers that professional development allows subject specialists to reflect, to learn and to share in the context of their subjects.

Teaching as a technical skill

Alternative models of enabling great teaching (such as the Oak National Academy[1] model) tend towards uniformity and standardisation. This does not appear to be based on a consideration of best practice or on the ability to improve levels of motivation and engagement, but on the simpler metrics of scalability and repeatability, as if teaching is more like a technical skill than a complex and dynamic interaction.

Pre-prepared lesson plans and materials might appear to focus on subject knowledge and do not attract the same criticisms that were levelled at the 'learning to learn' approach, but they do have many drawbacks, including the issue that they undermine the integrity, knowledge and understanding of the teacher. They narrow and reduce rather than broaden and elevate.

Simplified, repeatable, scalable methods of instruction are undeniably useful in certain circumstances, particularly in times of crisis, but they do lead not only to a one-size-fits-all, conveyor belt approach to teaching but also a similar attitude to education in children. Pupils and students will become very aware of being seen as instrumental in nature if the education they are offered can be reduced to a template.

Seemingly transformative solutions to one set of problems in a school can lead to serious consequences elsewhere, and these approaches have been roundly criticised by teachers and school leaders alike for lacking depth and breadth, limiting independent thinking, narrowing educational focus, and developing an assessment-driven and operational approach to education and people.

There is no doubt that the best teachers can deliver exceptional teaching based on such templates, usually by subverting them, but for many hard-pressed teachers, they appear to offer an escape route only to create a compliance-based, thought-limiting approach to planning and delivery which underutilises a teacher's knowledge and skills while undermining their fundamental role, belief and purpose.

A teacher's role is to believe

It must be remembered that teachers are specialists not only in their subject knowledge, but in their unique role as the representatives and advocates of their subject and their development in the school. A good teacher believes in what they are doing and in the ability of their pupils to improve. Template teaching strips teachers of this role and their agency, but it also fails to recognise, as pupils are quick to point out, that a teacher is more than someone who can deliver a lesson plan, but someone who cares deeply and passionately about the knowledge they are teaching and the children who are engaging and grappling with that knowledge. What we need in terms of subject knowledge is not a set of quick-fix, knowledge-lite, or crisis-ready solutions, but approaches that enable teachers to deepen their knowledge, reflect on and test subject-specific pedagogy, challenge themselves and develop their style.

Professional development

The impact that professional development can have on great subject teaching is far less talked about in educational circles because it is the more difficult and more time-consuming solution, and because of that, the solution that is the most lasting and transformative. Those schools that have the courage to put principles first and the transactional and instrumental to one side report the benefits in teacher motivation, pupil fulfilment, and achievement.

Time and time again, through the PTI, we have seen the positive impact of courses which focus on providing the time and space for teachers to think, reflect and share, engage with the latest research, and deepen their subject knowledge, while being pushed and challenged intellectually and in terms of their role as teachers. At a time when teacher recruitment and retention are in a state of crisis, this approach can return teachers to their sense of purpose and vocation, and remind them of their rewarding and vital intellectual and public role.

The views of teachers

It is important to take this opportunity to reflect not on the theories and debates, but on the experiences, principles and beliefs of those teachers who have faced challenges in school but have retained a belief in the transformative power that teaching can have on the lives of others. Over the years, many thousands of teachers have attended PTI courses, and the quotations below provide a brief outline of how subject-specific professional development can have a significant and lasting impact.

Subject knowledge and inspiration

Teachers repeatedly emphasised the importance of deepening their subject knowledge and rediscovering the importance and excitement of their disciplines:

> This simply was the best talk I have been to in years and years and years. I feel so lucky to have heard it, and it has reinvigorated my views of this topic.
> CPD Online Course participant

> Hearing academics speak and being guided by inspirational teacher leaders gave me the permission I needed to celebrate the beauty of my subject.
> Assistant Headteacher

Teaching and career impact

Teachers also noted how focusing on their subject rejuvenated their teaching practice, provided fresh ideas, and inspired them to embrace new challenges:

> The course has made me consider taking more risks and being braver in picking topics that are not areas of my direct expertise.
> Director of Music, Gordon's School

I have been reminded why I became a teacher and just how wonderful this profession truly is. I am returning to my department FULL of ideas to implement.

Attendee, Subject Enrichment Residential

Student engagement and outcomes

Teachers also reflected on how improved subject expertise and innovative teaching practices translated directly into higher student engagement and better learning outcomes:

> The poetry unit really improved students' overall appreciation of whole collections and the power of a poetic voice.
>
> Attendee, West Kirby Grammar School

> Pupils developed an enthusiasm for mathematics which led to a significant increase in students taking higher tier GCSE Mathematics and improved exam success.
>
> Curriculum Leader, Leeds West Academy

Collaboration and leadership

Teachers highlighted the value of networking and the opportunity to collaborate with colleagues across the country to share ideas and best practices:

> PTI has provided an incredible national network of colleagues who enthusiastically support one another by sharing best practice and inspiring ideas.
>
> Attendee, Bexley Grammar School

> The programme helped to develop and strengthen my subject knowledge of key areas in history, and also gave me practical ways to implement this into my classroom practice.
>
> Attendee, History Teacher

Leadership development

Teachers felt encouraged and enabled to take on leadership roles, innovate their curricula, and inspire their departments:

> The PTI has created a platform for research and debate on our everyday practice, and both myself and my department have hugely profited from this.
>
> Head of History, Hinchingbrooke School

The Certificate for Subject Leadership allowed me to think about and introduce topics that were completely new.

Head of History, Broadway Academy

Inspiration and creativity

Many teachers expressed a renewed passion for teaching and greater confidence in experimenting with creative approaches:

> The opportunities to share areas of common concern, ideas, resources, inspiration, and moral support were essential.
> Justine Greenhalgh, Ullswater Community College

> The PTI sessions have made me feel braver about trying new things, and my students are loving the change.
> PTI Workshop Attendee

All these teachers, and many more, agree that great subject teaching requires teachers to be enriched, supported and encouraged within their subject disciplines and by other teachers and lecturers. Great teachers are developed through engagement and innovation, trial and error, discussion and debate, and rich professional development rather than through pre-digested programmes and materials. Teachers who have attended PTI courses consistently report on the impact this approach has on their belief, practice and purpose, and how lasting such engagement can be.

In conclusion, while there will always be alternative approaches which seem to offer quick gains or simpler approaches, we should not forget that the primary purpose of a school is to educate each pupil and enable them to thrive, and that is not a simple or straightforward task. It requires a dynamic, caring, holistic approach, and the commitment, enthusiasm and expertise of many people, especially teachers. It is a human endeavour, a vocation, not merely a technical challenge. Our goal as teachers is to enable people to best serve their unique purpose in the world, and that requires that we engage with teachers in a similar manner and support them to embrace and deepen their sense of purpose and commitment.

Going back to the title of this piece, I would argue that it is difficult to conceive of a single good lesson without a great subject teacher, let alone a good school, but looking at it positively, what does this tell us? It tells us to consider the impact we might have if all lessons were taught by inspirational subject specialists, and great subject teaching was the very heart of a good school.

Note

1 Oak National Academy was created in April 2020 as a rapid response to the coronavirus outbreak and provides online resources to support teachers.

Section 2
Essay 5

Local curriculum development

John Wilkinson

In 2017, I accepted the prestigious opportunity to become the new Head of Geography at St Edward's College[1] in Liverpool, a co-educational state school in the north of the city. I immediately encountered multiple barriers, including low levels of recruitment and retention at Key Stages 4 and 5, a diaspora of Geography teachers and a built environment containing classrooms that were ultimately condemned. I reframed these challenges as blank canvas opportunities: my educational goal was to change the narrative, so students did not just come into lessons to learn about Geography, but learning experiences were part of a much bigger journey, where students were developing as Geographers. The silver bullet, which could achieve our ambitious objectives, was centred around the curriculum.

The approach we decided to take to curriculum development was shaped by the application of certain 'pillars'[2] – principles of curriculum development. The result has been a multifarious array of truly transformational outcomes for learners, enriching their personal geographies with awe and wonder. Classifying our curriculum into discrete pillars provided an effective working methodology to shape the evolution of our programme of study. We have deliberately focused on the local sense of place, lived experience, built environment, identity and the physical environment in our curriculum construction so we can achieve our educational goal of developing Geographers who think globally, act locally and live sustainably. Examples of how we use the pillars include:

Pillar 1: Developing a challenging, innovative and enriching curriculum

The Key Stage 3 Geography National Curriculum is a blank canvas and offers opportunities for creativity, dynamism and transformative learning and teaching. A combination of spirit and determination can ensure even the most esoteric of concepts and case studies transition from exclusive to accessible learning experiences, particularly when celebrating everyday geographies in the local environment, adding value to students' personal geographies.[3]

Liverpool is home to Everton and Liverpool Football Club. Everton is a founding member of the Football League, with Liverpool being the most successful English football club of all time. Sporting identity is the beating heart of our city. When constructing our Key Stage 3 curriculum (S2 Table E5.1), we knew it was essential to include everyday geographies which address the sporting identity of the lived experiences of our students' daily lives.

Our department developed a Soccernomics scheme of learning, the provenance of inspiration quarried from Kuper and Szymanski's seminal text.[4] Why should students not learn about football in Geography lessons? However, we needed to be aware of the demand for rigour, essentially: 'Where's the Geography?'[5] Soccernomics uses football as a vehicle to consider the global intersectionality of money, power and identity in the 21st century,[6] with students learning about social inequalities, economic change and environmental sustainability.

Soccernomics has provided the Geography department at St Edwards College with a sustainable competitive advantage. Our current three-year trend shows a 50.5% increase in the recruitment of GCSE Geographers in a competitive marketplace with a diverse selection of options. How? Schemes of learning like Soccernomics provide challenging yet engaging and exciting activities[7], and students are enthusiastic about developing hinterland knowledge about their place, a key stepping stone in their evolution as Geographers.

Local curriculum development is a challenge: colleagues who can access materials about their local place in textbooks are both in the minority and incredibly lucky. However, the time and effort ploughed into developing sequences of lessons and schemes of learning about local concepts and case studies is an investment in success and offers an authenticity that learners will inevitably buy into, securing rapid and sustained progress.

Pillar 2: Enthusing pupils through subject-based activities beyond the curriculum

We made a conscious decision to exploit educators' cross-curricular expertise in the department to enrich learners' experiences through the integration of adjacent complementary disciplines into our supra-curricular programme of study. Geology

S2 Table E5.1 St Edward's College Geography Department KS3 Programme of Study 2024–25

	Unit 1	Unit 2	Unit 3	Unit 4	Unit 5
Year 7	**An Introduction to Geography** Geographical skills, regeneration, rebranding, reimagining	**Rivers and flooding** Processes, landforms, flooding Fieldwork@ Sandstone Trail.	**Prisoners of Geography** Development: challenges & opportunities	**Climate change** Causes, impacts, responses	**SEC Fieldwork** Weather & Climate
Year 8	**Addressing Africa** Conflict, poverty, health	**Cold Environments** Processes, landforms and climate change	**Soccernomics** Social inequalities and economic change	**Coastal Environmental Change** Processes, landforms, sea level change Fieldwork@ Sefton Coast	**SEC Fieldwork** Biogeography
Year 9	**Extreme Environments** Mountains, deserts, polar Fieldwork@ Moel Famau	**Globalisation & Development** Concepts, case studies, social media	**Hazards** Tectonic, atmospheric, multi-hazardous environments	**The Beatles: Music, Money & Macca** Social inequalities, economic change & sustainability	**SEC Fieldwork** Forestry

S2 Table E5.2 St Edward's College Geography Department's five-year Geology plan

Year	Key characteristics
1	Key Stage 3 extra – curricular Geology club: 'the school of rock' – an introduction to Geology
2	Year 10 GCSE Geology, 30 minutes/week – analysing and interpreting rock exposures
3	Year 11 GCSE Geology, 1 hour/week – big ideas, planetary geology, human interactions
4	Year 12 AS Geology, 2 hours/week – foundations in geology
5	Year 13 AS Geology, 2 hours/week – global tectonics, interpreting the past

was the obvious choice. In 2025, the Geographical Association's educational goal is to promote connected geographies, highlighting tangible links between adjacent disciplines.[8]

S2 Table E5.2 shows our five-year plan.
Each of the five years' facets is cumulative. The staggered staging has cultivated capacity across the department, which has allowed all experiences to be active simultaneously.

Data has produced some interesting outcomes, including examination results, recruitment and retention. In 2023, GCSE Geology grade 7–9s scored 37.5%, with 50% of our student cohort being girls, in a subject where there has been a traditional gender inequality (nationally, on average, 7 out of 10 examination entries are boys). In 2024, our students achieved 83% grades 7–9, significantly above the national average. Furthermore, examination results in physical Geography exams improved by 8% in 2024 compared to 12 months previously – a marginal gain, the product of the presence of Geology within the department improving outcomes for GCSE Geographers. We currently have 31 students at St Edwards College attending Year 10 GCSE Geology lessons in their own time in twilight sessions – this is the real success story. Last year, only 590 students were entered for GCSE Geology across the UK.

All colleagues have qualities which they can supply for departmental development across the curriculum in adjacent disciplines, regardless of context. Our five-year model offers a framework colleagues can adopt elementally or in its entirety to add value to learners' experiences and develop their subject's culture across the curriculum.

Pillar 3: Enriching the subject knowledge and impact of all teachers within the department

Teachers can always upskill and develop their tradecraft. Educators constantly adapting[9] to the ebb and flow of pedagogy and the dynamics of their discipline make sigmoid leaps in terms of learning and teaching,[10] ensuring their students

Local curriculum development **93**

enjoy and achieve. A sigmoid leap involves identifying when learning experiences are no longer lucrative for learners and require maintenance, modernisation and/or wholesale change. As a consequence, educators jump onto the upward trajectory of the ensuing curve. CPD is the key to successful sigmoid leaps as illustrated in S2 Figure E5.1.

As a part-time PhD student at the University of Liverpool studying sea level change in the Mersey-Lowlands, I was excited by the opportunity to use my research to add value to St Edward's Geographers' learning experiences through the integration of high-order concepts, case studies and skills.

My thesis focuses on fieldwork in an ancient coastal environment using short cores to access sediments which can be analysed and interpreted to show a range of paleo-coastal environments evidencing sea level change – it uses a selection of progressive data collection, presentation and analytical techniques and is a terrific mechanism to segue A Level into undergraduate Geography. My academic experiences supported students' coursework and core content across all syllabuses, particularly regarding coastal systems and landscapes, increasing percentages of As and A*s – in 2024, 39% of students secured As and A*s. Examination outcomes are influenced by a deeper, academic, undergraduate knowledge and understanding. The ability to model the value of academia, essentially my commitment to study 20 years into my career, offered authenticity and consequently 'buy-in' from students – in 2023, 33% of our A-level cohort progressed to study Geography in Higher Education.

A PhD is a terrific opportunity, but I am the first to admit this is a finite form of CPD. However, any CPD will add value to learners' academic experiences and invariably increase their cultural currency, especially when concepts and case

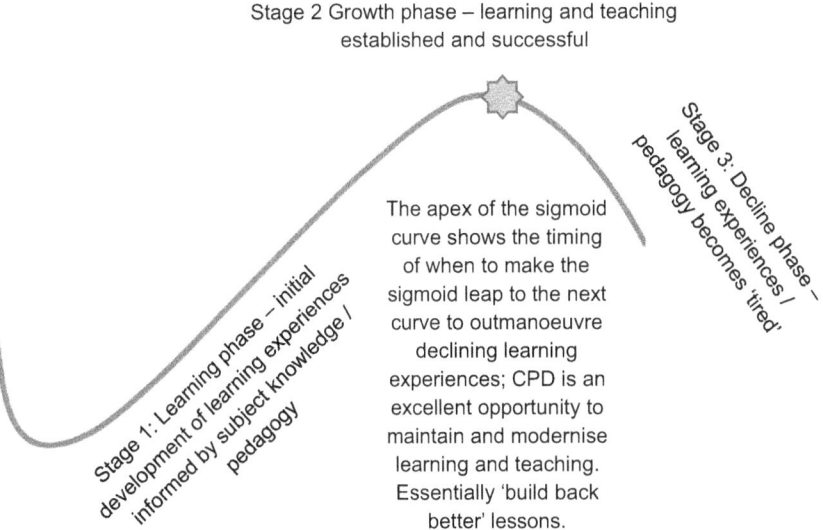

S2 Figure E5.1   Sigmoid curve application to CPD engagement (inspired by Handy, 1995).

studies supersede conventional curricula. Local knowledge and understanding in terms of the intricacies of concepts and case studies is a sure-fire guarantee of success.

Pillar 4: Encouraging links within/beyond school, including universities/professional bodies

Interconnectivity with external agencies generates interdisciplinarity and opens us to extraordinary opportunities to contribute to learners' cultural currency. The nexus of a diverse array of local stakeholders has the power to seamlessly transition the mundane into the mesmerising, lighting the fires of community cohesion.

The school grounds at St Edward's College contain ancient woodland where, historically, there was a rudimentary trail approximately 1km in length, which was no longer accessible due to colonisation by vegetation / excessive overgrown foliage. The Geography Department led the effort to cultivate the Milankovitch Woodland Trail, which is now a 670-metre stretch of forest in the heart of the city fit for purpose for academic and pastoral utility (S2 Figure E5.2).

S2 Figure E5.2 The Milankovitch Woodland Trail at St Edward's College in North Liverpool. Only 15% of the city's green space is situated in the north of the city – our initiative is an effort to address environmental inequalities and associated quality of life/standard of living impacts for our college community.

Geography fieldwork experiences are now integrated into all year groups' programme of study on the college campus in the woodland, including micro-climate, biodiversity and the carbon cycle. The St Edward's Environmental Expedition, a team of 6th formers and staff, have cleared the trail of pollution/contamination and is a stakeholder in the development, governance and decision-making of the woodland moving forward – an investment in success and sustainability. This supports our *raison d'être* that students' contributions were becoming part of their lived experience, that they were truly developing as geographers exercising a critical thinking skillset.[11] Regenerating and re-wilding the woodland, supporting our community's mental health through the provision of a safe space while allowing for market-gardening/ornithology on site, are some of the ambitious, achievable aims of the project.

External agencies are keen to contribute to educational initiatives – blue sky thinking is an asset, and accessing links and connections with local government, corporate bodies and community groups can provide expertise, technology and resources which are not available in schools. This can lead to transformational change, experiences and ultimately, exciting outcomes. A speculative email is a great place to start.

Conclusion

Sustainable curriculum development is rooted in integrity. Honour, loyalty and trust are in short supply when we consider the intersectionality of population change and climate change – the two greatest challenges of the 21st century, two challenges which can be addressed by Geography. The PTI's pillars are a first-class vehicle which provides the framework to achieve our department's educational goals, the slick dexterity of learners and educators working together to be good ancestors, leaving the jersey in a better place, planting trees we will never see.[12] St Edward's geographers think globally and act locally, future-proofing the global village with forward-thinking, outward-facing values, the result of intellectual and emotional investment in local curriculum development.

Notes

1 St Edward's College (SEC) is an 11-18 co-educational, Catholic comprehensive school, in West Derby, Liverpool. 1171 students are on roll. 60% of students would be eligible for grammar schools, while there are average Pupil Premium and SEND numbers compared to other educational settings outside of the Liverpool City Region.
2 The 'Pillars' were taken from the Professional Teaching Institute (PTI). www.ptieducation.org - a first-class framework for curriculum development from the PTI's Departmental Development Programme.
3 Parkinson A, 'Everyday geographies: the power of the quotidian', *Teaching Geography*, 47(2), 2022, pp 53–55.

4 Kuper S and Szymanski S, *Soccernomics: Why England loses, why Germany and Brazil win, and why the US, Japan, Australia, Turkey - and even Iraq - are destined to become the kings of the world's most popular sport*, Hachette, 2018.
5 Roberts M, 'Where's the geography? Reflections on being an external examiner', *Teaching Geography*, 35(3), 2010, p 112.
6 Goldblatt D, *The age of football: The global game in the twenty-first century*, Pan Macmillan, 2019.
7 Hughes M, *The Magenta Principles: Engagement, Depth and Challenge in the Classroom*. Magenta Principles Limited, 2014.
8 Bustin R, 'Editorial', *Teaching Geography*, 49(2), 2024, p 49.
9 Kerr J, *Legacy,* Hachette, 2013.
10 Handy C, *The empty raincoat: Making sense of the future*, Random House, 1995.
11 Leat D, *Thinking Through Geography*, Chris Kington Publishing, 1998.
12 Kerr J, *Legacy,* Hachette, 2013.

Section 2
Essay 6

Education as transmitting knowledge, values and cultural identity

Erika Podmore

There is no doubt that a core purpose of education is to teach or transmit knowledge, but in schools, we transmit far more than just knowledge. Through the hidden as well as the taught curriculum, we can significantly impact the values and cultural identity of the students we teach. Reflecting on a career spanning over 30 years of teaching and leading in Inner London secondary schools, my experience has shown me that school leaders and teachers are in a powerful position to impact positively not just on students but on their communities and wider society in ways that go far deeper than just academic outcomes.

It was 1989 when I started training to become a history teacher, in a time pre-National Curriculum when the Inner London Education Authority (ILEA) still directed teachers to London schools and the main tools of the trade were blackboards, chalk and the Banda machine.[1] I have worked in four different schools since then and spent the last seven as headteacher of a local authority-controlled comprehensive girls' school in Eltham, South East London. I went into teaching not because of any great sense of vocation but because I wanted to carry on studying history and could not afford to stay in education any longer. I also had a vague sense of being able to make a difference as a teacher, to impact on the development of the next generation and even in some way to make the world a better place. I was also inspired by a great teacher, John Hite, my teacher for O

Level and A Level history at a comprehensive school in Sussex, who was one of the brilliant minds behind the Schools History Project (SHP) in the 1980s.[2] He created challenging resources focused on analysing evidence and historical investigation at a time when many history teachers were still just dictating information, and his lessons made me think deeply and question everything. As a rebellious teenager, I very nearly dropped out of school in the 6th form and only went on to study history at King's College London because of the inspiration he offered. The knowledge he and a few other teachers transmitted was powerful: it opened a world of ideas in terms of politics and philosophy and gave me the tools to understand and interpret the world. It is why, as a school leader, I invest heavily in supporting teachers to develop their subject knowledge and become experts in their fields. Great teachers change lives with the knowledge and values they transmit, and every adult should be able to tell you about at least one who changed theirs for the better.

Deciding on precisely what knowledge to transmit to students is a challenge for both school leaders and governments. I entered the teaching profession in June 1990, starting work as a history teacher in a South London girls' school. It was a time of real change; the ILEA had been abolished in April 1990, and the first National Curriculum had just been brought in following the 1988 Education Reform Act.[3] We used our 'Baker days' (INSET days named after the architect of the Act, Conservative Minister Kenneth Baker) to plan the implementation of the new required knowledge. Before that, teachers had free rein to choose what they taught outside of exam syllabi and from my teaching practice experiences, I knew that could lead to very inconsistent experiences for students. At one school I was at, Year 9 spent a term studying the assassination of President Kennedy and later did a term on the history of smoking, so although I did not support many of the education reforms brought in by Margaret Thatcher's government, I did see the value of having a coherent curriculum plan that allowed some choice within an agreed structure. Of course, since 2013, we have had the revised National Curriculum devised by Michael Gove, which was intended to ensure 'that all children have the opportunity to acquire a core of essential knowledge in key subjects'.[4] In reality, now, as Academies are exempt from following that curriculum and, as of January 2023, 80.4% of secondary schools are Academies or Free Schools, it is not a 'national' curriculum at all. Sadly, in many schools, the reality is that the breadth of knowledge taught has decreased significantly because of the focus on league tables; consequently, children are back in an education lottery, and some lose out when it comes to wider learning or just learning for the love of it.

One thing I learnt early on in my career is that the choices school leaders make about what knowledge to transmit and how to do so, both communicate our values and can contribute to the sense of cultural identity for students in schools. Leading a history department in a girls' school in Brixton for seven years in the 1990s, it was apparent that virtually none of the students we taught felt their cultural identity was valued within the education system. Whether from a black Caribbean, black African or white working-class background, there was a sense of disconnect from the curriculum and the values of the school. It became crucial in history to look at our schemes of learning and make sure we were using our choice of content to show our students we valued them and to build a positive sense of identity. Choosing to study apartheid in South Africa, the role of empire in Africa and slave revolts alongside the units on slavery and the role of women and working-class communities in bringing about social and political change, made a massive difference to how the students viewed history and their own role within it. It has been a joy in recent years to see how many of those students have gone on to become school leaders in London themselves, inspired by their education to give back to their communities.

My experience as Head of Humanities and then as Assistant Headteacher on the Isle of Dogs between 1997 and 2008 made it clear to me how the ability to make choices about what is communicated can impact not just individuals but a whole community. It was an exciting time to be in education, when Excellence in Cities was transforming London schools, and education was a top priority for the Labour government, but the development of the Docklands had resulted in huge tensions in that part of London. We were able to use our history teaching there to question the narrative being pushed by the far-right British National Party, who had managed to get a councillor elected in the East End in 1993.[5] It was a time when there was a huge divide and massive mistrust between the white working-class community and the Bengali community, so an understanding of Empire, learning about the history of the docks and of London's diverse history, was crucial in changing attitudes. Equally important was teaching students that being proud of being British did not mean hating immigrants and that being a British Muslim was not a contradiction in terms. The values we were transmitting as a school at that time were often unpopular with sections of the local community, but the positive impact on students and their relationships with each other was clear to see. The brave leadership of Headteacher Kenny Frederick and her simple but effective vision of 'All Different, All Equal' inspired at least eight of her middle leaders at that time to go on to headship and helped to create a whole generation of forward-thinking community leaders from the student body.

In 2002, citizenship was introduced into the National Curriculum, and as Head of Humanities, I led on its development.[6] There was much discussion about how best to teach the values of democracy, the rule of law and respect and tolerance for diversity, and we established a new GCSE course as well as lots of assemblies and drop-down days. What became clear to me over time, however, was that those values could not be taught in the same way as we deliver knowledge. The values students learn in school are those that they soak up through the choices school leaders make about their curriculum, the opportunities they are given, the way they are treated and the way the adults in the school community treat each other. The behaviour policy and approach to Special Educational Needs and Disabilities (SEND) in a school are often better indicators of the values being transmitted to students than the headteacher's statement about 'our values' on the website. The staff structures created and the allocation of funds within a school to certain areas over others build the framework from which the values of a school are made a reality. For example, it is a conscious choice to allocate funds towards a wide range of activities to celebrate Black History Month, including a staff-and-student-led two-day conference, but in a school that celebrates the diversity of our society, it is a vital part of communicating that value.

As a school leader, you can have a massive impact on how knowledge, values and cultural identity are communicated and taught within your school. You set out the values of the school and recruit those who share your vision. Each school can develop its own distinct identity, and if you get it right, the students and staff feel a real pride in being part of that community. In my school, we have spent the last five years focusing on getting Key Stage 3 right, ensuring the curriculum develops deep subject knowledge and that teachers can recognise and explain the links between subjects. We define the vocabulary we want students to be confident in understanding and using, then fine-tune the connections between subjects so that schemata are carefully built up and reinforced over time. This allows students to build up a sophisticated understanding of the world rather than just learning the facts required to pass exams, but also communicates the fact that we value learning for its own sake.

It is vital that subject leaders are given the time to think carefully about what they choose to teach and how they deliver that content. We work within the National Curriculum but make choices that support us in communicating our values and in validating the cultural identity of our students. For example, in history, we choose to study the empires in Ghana and Mali alongside the required study of Norman England and the Angevin Empire so that we challenge the misconception that African history began with the slave trade. We also choose to deliver knowledge-rich drop-down days to focus on areas of the world or human experience that are relevant to our students but are not covered in the timetabled curriculum. We choose to value creativity alongside the EBacc by having a compulsory creative option for all students at Key Stage 4, to subsidise instrumental lessons and prioritise an annual production and termly concerts.

In a diverse South London school, cultural identity is often excitingly complicated, and the fastest growing ethnic group are those who would describe themselves as mixed heritage. We teach our students through the curriculum that we are a nation of immigrants with different groups moving into this island from the Stone Age onwards. We actively challenge racist ideas, particularly important in an area most renowned for the racist murder of Stephen Lawrence in 1993.[7] As a school, we are in a powerful position to help students develop an understanding of and pride in their often very complicated cultural identity, which includes feeling proud of where their family originated from, proud of being British and of being a Londoner. The knowledge we teach in our curriculum, consciously decolonised and celebrating diversity, supports this understanding. Outside of the curriculum, we also have termly cultural celebration weeks which provide a real opportunity to learn about and celebrate the cultures of members of our community; last year, that included celebrating the cultures of both Ukraine and Russia, an important lesson that you can be proud of your culture without supporting the actions of the politicians in charge. This year, we are looking at Afghanistan and Scotland amongst others, and England is on the plan to be celebrated too, making it clear that the use of the St George's flag by the far right does not mean that we cannot be proud of and celebrate English culture and history.

Our commitment to inclusivity is communicated through our very clear vision to be a highly successful comprehensive community school where every student is supported to achieve their very best, whatever their starting point. Democratic values are clearly communicated through our approach to student leadership and response to student voice, as well as being explored through the curriculum. Rules are clear and expectations are high, but students are supported to be consistently kind, to learn how to behave well and to resolve difficulties with their peers. Importantly, staff model this in their interactions with students and with each other. A whole school focus on oracy, critical thinking and developing public speaking and debating skills supports students to feel empowered to make sense of their world and to go out and make a difference in it.

Working in London schools for over 30 years, I have seen the impact of education on a generation of young people and have watched them become more tolerant, open-minded and increasingly less likely to be influenced by ideologies of hate and division. It fills me with optimism about the ways in which the knowledge, values and sense of cultural identity that we communicate as teachers and leaders can help to transform our communities and our country.

Notes

1 The Banda machine was a spirit duplicator - also known as a Rexograph, Ditto machine or Fordigraph.
2 'Interview with John Hite, 11 July 2010', *The History in Education Project*, https://archives.history.ac.uk/history-in-education/browse/interviews/interview-john-hite-11-july-2010.
3 *Education Reform Act 1988*, www.legislation.gov.uk.
4 'Education Reform: New National Curriculum for Schools', www.gov.uk, 12 September 2013.
5 '1993: Shock as Racist Wins Council Seat', BBC On This Day, 17 September 1993. http://news.bbc.co.uk/onthisday.
6 *Citizenship Education in England 2001 to 2010*, Department for Education, 25 November 2010.
7 'Stephen Lawrence Would Have Been 50 Today. Is There Still a Chance to Get Justice for Him?' BBC InDepth, 13 September 2024, www.bbc.co.uk/news/articles/ce8083pzrpdo.

Section 2
Essay 7

Rendering tensions productive: Finding joy and seeking wisdom in the intellectual enterprise of the curriculum

Richard Kueh

Leadership of the curriculum is tough. It goes way beyond the managerial. It goes to the very heart of the 'what' and the 'why' of education. As such, leadership of the curriculum is an intrinsically intellectual enterprise. The curriculum (from the Latin '*currere*', 'to run' as in 'to run a racecourse') is the journey that leaders set out for pupils to explore, to navigate and – as I will touch on later – to ascend. It is a privilege and joy to bear the responsibility for designing, constructing and continually renewing it. It is not, however, without its challenges.

It is precisely to these intellectual challenges of continual curriculum formation that this chapter attends. In it, I will explore four high-level challenges that curriculum leaders and those with senior curriculum oversight face. In fact, these challenges are more like 'tensions' that exist in all curriculums, and are embodied within the decisions of design and perceived in the experience of enactment.

The purpose of this chapter is not to offer simple solutions to such tensions, but to cast a light on them. Indeed, the range and depth of issues often at stake within each set of tensions should cause the reader to be suspicious of those offering simple solutions to them. Instead, my aim here is to signpost and to map out aspects of their conceptual geography; to consider the framework of their architecture; and to offer broad brushstrokes to facilitate their visualisation. Following this, I shall reflect on the kinds of values and competencies that these questions *demand* of us as curriculum leaders.

So, what are the curriculum tensions that permeate? I offer four, but make no claims as to their totality or comprehensiveness. I am sure that there are a multitude of curriculum tensions experienced by leaders and thinkers working in education. The four I have selected are as follows:

- Tensions that sit at the core of curriculum decision-making, frequently appearing in debates about content choices (the challenge of curriculum purpose)
- Tensions that play out when wrestling with the idea of progression (the challenge of curriculum progression)
- Tensions that arise in considering how the curriculum is to be taught (the challenge of curriculum pedagogy)
- Tensions that appear, often in practice, between curriculum and assessment (the challenge of curriculum 'processed')

I will explore each of these, in turn, considering some of the key issues at stake. A word of warning, however: a common problem that applies to any kind of abstract discussions about the curriculum is that it too quickly gets divorced from the subjects and phases within the curriculum. I will aim to earth some of the tensions in practical subject examples, but it is important to acknowledge that not all curriculum tensions apply to, say, different subjects in the same way (for instance, some of the issues that apply to secondary history curriculum debates may not translate directly to the teaching of computing at primary). I will, however, make no apology for using some key examples and illustrations from my own subject – religious education – which, too often, gets a rotten deal in the curriculum.

Curriculum purpose

What might three European philosophers from the late twentieth century have to do with the purpose of the curriculum? A short, brief, philosophical excursus, I think, nicely portrays the *tension* at the centre of contemporary debates about curriculum purpose.

There are, of course, various rationales that educational thinkers have posited about curriculum purpose. Some of these include debates about whether the curriculum should have intrinsic or extrinsic value: do we educate for inherent reasons of worth, or do we educate in order to serve economic needs, for instance? Certainly, whatever curriculum approach a school alights on, it is likely to hold these kinds of considerations in *tension*.

But even within circles that value and prioritise the intrinsic worth of the knowledge and skills that pupils develop through the curriculum, the question of 'which knowledge?' and the 'quality' of the knowledge taught is far from clear. To what extent should the selection of the content of the curriculum reflect the social and political issues of the day, and why does this matter?

So, I ask again, what might Hans-Georg Gadamer, Jurgen Habermas and Paul Ricoeur contribute to this question? Let me first introduce Gadamer, who lived to the ripe old age of 102. In fact, had he been born a few months earlier would have had a life that spanned three centuries! He was a philosopher who considered what happens when we *interpret* something. We might *interpret* a novel, a piece of art, a gesture or a symphony. He suggested that when we interpret something, the 'past' – that which has gone before us in the history of culture and civilisation – bears down upon us. Our 'interpretation' is what he called a 'fusion of horizons': the horizon of the text (or novel, or art, or gesture, or symphony) meeting our own horizon shaped by our cultural background.[1]

Habermas, who was part of the Frankfurt School of philosophy, queried this. What troubled Habermas was the way that Gadamer's account of interpretation was too idealistic. In his key works, he outlines his concerns that Gadamer was essentially uncritical.[2] Unlike Gadamer's account of, say, interpreting a text, Habermas thinks that there are forces at work, which means that interpretation needs to be more critical. Inasmuch as we need to consider the ways in which the past empowers us to interpret the text, we also need to consider, for instance, the ways that the text may be a force for oppression or may be rooted in spurious motives of writers and readers.

Our third philosopher, Paul Ricoeur, then interjected into the Gadamer/Habermas debate, and did what all good philosophers do: he sees the tensions between the two, renders them productive and finds a middle way. Ricoeur essentially says that the previous two philosophers are both correct. He says that they reflect two sides of the same coin. In a famous passage in his work, *Freud and Philosophy: An Essay on Interpretation*, he says that these two opposing views express a 'double motivation', a 'willingness to listen' (in the case of Gadamer) as well as a 'willingness to suspect' (in the case of Habermas) and, again, a respective 'vow of obedience' and 'vow or rigour'.[3] In a famous passage, he says:

> In our time we have not finished doing away with idols and we have barely begun to listen to symbols.[4]

I find these words quite revealing of curriculum discussions taking place at the moment. For instance, in considering curriculum choices around representation, ethnic diversity, minority groups and themes linked to suspicion of institutions on matters such as liberty, the enforcement of the law and the sustainability of the planet, we see some of these Gadamer versus Habermas themes playing out in education. 'Past curriculum choices were well-and-good for that time and place, but the curriculum needs to teach pupils how they should respond to these issues now' and 'we cannot put the curriculum in the service of changeable, controversial and sensitive social issues' are apparently contradictory slogans from diametrically opposed camps.

So, what are curriculum leaders to do? They may well take a lesson in rendering a tension productive from Paul Ricoeur: yes, we may well need to do away with idols of the past, but we shouldn't do that at the expense of listening to symbols. The curriculum leader does well to consider, in the subjects and phases they teach, how to enact both a 'vow of obedience' as well as a 'vow of rigour'.

Curriculum progression

Next, let us bridge the abstract and the practical through exploring curriculum progression. One way of considering challenges and tensions within curriculum progression is to consider the tension between the simple and the complex. Or, better, the tensions between the desire to simplify curriculum progression in order to understand it and to represent it (on the one hand) and the inherent complexities involved in articulating an answer to the question 'what does it mean to *get better* at this or that part of the curriculum?' (on the other hand).

Certainly, there is a deceptively simple aspect to 'progression'. One aspect of progression is overall accumulation: a pupil, one would expect, would know and be able to do more than they did previously as they journey through the curriculum. But that really is not a mark of *curriculum progression*; it is more a mark of *temporal progression* – just learning more through exposure over time, irrespective of the substance of what is planned.

What is needed to fill the missing gap, therefore, is for each domain or 'family' of content within the curriculum to be shaped around a plausible theory of 'getting better'. Given that the vast majority of schools in England base their curriculums around specialised domains of subjects, in this context, what matters is the subject-specific journey.

In the past ten years, in particular, engagement with theories and research into educational cognitive psychology has been a focus of teacher development in England. One aspect of this is schema theory: the representation of webs of knowledge in the mind. This is helpful in illustrating the difference between 'temporal progression' and 'curriculum progression' above. Whereas the former might lead to an overall growth in knowledge, the distinguishing feature of the latter is the curriculum-led, teacherly-guided *particular set of connections that sit in the mind*. It is the *particular set of exciting stories* from *particular curriculums* in humanities' subjects that furnishes a *particularly enriched conception* of, say, 'parliament', or 'capital city', or 'creed'. Without that, such words are, for pupils, mere common nouns for which they have a rather incidental set of associations.

So, what matters is a subject-specific journey. That journey can be experienced with excitement, affection and joy by pupils, but it does require thoughtful consideration by leaders of the curriculum. Drawing on schema theory above, Michael Fordham describes this as 'the mental map of the subject you [the teacher or curriculum leader] have in your head'.[5] Here, Fordham is talking about the way that subject knowledge is represented in the mind, and the 'map' is one that leads pupils from their current state (perhaps as novices) to a goal state (as having greater degrees of expertise). It is a subject-specific journey, where the journey is a series of interconnected knowledge steps that, if learned, move pupils from their current state to the teacherly goal state.

The idea of a 'map' is both compelling and helpful. It reminds us not only of a departure point and a destination, but also that the contours of the terrain matter too. Daisy Christodoulou makes this point too: 'the model of progression… [involves] not just the starting point and the end goal but *the steps along the way*'.[6] Earlier, I mentioned pupils exploring, navigating and *ascending* through the curriculum journey. In the context of curriculum, Professor Christopher Winch uses the language of 'epistemic *ascent*'. This can be thought of as a process by which pupils' received understanding is brought into a fresh set of relationships, with knowledge contextualised in subject-specific abstractions and generalisations. A curriculum leader's 'mental map of the subject' is not a flat terrain; it is an upward ascent, towards a summit that represents subject-specific progress.

Now, what constitutes a mental map of a subject, an upward ascent, the steps along the way, will absolutely depend on the nature of the subject. Ruth Ashbee calls this the 'manthanology' of a subject. Some subjects require essential prior knowledge components in order to access other components; other subjects do not require something logically prior. She points out that '[i]n some subjects with strong integrations, such as maths and languages, there are specific components that must be mastered in order to access a particular piece of new knowledge…'[7] To use a rather obvious example from mathematics: in order to be able to multiply fractions, one requires functional knowledge of times tables.

But other subjects are not so straightforward. In subjects where there are more aesthetic choices, such as in the humanities or areas of the arts, there is a range of choices that can be made, often with no obvious starting point. Let us consider an illustration from religious education to help.

Consider the approach of three curriculum leaders: leader A, leader B and leader C:

- Leader A has noticed that there are six half terms in the year and considers there to be six main religious traditions for pupils to study (Buddhist, Christian, Hindu, Islamic, Jewish and Sikh traditions). Pupils study each tradition, one per half term, each year throughout primary.

- Leader B also wants pupils to study these six traditions, but groups them according to familial relations of the traditions. So, pupils learn about the 'Abrahamic' traditions in the order in which they appeared in world history

(Jewish, Christian and Islamic traditions) and similarly for 'Dharmic' traditions (Hindu, Buddhist and Sikh traditions), for half the year each.

- Leader C thinks that Leader B's model is a helpful starting point, but wants pupils to recognise by the end of the course that the world's religious landscape is more complex and, in some parts of the world, such as Nepal, the lines between different religious traditions are quite blurred.

Which of these gives the appearance of progression, and which of these offers a more credible account of subject-based epistemic ascent? It is Leader C who considers the steps along the way that lead to an overall more-complex, subject-specific goal.

In wrestling with the challenges and tensions within 'curriculum progression', curriculum leaders can begin to consider the pitfalls and deceptions that might best be avoided. And there are lots out there that are best avoided: curriculums shaped around hierarchies of command words that suggest progress ('describe', 'explain', 'evaluate') unhelpfully avert the eyes of curriculum leaders (and pupils) away from the subject journey. Similarly, the idea of 'age-related expectations' gives the appearance of simplicity of progression, but may not actually reflect the journey, the ascent, set out in the 'mental map of the subject'.

Curriculum pedagogy

What might we mean by 'curriculum pedagogy'? Why not just 'pedagogy'? A little bit of an explanation for clarification and interest, before we move on.

First, pedagogy itself is a fascinating term. From two Greek words for 'child' (as a noun) and (the verb) 'to lead or bring', pedagogy is frequently in UK educational practice understood to mean teaching practices and techniques. Interestingly, on the continent, pedagogy often takes on the wider sense of aims and purposes of education, with 'didactics' used instead as the term that refers to teaching practices and techniques.

Second, the way that pedagogy is discussed, explored and treated by teachers in England, particularly with the aforementioned rise and development of educational cognitive psychology, is also fascinating. Part of the way that teaching as a profession has developed has been through an increasing focus on research. Making 'research-informed' teaching decisions has been supported by a range of initiatives, from resurrecting Barak Rosenshine's work on teaching functions in instructional programmes from the 1980s to current evidence collections by the Education Endowment Foundation (EEF).[8]

Whilst these developments are, in a number of important ways, positive and laudable, there is one key challenge that they pose for curriculum leaders. The challenge is one that is seen in the *tension between curriculum and pedagogy*. Taken on its own terms, principles of instruction, perhaps supported by teaching and learning toolkits, might inform curriculum leaders as they answer the question of 'how' to teach. What principles of instruction are unable to do is answer the question of 'what' to teach.

When senior school leaders tackle issues concerning weaknesses in curriculum, teaching and assessment, taking a prescriptive approach to 'teaching' often seems like a quick win. It's a way of getting the appearance of consistency; it enables claims such as 'x or y percent of teachers are effective in using retrieval practice'. Yet this is problematic if the quality of what is to be learned is bypassed. Curriculum collapses into pedagogy. As Christine Counsell remarked, you can't 'Rosenshine' (used as a verb!) your way out of a curriculum matter: Rosenshine techniques will not help the curriculum leader to weigh, choose, arrange, configure and shape curriculum content.[9]

The tension between curriculum and pedagogy is at its most extreme when they are really considered incidental to each other. In the most egregious cases, they are considered as 'non-overlapping magisteria' (to misquote the historian of science Stephen Jay Gould). The phrase 'non-overlapping magisteria' is sometimes used to denote a position that contends that science answers one type of question, and religions answer another, but fundamentally have little bearing on each other.

Applying that kind of distinction to curriculum and pedagogy, there is an interesting parallel. Whilst it is quite correct that pedagogy cannot answer curriculum questions, it is the curriculum – and the content choices therein – that provides the basis for what is the appropriate pedagogy (or didactic!). Though curriculum and pedagogy both answer different questions, curriculum should be the driver for pedagogical decisions. For this reason, the tension of curriculum and pedagogy can be rendered productive when pedagogy is considered as 'curriculum pedagogy'.

It is curriculum that mediates and moderates pedagogy. Let us take an example of a pedagogical approach involving 'retrieval practice'. Imagine three curriculum leaders for science, music and (as you might expect) religious education in School A, and the curriculum leaders of the same subjects in School B. Each of these curriculum leaders has been directed to ensure that retrieval practice is embedded within their practice:

- In School A, the three curriculum leaders all do a low-stakes quiz in every lesson that revisits key definitions of 'evaporation' (in science), 'hemiola' (in music) and 'dharma' (in religious education).
- In School B, the curriculum leader in science sets a quiz to check pupils' knowledge of evaporation; in music, the curriculum leader plans for pupils to clap a hemiola rhythm for their teachers to check; and in RE, pupils narrate a story that shows the concept of dharma.

Both schools are pursuing a pedagogy that includes retrieval practice, but it is School B that recognises that the way in which retrieval practice depends on subject-specific considerations. Pedagogy without subject-specific and content-specific curriculum considerations becomes a blunt tool. Curriculum choices matter. Pedagogical choices matter too: they matter not just in the sense of being 'warranted', but also in the sense that they are 'curriculum driven'. Curriculum leaders render the tensions between curriculum and pedagogy when they place 'curriculum pedagogy' front and centre.

Curriculum processed?

If curriculum pertains to the substance or content of what is taught, assessment pertains to the extent to which one could claim that the curriculum has been learned: has the pupil inwardly digested the substance of what was intended to be learned? Has the curriculum been processed?

Finally, then, let us consider the tensions that arise between curriculum and assessment, and how they, too, can be rendered productive. Why might there be a tension between curriculum and assessment?

Earlier, in the section above on 'curriculum progression', I alluded to some pitfalls that ultimately collapse curriculum into assessment. Different taxonomies (I mentioned Bloom's 'describe', 'explain', 'analyse' previously) when used to denote progression in the subject can unhelpfully distract curriculum leaders from the subject-specific journey through which they want their pupils to progress.

But there are other ways, too, that an over- or premature emphasis on assessment can lead to curriculum distortions. Some are more embedded than others (in the most worrying cases, they are *normalised* by teachers), but they are all problematic. A classic example, evident across a range of subjects, is using end of Key Stage 4 terminal examination descriptors as assessment criteria in other, often earlier, key stages. The problem with this *should* be obvious. Those examination descriptors were designed to assess whether pupils have learned the 'domain' of the Key Stage 4 programme of study. Pupils in other key stages simply will not have had the opportunity to learn the very domain those descriptors were designed to assess.

In some of the most problematic cases, the key stage examination grade descriptors are not just *used to assess* other key stages but actually *distort or twist* the curriculum that pupils learn. For example, in text-based subjects that examine pupils' knowledge of the programme of study through shorter extracts or gobbets, distortions happen when curriculum leaders think that it is appropriate to prepare pupils throughout their subject education with an inadequate diet comprised solely of quotes and short extracts. In being driven by assessment in this way, pupils are deprived of the richness and nourishment that comes through experiencing, reading and learning from extended texts, such as academic texts and quality literature.

Another very interesting way in which assessment can distort the curriculum can be seen through the (perhaps unintended) impact of question types used in examinations. One last example from religious education. Professor Bob Bowie has highlighted that the questions used in the GCSE religious studies examinations have a specific and implicit 'knowledge structure'.[10] The GCSE is based on the assumption that religious viewpoints are designed either to be 'supported' or 'opposed'. This becomes problematic when curriculum leaders orient their curriculum decisions to this kind of end. In this (very real) scenario, religious education ends up being all about finding oppositional viewpoints. In doing so, what is lost from the curriculum is all the other ways in which humans express being 'religious': narrative, myth, dialogue, tradition, culture, expression, revelation and scripture. Instead, pupils are given an assessment-driven diet of an impoverished view of religion. When the assessment tail wags the curriculum dog, the very content which pupils are taught can become malformed.

For curriculum leaders dealing with how to assess, the tension can only really be rendered productive when the limitations of assessment are understood, and the lethal mutations of curriculum-driven-by-assessment are avoided.

What does curriculum demand of us?

A curriculum leader is someone trusted with a great, but not impossible, task. The task is not dissimilar to that of a curator, who acts as an intermediary – acquiring, caring for and developing artefacts of content – ultimately, for the benefit and enrichment of others. In taking on this mantle, the curriculum leader mediates subjects (and subject content therein) for the ages and phases of the pupils who learn the curriculum. So, what does this task demand of them as curriculum leaders?

As we have seen in exploring some of the various tensions that they face, much of the task of curriculum formation is rooted in the strength of subject knowledge. Love of the subject being taught, combined with a willingness to learn more, invariably leads to curriculum leaders (and teachers) with such a strength of knowledge that ends up replicated in the richness of the curriculums taught. In many ways, curriculum choices represented in the subject map are a kenotic (from the Greek 'kenosis', a self-overflowing) embodiment of the curriculum leader's own grasp of the subject; its contours, the way it is conceived, and the misconceptions that inhabit it, too.[11]

But there is at least another one other dimension to curriculum as well, of which Paul Ricoeur helpfully reminds us. This dimension involves navigating the choices that curriculum leaders face: (on the one hand) 'listening to symbols' by recapitulating and drawing on those things we inherit from previous generations' knowledge and previous curriculum iterations and (on the other hand) 'tearing down idols' by challenging those things that are no longer tenable and by seeking something better. These are not just aesthetic judgements that curriculum leaders have to make; there are also ones that navigate human values, sensitivities and morals. These judgements are not easy ones, and so curriculum leaders also need *wisdom* to guide the choices they make.

Joy and wisdom: joy through love of subject, and wisdom through discerning judgement. It is joy and wisdom that will be the faithful companions of leaders navigating the tensions and challenges of the curriculum.

Notes

1. Gadamer H-G, *Truth and Method*, tr Marshall D and Weinsheimer J, Continuum,1989.
2. Habermas J, *On the Logic of the Social Sciences*, Polity, 1988. See also, Habermas J, 'On Hermeneutics' Claim to Universality' in Mueller-Vollmer K (ed), *Hermeneutics Reader: Texts of the German Tradition from the Enlightenment to the Present*, Continuum, 1988, pp 294–319.
3. Ricoeur P, *Freud and Philosophy: An Essay on Interpretation*, tr Savage D, Yale University Press, 1977.
4. Ricoeur P, *Freud and Philosophy: An Essay on Interpretation*, tr Savage D, Yale University Press, 1977.
5. Fordham M, 'Subject knowledge and mentoring: my talk at Teach First', https://clioetcetera.com/. 2017.
6. Christodoulou D, *Making Good Progress?: The future of Assessment for Learning*, 2017.
7. Ashbee, R, *Curriculum: Theory, Culture and the Subject Specialisms*, Routledge, 2021.
8. See, for example, copies of Rosenshine's typed works at ed221538.tif.pdf; see also, for instance, the EEF's 'Teaching and Learning Toolkit', https://educationendowmentfoundation.org.uk.
9. Counsell C, 'Teaching as text and texture: why knowledge needs subject difference', a conference speech given at REsearchED National Conference, 7 September 2024.
10. Bowie B, 'The implicit knowledge structure preferred by questions in English religious studies public exams', G Biesta G and P Hannam P (eds), *Religion and education: the forgotten dimensions of religious education*, Brill, 2019.
11. Fordham beautifully shows how this kind of conceptualisation of curriculum as a mental map of the subject applies, if not especially, to assessment: 'But what is actually going on when you assess someone's knowledge? In short, it involves a comparison, between the mental map of the subject you have in your head and the mental map they have in their head. In making an assessment, a teacher is trying to diagnose where the gaps in that mental map are, so that he or she can then do something about it.' See Fordham M, 'Subject knowledge and mentoring: my talk at Teach First', https://clioetcetera.com/. 2017.

Section 2 Essay 8

What is a quality curriculum?

Dan Whieldon

Maya Angelou once said, 'I've learned that people will forget what you said, people will forget what you did, but people will never forget how you made them feel'. This speaks to the lasting impact of an emotional connection in our interactions with others. Words and actions, though important in the moment, often fade from memory.

If I am asked what I remember of my own experience of school, specifically my initial 7 years of primary and secondary education, certain things immediately leap to mind. I have to confess, when considered extemporaneously, few of these are to do with the subject content of the curriculum we followed, but rather, predominantly, they are entrenched in other artefacts of the school experience. The teachers (in my case, the Christian Brothers of St. Joseph's Catholic College in Stoke-on-Trent) remain indelible in the memory. The building we inhabited I can faithfully evoke; its classrooms and wooden desks with the flip top lids and defunct ink wells; the amusing student scripture that adorned the toilet cubicles – many worthy of publication themselves; as well as the names for the various 'instruments' used to enact the doctrines of the behaviour 'policy' and the indelible marks they left. Much of the residing infrastructure could be considered indicative of the Victorian paradigm of education, preparing pupils for life in the industrial economy of Britain, which was, at the time, rapidly disappearing.

Once excommunicated from the doctrines of a Christian Brother's education system and normalised into a more traditional secondary provision of the time, my most immediate and acute recollection is the ability, still, decades later, to name every single individual in my form in perfect alphabetical order. The party trick no one knew they needed (because they do not).

Yet, as I write this, after a brief foray into a career in the media, I have dedicated my life to education and now have the privilege to lead a secondary school in Leeds in the north of England as a principal and continue to be deeply committed, not just to the educational experience of the students in my school, but to the global mission of education to transform lives through a full rich educational provision as right for all young people. My career has been underpinned by a desire to work with the most vulnerable pupils. Each of the schools I have worked in has predominantly been characterised by significant proportions of vulnerability and disadvantage. I am humbled and privileged to have that purpose each day, and this purpose defines the culture of my school.

So, where, after what seems a trivialising of my own school experience, does that come from? What lit the votive candle of devotion to the educational experience? Each of the seemingly trivialised memories comes from a powerful association with school, and these seeming trivialities can still, to this day, open up a powerful mental storybook of learning. Evocation of Victorian architecture, wooden desks and cassocked teachers opens the portal to the infinite textbook of my education. I can then flip at will, like the lid of an antiquated desk, to myriad chapters of a rich learning experience where there is instant access to memories of reading Shakespeare, Keats, Yeats for the very first time; or of our communal wonder as Brother Manley's baritone extolled the mathematical symmetry of nature and its hexagonal structures from honey cones to snowflakes. Even the seemingly dry automaticity of a list of names in alphabetical order elicits recollections of individuals, shared experiences and values; learning to empathise and diversify in thoughts, ideas and cultures.

Undoubtedly, the power of memory in learning has been recognised as the crux of building knowledge and skills over time within a quality curriculum. In England, at a regulatory level with Ofsted's 'research into research' of what makes an effective curriculum, memory is now the thing to remember in curriculum design and inspection. The accumulation of knowledge and skills over time, and building composite knowledge through securing component knowledge, schema, knowing more and remembering more are all mantras across the educational landscape.

Memories of my own start in education as a teacher of English in 2001, just a few miles from where my current academy is in the west of Leeds, were not of the necessity to consider how best to define and then secure the right knowledge and skills over time and embed these in long-term memory. I do not recall any architecture of Bruner's spiral curriculum model or any direction to revisit defined knowledge and skills with increasing complexity over time. Rather, this time was defined by a personal sense of freedom to pick my own texts, develop my own schemes and lesson plans, and with the support of an A4 sheet with Bloom's

Taxonomy sellotaped to my desk, decide on the content and pedagogical strategies I wanted to employ to ensure successful end points. End points were defined by the assessment objectives in the internal termly summative assessments, or the externally prescribed Year 9 SATs, GCSEs and A-Levels. With the power of hindsight and a particular lens on this time, the approach seemed somewhat chaotic but personally empowering as the leader of the educational approach, the master of one's own curriculum and engendering a sense of individual leadership and autonomy in the classroom.

Changes within the educational landscape, however, with the dawn of academisation and the growth of Trusts seeking to create through a central hegemony a homogenised and autocratic set of structures, seemed a necessary response to high levels of autonomy at the individual teacher level, which produced at times chaotic approaches within individual organisations. Large organisations require a set of organising principles to provide a backbone to align systems, procedures and efficiencies. Many early trust models would respond with what could be argued was an overzealous alignment across their academies. Their organisational systems, infrastructure and curriculum created a different factory setting from that of the anachronistic late twentieth-century model and my own personal educational experience; a factory of examination results and strong league table standings. Pupils could now be provided with examination success through high alignment and high accountability, facilitated by a centrally prescribed curriculum with a set of success criteria and performance indicators that removed chaotic, elevated levels of autonomy in an attempt to efficiently manage large educational organisations.

During my formative leadership journey, I worked across this churn in education within high levels of autonomy and with high levels of alignment in different settings. Depending on the career stage, experience, and educational philosophy, both could be an anathema to teachers within each setting. In the background, with growing traction, would come research. Initially confined to academia beyond school settings, research seemed defined by gimmickry and designation and an almost tokenistic approach to justification for pedagogical implementation within a school. If a new idea wanted to establish currency with immediacy, it could often be defined as 'research' within schools to validate its implementation without a measure of its efficacy or a data set to prove its worth. Little peer or literary review or impact data was presented as schools diligently relabelled schemes of learning and lesson plans with a V, an A or a K, as a resurgent 1920s theory in supporting pupils with dyslexia became a mainstream expectation across schools in the UK. We were now able to use the tripartite of learning styles (visual, audio, kinaesthetic) to support curriculum delivery. A veritable Bermuda Triangle of lost time and learning ensued. Spending an INSET day doing nothing other than this labelling task did not seem to result in any improvements in engagement or results with my own classes at the time. See no learning, hear no learning…

In 2011, the nascent Educational Endowment Foundation (EEF), formed by Sir Peter Lampi's The Sutton Trust, sought not just to bridge the gap between research and school strategy but to provide a platform for schools to implement their own research projects within an established framework and provided a measure to judge efficiencies of cost and level of impact. The defining Sutton Trust report, 'What Makes Great Teaching' reviewed over 200 pieces of research to identify the elements of teaching with the strongest evidence of improving attainment and seeking to dispel established, common practices that could actually be harmful to learning with no grounding in research. The report concluded that the two factors with the strongest evidence of improving pupil attainment are: (1) teachers' content knowledge, including their ability to understand how students think about a subject and identify common misconceptions; and (2) quality of instruction, which includes using strategies like effective questioning and the use of assessment. Interestingly, the report mentions 'curriculum' just four times.

By the time of the publication of The Sutton Trust Report in 2014 I had completed a Masters in Leadership and Management in Education with a focused dissertation on research and curriculum, and was now an Assistant Principal for Teaching, Learning and Assessment and Research Lead and was just about to engage on behalf of my school in the RISE project jointly funded by the EEF and the Department for Education. I had also started a research project specifically around the impact of one-to-one devices in supporting a Key Stage 3 thematic curriculum for the Professional Teaching Institute (PTI) Leadership Mark. The RISE project was specifically around Research-leads Improving Students' Education (RISE) and worked through a structured school improvement process, involving external research and evaluation. It ran for four years and provided the development opportunity to work with some luminaries of education, like minded colleagues at similar career stages, and combined with my Masters, was formative in shaping my own vision for how research and an understanding of the good and the bad in its utility in shaping a curriculum impacts on attainment, with a particular focus on pupils with disadvantage. A very pertinent area and demographic for my career focus and pathway. But attainment, as a focus, was still the prevailing measure of great teaching. The Sutton Report was clear, however, that teachers' subject content knowledge was critical in being able to address misconceptions for pupils, something in my current school we really value and develop. But for my own personal philosophy of learning this, combined with the exam-defined approach to success, seemed to narrow the professional experience of teachers. Subject content knowledge – the content seemingly being that which was relevant to the exam specifications. Subject expertise risked solely being assessed through the predetermined criteria of assessment, the National Curriculum and resultant examination performance of teachers. Whether this was entirely true or not, at that stage of my career, this felt as though teaching and subject experts were under-resourced and underdeveloped. Whilst initially driven by an idealism about developing subject specialists as the senior leader for teaching and learning as a principal of a school, I am now acutely aware of the power of inspirational teaching in engaging pupils in their learning, and the power of investing in colleagues to develop a breadth of subject expertise.

By doing so, they remain in love with their subject. I still subscribe to the philosophy that to create inspirational learning, you must inspire teachers to teach, not forsaking the importance of examination results, but to symbiotically create breadth of experience for teachers and pupils alike. Investing in teachers will often mean they become invested in their school, retaining and developing the very best educators for the pupils of your school.

Leeds West Academy, the building, was constructed and opened in 2011 on the site of Intake School. I have been at the school since 2017, starting initially as Vice Principal before taking on the leadership of the academy, firstly as Head of School in January 2020, before being appointed as Principal. The building itself, from approach, sits like a marooned ocean liner on Intake Lane and upon entering, you discover you are on the third floor of a large and modern building. The academy predominantly serves the communities of Bramley, Rodley and Stanningley in the west of Leeds. As Intake School before us, we have a Performing Arts specialism with the predecessor school producing a number of soap opera actors and a Spice Girl, to name but a few. The academy's catchment is varied, but there are approximately double the national averages for disadvantaged pupils and those with special educational needs and disabilities. We are now an 11-16 provision and have expanded to a capacity of 1500 pupils since 2017. Our Ofsted in October 2024 opens with the line, 'This is a happy and inclusive school.' Since opening, there have been four principals in post, so as I write this, I am now the academy's longest-serving principal. Taking on the leadership of the academy at the start of the COVID pandemic, supporting high levels of vulnerable pupils and navigating a five-million-pound expansion with pandemic-hit delays as the school grew seemingly exponentially each year has been a challenge. This liner has at times hit some stormy seas since I joined in 2017, but we have continued to shape a school for our community built on a clear vision and set of values that provide our compass and anchor.

Our vision is to be an Academy that *'unites and inspires our community through the power of education, opportunity and inspiration to secure successful futures for the children of the west of Leeds'*. When writing the vision for the school, I was keen to ensure a non-insular approach. Whilst Leeds West Academy was the priority, it was important to me that our vision incorporated not just the children who attended the academy but was broader for all of the children of the west of Leeds, with a commitment to work in partnership with neighbouring schools at different phases. During my journey through education and encountering different organisations with at times a parochial and competitive approach to education, forged in the political culture of league tables, exam results and trust-led hegemonic systems, this often seemed, to me, to pit schools against one another. Leeds West Academy sits within a small trust, where collaboration, co-construction and relationships underpin the organising structures, thus providing an optimal balance of autonomy and alignment – the two defining collocations of my own educational organisational outlook. I have been able to support the development and ethos as a leader within the Trust in helping shape and define this approach, and creating this ethos and culture.

Ethos and culture are the stratum and adhesive to the roadmap at Leeds West Academy. Curriculum is no exception. In the early stages of my association with the school, the necessity was for a compliance-based approach to schemes of learning, curriculum content and delivery methodology to get things 'ship shape'. But at the same time, the next iteration of the curriculum was being constructed in the background, built on the ethos and culture now defined across the academy. Two key pillars support our culture: professional excellence and organisational clarity. Two structural pillars to support a culture of high ambition and high support.

Professional excellence we defined as doing the ordinary things extraordinarily well. Small aggregated marginal gains in our individual practice, achievable but requiring little training other than repetitious implementation, all colleagues, all roles. Essentially starting with the basics – a professional expectation of the small things, but augmenting through elevating the basics through refinement and exposition. Expectations of professional excellence become habitual. An alignment of excellence, but with the autonomous ownership of your role. Outside every classroom, there is a professional excellence logo, and colleagues all wear pin badges of the same design with pride – it is a defined and aligned commitment. But with disparate roles and a diversity of colleagues, organisational clarity in the definition of professional excellence across the academy was an essential unifying pillar. Organisational clarity defined the why, the what, the how, and the who. It provided the guidance, principles and measures for success as we defined it.

So, calming the organisational tempest with clear environmental expectations, aligning systems and clarifying the organisation's culture, the next imminent risk is the doldrums. These organising structures are cancelling out the potential for inspiring lessons, filling the sails of education to propel the learning experience. Or the political battle inherent in ensuring both knowledge and skills, and then the right knowledge and skills, and how to navigate these through the construction of a quality curriculum for the pupils of a school. Knowledge, to me, has always seemed to be created within specific historical and cultural contexts of those bestowing this knowledge. Knowledge risks being rooted in how power and perspective create and prioritise it. As our curriculum evolved, we talked of its decolonisation, but again, balancing this with an understanding of a consideration of approach and not blind acceptance. Much of this work, therefore, required the co-collaboration and research to ensure a diverse range of viewpoints supported this creation of our curriculum intent, which did not fuel a specific agenda but opened up thinking underpinned by the development of character and values.

At Leeds West Academy, we had inherited a sense of rapid improvement, with our strategic plans lasting one academic year. We often considered it as trying to fix a plane whilst it was still in the air and flying at 400 miles an hour. This did work for the context at the time, improving our Ofsted grading and results. By the time I became principal, I was keen to look at something more stabilising that did not diminish our better-never-stops, high-flying approach to improvement, but took the right things and considered these over a longer period of time. So, whilst we flew on in the final year of an annual plan, we considered more fully how we would approach a more long-haul flight, which may take longer, but will always take you further and to more interesting and harder-to-reach destinations. Effectively, now, we were creating a shiny new plane in the hangar and could really consider the 'why, what, how, who?' and the destination we wanted to reach. As an English student and with a love of the devilish Shakespearean Dogberryistic approach to language, I take great joy in mixing metaphors and analogies and enjoy the turbulence of language. I, therefore, make no excuses for the fact that once we had created our plane, decided our direction, briefed the crew, decided our altitude, speed and destination, applied and tested our sophisticated navigation and warning systems... We ditched the plane analogy and created a roadmap. Specifically, a 'Roadmap for Embedding Excellence'. It is important, I decided, with any strategy, to stay grounded!

Our Roadmap was a three-year strategic approach that was designed to ensure we kept doing what works based on strong foundations and increase its complexity over time. We had clearly defined endpoints, which we would assess and evaluate using success criteria or assessment objectives for their impact. Through the duration of the Roadmap, we would revisit the fundamentals with regularity and always be supported by strong, simple values. Our strategy was built mirroring our approach to how a quality curriculum is constructed. In fact, most of what we do at Leeds West is. We created the plan through a strategic planning event in which three-quarters of colleagues from the school attended and planned our approach collaboratively – everyone owned our plan and had a voice in its creation. We had three clear strategic goals, and the plan was to last for three years.

Strategic goal 1 – Leadership and Management

An inclusive community culture that promotes personal wellbeing, professional development and strong community engagement, with high levels of support and advocacy for all.

Strategic goal 2 – Quality of Education

An inclusive, coherently sequenced and diverse curriculum that promotes the accumulation of knowledge, skills and cultural capital delivered through inspirational lessons.

Strategic goal 3 – Personal Development, Behaviour and Attitudes

An inclusive and developmental student culture in which all students are known, valued, and understood; promoting strong attendance and positive behaviours; and underpinned by a strong personal development curriculum to support successful futures.

Once we had decided what we wanted to achieve, it was then that we looked at it through the Ofsted lens to ensure that our approach fulfilled the regulatory criteria of the Education Inspection Framework, using their categories to frame our goals to ensure clear direction and understanding for our next inspection team. Supported by a clear culture and ethos we had established through ensuring professional excellence in doing the ordinary extraordinarily well; organisational clarity to provide clear direction and support; and augmented by establishing the optimal balance of alignment and autonomy within our cultural fabric; we had established the foundation to embed excellence at Leeds West Academy and our Strategic Goal 2 was all about how we would do that through our curriculum.

> *An inclusive coherently sequenced and diverse curriculum that promotes the accumulation of knowledge, skills and cultural capital delivered through inspirational lessons.*

By the time of becoming principal, I had developed lots of different curricula as Head of English, Assistant Head for Teaching and Learning and Vice Principal for Quality of Education. Building new models and an approach to curriculum was a constant iterative process. We wanted to create a structure informed by the spiral model but retaining a fluidity and adaptability to mitigate any risk of a fixed approach of constant forward motion without making any adaptations. Rather than simply ploughing ahead with the next learning episode regardless, we would source information along the way through assessment, evaluation and review to ensure that the curriculum worked for all students.

Along the way, I had adopted the ideal John Dewey espoused into my educational philosophy, 'We do not learn from experience… we learn from reflecting on experience' – this was, in many ways, my guiding premise. I wanted a curriculum that was vibrant and multilayered but built on an architecture and framework for exploration and a sense of clarity of its utility.

What had been so evocative for my own educational experience that from seemingly innate memories I could still access a cache of knowledge across a range of subjects? But more than that, these had been the foundational building blocks that had made me search, question, and ultimately led me to my current position. What curriculum model would be right for these children in the west of Leeds to give them the very best future? Once again, as a principal, the weight of responsibility presses down, but so too the opportunity to make a remarkable difference and lead and shape the learning experience of our community. Reflecting on the experience and opportunities my time in education had provided, and the knowledge I had been exposed to through these experiences and considerations of theories and research, was critical in defining my own view of quality within a curriculum. As Dewey asked, what were my reflections on experience?

'Knowledge is not for understanding; it is for cutting', Michel Foucault suggested that knowledge should be a tool for questioning and challenging dominant narratives. The natural rebel in me loves this sentiment – decentralise knowledge and encourage, in effect, a more inclusive and pluralistic educational experience. Active, critical thinkers, not just listening to what they are told! But there is a risk with a thin layer reading of such sentiment, and it is the assumption of the foundational experience and character to allow this to happen – the platform. If not established, then the critical thinking could evaporate into an ether of a lack of reference points. I love the thought of liberating education from its dominant narratives, but Foucault's sentiment needs a sturdy platform to make it effective. It is all well and good to encourage critical thinking, but without a solid foundation, that free-thinking can easily drift into a disorienting abyss of confusion. You cannot build a house without solid foundations. But there was something there – a foundation of rebellious learning, but a responsibility to scaffold knowledge so that students do not just spin around aimlessly, lost in a sea of ideas and rebellion, quixotically charging. Scaffolding is synonymous with construction, so probably constructive to segue into constructivist theory.

Jean Piaget and Lev Vygotsky, the dynamic duo of learning theory, championed the notion that learning is an active process of constructing new knowledge, building on what we already know. Perhaps crucial for creating a curriculum that does not just throw students into the deep end of independent thinking, but rather helps them gradually build up their cognitive scaffolding. Students engage actively in constructing meaning through problem-solving, collaboration, or simply reflecting on their prior experiences – they not only retain more information but can apply it far more effectively. Memory, therefore, becomes not a passive repository but an active part of the learning process. Building systematically from the foundations upwards with scaffolding to support the construction.

Sweller's Cognitive Load Theory offers a nice reminder that working memory has a limit. So the design of the curriculum needs to work systematically in a sequence that builds gradually, allowing students to connect it to what they already know. Building up long-term memory in a way that fosters deeper learning. Memorable, too, is the research around long-term memory in building expertise. Researchers like Ericsson have shown that learning is most effective when new information is integrated into our existing mental frameworks. So, when we revisit material over time, we are helping students reinforce these connections, ensuring better retention and the ability to apply what they have learned in new contexts.

Add to that the benefits of retrieval practice, where regularly pulling information from memory actually strengthens it (this is not just a drill, it is a key to mastery!). Studies indicate that retrieval practice not only enhances retention but also helps students organise and make sense of the material, making it easier to recall when needed.

The role of working memory and executive functions, such as attention control and cognitive flexibility, also deserves a mention. If students can juggle multiple pieces of information at once, make connections between them, and switch between tasks with ease, they are going to thrive. This brings us full circle to the importance of a well-structured curriculum that does not overload working memory but rather builds it up strategically, like weight training for the brain.

Ultimately, all these ideas come together with one big takeaway: learning should be a dynamic, interactive process, where knowledge is not just memorised, but actively constructed, connected and applied. And for leaders building curricula, this means understanding that a robust, well-supported foundation is key to enabling students to develop the critical thinking skills they need to question, challenge, and ultimately cut through the clutter of dominant narratives. You cannot just tell them what to think – you have got to give them the tools and the context to think for themselves. After all, if knowledge is the tool for cutting, we need to make sure it is sharp and well-crafted.

Maya Angelou's words, once more, 'I've learned that people will forget what you said, people will forget what you did, but people will never forget how you made them feel', resonate profoundly when reflecting on the nature of memory in education. As I think back again on my own school experiences, I realise that what truly lingers is not necessarily the knowledge I acquired, but rather the emotions those experiences provoked and from there I access that well of knowledge. This connection between emotion and memory is not just my over-sentimentality; it is grounded in neuroscience – the brain's remarkable ability to form stronger, more enduring memories when emotion is involved. When learning is paired with emotional engagement, it does not just lead to academic success – it shapes character, too.

Recalling an academic lecture on the science of learning, the brain is not a passive recipient of information, but rather an active processor, drawing on multiple regions responsible for memory, emotional processing and learning. The hippocampus encodes new memories, while the amygdala, the brain's emotional centre, ensures that emotionally charged experiences are stored with heightened intensity and longevity. That is why emotionally engaging moments, whether sparked by an inspiring teacher, a captivating story, or an exciting intellectual discovery, are more likely to be retained deeply. John Dewey, ever the advocate for experiential learning, said, 'If we teach today's students as we taught yesterday's, we rob them of tomorrow'. This sentiment ties directly to the idea that memories made through emotional and meaningful experiences are more likely to last and, in turn, foster both academic achievement and character growth.

The science behind this is fascinating (and frankly, it is a good excuse for those sentimental memories of school, which I keep returning to). When emotions are engaged, neurotransmitters like dopamine and serotonin are released, strengthening neural connections. This means that the impact of a passionate teacher or a room of engaged learners lingers long after the subject matter has slipped from the mind. When students connect emotionally with the content – whether through empathy for a character or the thrill of problem-solving – their brains form deeper, more lasting memories. As an educator, I have learned that it is not just the material that matters, but how students feel while engaging with it. So, all of the clever construction is enhanced by the way we feel when engaging with learning. So, to inspire students along the way is critical. To inspire students, we must first inspire teachers, and my association with the PTI has remained a constant in delivering this.

We were told that the brain's ability to remember more and know more depends on strategies that support memory retention – that is, the construction and the delivery methodology and pedagogical approaches. Approaches like spaced repetition, retrieval practice, and active engagement are essential in helping students retain and apply knowledge. They really work. Spaced repetition, where material is revisited at increasing intervals, taps into the brain's natural tendency to solidify memories over time. Retrieval practice, which prompts students to actively recall information, strengthens neural pathways, deepening learning. These strategies don't just improve academic outcomes; they build confidence and resilience, turning students into independent thinkers who can apply their knowledge in new contexts. We ensure that within our implementation and pedagogical approach, these aligned learning approaches are consistently implemented but nuanced for effective application, dependent on subject, content and desired outcome. Aligning the approach with the autonomy of implementation.

Equally important is the development of character through a well-rounded curriculum. Howard Gardner's theory of multiple intelligences posits that students possess different kinds of intelligences – interpersonal, intrapersonal and others – that contribute to emotional and social growth. A curriculum that integrates these aspects does not just focus on knowledge; it helps students develop the emotional and ethical frameworks to use that knowledge wisely. Memories created through experiences like collaborative teamwork or respectful debate leave lasting impressions that shape how students navigate life's challenges. The curriculum extending beyond the academic is another 6,000 words worth of writing on its own, but it has been implicit in all the musings and explicit in the connections of experience and emotional impact as subject content is brought to life, eliciting engagement and interaction. Equally compelling is the process of character-building influences the brain's neuroplasticity, its ability to adapt and rewire itself. Studies have shown that practising empathy, perseverance, and kindness can foster both cognitive growth and emotional development. This is why a curriculum that balances academic and character education is crucial. It creates a foundation for lifelong learning that is grounded not just in knowledge but in values that guide individuals through life's complexities.

If I take a step back and reflect on how these ideas come together in a quality curriculum (the question I was seeking to answer through these educational meanderings). Perhaps it is not just about the content or the curriculum structure – it is about the integration of knowledge, emotional engagement, and character-building in a coherent, inclusive, and well-sequenced way with an underlying understanding of the science of learning. A curriculum that is designed thoughtfully, drawing on the principles of educational research and creating an environment where both intellectual and emotional growth are nurtured and learning is inspired, will set students up for success in both academic and personal spheres of their futures. Real legacy.

A lot of ground has been covered, but what I hoped to have done to some degree is to emphasise the complex and varied nature of education. Independent thinking is often most effective and perhaps only achievable when it is built on a solid foundation of knowledge and intellectual depth. As Albert Einstein once said, 'Intellectual growth should commence at birth and cease only at death'. That idea of lifelong learning is engendered through a curriculum that creates the rebellious learners who are engaged, critical, thoughtful and ultimately successful. There is clearly a crucial importance in fostering a deep understanding of subjects as a precursor to critical and independent thought – scaffolding the rebellion! Students grounded in knowledge can develop the ability to think critically and creatively, leading to a more profound understanding of the world around them. Moreover, the emotional and inspirational aspects of learning are essential for success. Teaching is not just about delivering facts; it also encompasses fostering curiosity and passion among students.

The late Sir Ken Robinson noted, 'Education is about learning rather than teaching'. This underscores the significance of engaging students emotionally so that they become active participants in their own learning journey. Though important meaningful learning extends beyond simple memorisation, it involves understanding, critical reflection, meaningful connections and emotional involvement.

So back one final time to Dewey, 'If we teach today's students as we taught yesterday's, we rob them of tomorrow'. This serves as a reminder that education must adapt and evolve, encouraging students to connect their learning to real-world experiences and think deeply about the implications of their knowledge. Encouraging students to explore the 'why' and 'how' of information, rather than just the 'what', leads to richer educational experiences. Finding the right balance between student autonomy and teacher guidance is crucial for effective education, much like the organising principle in alignment and autonomy we have adopted within Leeds West Academy. This balance ensures that both students and teachers remain focused and directed, avoiding aimless or unproductive efforts. In the words of educator HJ Eysenck, 'The teacher is not only a guide but must also become a partner in student learning'. This approach emphasises the importance of collaboration in the classroom. Achieving this equilibrium allows students to take ownership of their education while providing them with the necessary support and direction. Consider how a well-structured group project can foster independence while allowing the teacher to monitor progress and offer feedback. Students may feel empowered to tackle a challenging subject matter, knowing they have a partner guiding them along the way.

So, with a final detour into nostalgia once more and the desks, the corridors, the smell of old books and polished floors all those years ago, evokes a powerful sense of memory. When I reflect on my time at school, it is not always the exact curriculum that comes to mind. Let us face it, some of those lessons were not always inspirational, and I was certainly not always engaged. But what I do remember is the passion of the teachers as a whole – a positive culture not just of teachers but geographers, mathematicians, scientists, athletes (and actual priests). There was a sense of an impassioned educational experience delivered by professionals in love with the subject. Their enthusiasm did not just make the lessons memorable; it made us feel engaged, it made us think critically, and it made us feel that what we were learning mattered. It was through these emotionally engaging experiences that our brains formed memories, not just of the content, but of the connection to the subject and the teacher.

A quality curriculum, for me, then, is a multifaceted construct. It is the science of learning. The research and sequencing, interleaving and revisiting. It is the independence and the guidance, the alignment and the autonomy. It is the sum of experiences that are not only planned but lived. It is the interplay of knowledge and emotion, content and character, academic rigour and personal growth. And while the setting, whether in the corridors of a Christian Brother school in the late twentieth century or Leeds West Academy today, the real value lies in how these elements are brought together into a curriculum that makes learning not just memorable, but transformative.

In the end, as much as we focus on the academic structure, it is the assimilation of these experiences, alongside the informed application of educational research, that defines a truly quality curriculum. And perhaps, just maybe, it is those feelings of engagement and passion from our teachers that remain the most vivid, long after the lessons themselves have faded into the background of our lives. Or until someone asks you if you remember anyone from your form when you were at school…

SECTION 3
Is assessment fit for purpose?

This section looks at the question dominating English educators. If our system is controlled by assessment, how accurately does it actually measure learning? Test results are said to be the clearest and fairest way to represent schools' effectiveness, giving accurate and intelligible information to taxpayers. How is that used? What contribution should assessment make to social justice? How does it affect the role of the teacher?

Think

1. Why examine? How important are exam results? Who to?
2. What risks does high-stakes accountability pose to school leaders' behaviour?
3. Have standards risen or fallen over time? How do we know? Does it matter?
4. What is the answer to 'is it on the test?'
5. What is the relationship between monitoring, checking and learning opportunities?
6. How are assessment techniques used in your classrooms? How do you know?
7. What are your exam trade-offs? Are you happy?
8. What should educational success look like?

Section 3
Essay 1

Assessment and children's experience of learning

Clare O'Sullivan

The tail wagging the dog

Education in the UK has undergone significant changes in recent years, particularly in the area of assessment and particularly following the impact of school closures during the pandemic. The Education Policy Institute (EPI) reported '…the attainment gap between disadvantaged pupils and their peers has widened across all educational phases since 2019. The analysis, based on attainment data from 2022, shows that some student groups have fallen further behind their peers'.[1] Almost a decade's worth of progress made by schools since 2011, on narrowing the attainment gap between disadvantaged children and their peers, had been reversed. On top of this, concerns over the pressure exerted on pupils by high-stakes testing and the importance placed on measurable outcomes, the experience of learning for children has become a complex one. The way pupils are assessed influences not only their academic achievement but also their well-being and sense of self-worth. As such, there needs to be a balance between high-stakes summative testing and the more formative, holistic approaches to assessing pupil progress.

EPI research highlights several problems with the current assessment system, including the overemphasis on summative assessment and the limited feedback that many pupils receive from their assessments. According to their 2020 report, the UK is one of the few countries where formal, high-stakes assessments are introduced at such an early age, putting considerable pressure on children to perform well before they have had time to fully develop their cognitive and emotional skills.[2] For decades, the reliance on heavily standardised assessment has been the key means of evaluating pupil progress. From Key Stage 1 assessments to GCSEs and A-Levels, exams are a dominant feature of the educational experience for children. While these assessments provide a clear snapshot of academic achievement, they have also been criticised for their narrow focus on academic content, their tendency to cause anxiety for pupils (and teachers, and parents) and their failure to reflect the full range of knowledge and skills contributing to a child's overall development. Furthermore, when assessment becomes part of 'public accountability...assessment can begin to dominate the curriculum, and incentives to 'cheat' can become overwhelming'.[3]

Tim Oates, Group Director of Assessment Research and Development at Cambridge Assessment, calls for a more balanced approach to assessment combining both summative and formative elements. He argues that while standardised tests are useful for accountability and benchmarking, they should be complemented by assessments that promote critical thinking, problem-solving, and creativity.[4] Geoff Barton, Chair of the Oracy Commission and former General Secretary of the Association of School and College Leaders (ASCL), argues that pressure to perform in exams often leads to test anxiety,[5] reduced motivation for learning, and a diminished sense of self-esteem for many pupils, especially those who may struggle with traditional exam formats. Barton goes further to suggest that while summative assessments are necessary, they should not dominate the educational experience or overshadow other forms of learning.[6]

The direct impact of the pandemic has exacerbated concerns further. Lost learning, alternative arrangements and various concessions around summative testing at GCSE and A-Level, along with budget cuts, and an alarming recruitment and retention crisis in the teaching profession and school leadership, contribute to a general sense of unsettledness. Not only is there anxiety around the function and execution of assessment practices, but also a complete collapse of the social contract between schools and families.[7]

In a report of assessment in primary schools, Wyse and Bradbury found, 'the majority of parents and teachers are dissatisfied with the current assessment system'.[8] Similarly, the EPI highlights the attainment gap between disadvantaged pupils and their more affluent peers, noting that traditional assessment methods may exacerbate these inequalities.[9] As a result, there is a push for more inclusive assessment practices that allow all children to demonstrate their knowledge and skills in a variety of ways. This might include project-based assessments, portfolios, verbal assessments and the use of digital tools, which may give a more comprehensive picture of a learner's abilities. Professor Bill Lucas of the University of Winchester and Director of the Centre for Real-World Learning (CRL) says in his work *Rethinking Assessment in Schools*, 'assessment is out of sync with curriculum and pedagogy. Where we have become increasingly evidence-based in teaching and learning, we are failing to keep up with the science of assessment, preferring to rely on outdated, outmoded and unsubtle methods'.[10] He highlights the opportunities that digital assessments present for creating more personalised learning experiences. This can lead to greater pupil engagement and more meaningful learning experiences, as pupils are able to work at their own pace and receive feedback tailored to their individual needs.[11]

There is a danger here and, therefore, a warning. What if, in our mission to address the issues of, as Lucas says, outdated and outmoded methods of assessment, we accidentally prioritise monitoring and checking over and above learning opportunities? We could switch the curiosity of children 'off' instead of 'on', valuing reporting over experience. We could risk burnout for already overstretched teachers. If we need to check interventions are working and money is being well spent, if we are worried about our public accountability, could we find ourselves in a situation whereby, as Oates warns, assessment and monitoring begin to eclipse learning and enrichment; a situation where the tail is wagging the dog.

The purpose of school

All children, regardless of background or ability, are entitled to a challenging and enriching educational experience. That this should be delivered by subject passionate expert teachers who are highly regarded and valued in society. That assessment should be integrated in such a way as to maximise learning and mitigate limitations. That it should be fair. I do not believe I have met anyone in the schools I have worked in or on my travels to schools up and down the country who would disagree. What is the point of school if not to furnish children with knowledge, inspire curiosity to develop that further and cultivate citizens who hope to leave the world in a better place than they found it? As Michael Young put it, 'Powerful Knowledge is not just knowledge that is useful for getting a job; it is knowledge that enables individuals to understand and transform the world around them'.[12] Young emphasised the role of schools in promoting knowledge that would enable social justice. We want our children to understand they can influence change and believe they have something to offer. And we also want them to be excited and find joy in their learning.

It is interesting why we might consider assessment and the experience children have in learning as if they are two separate parts of school life. Often, in schools, curriculum and progress responsibilities are split, with assessment schedules being dictated by a monitoring cycle consistent across the school, irrespective of whether it fits with particular subject areas or topics being covered. The purpose of this, of course, is to ensure pupils are making expected progress or better, and also to ensure the curriculum is fit for purpose. A clear monitoring cycle also helps to manage (or at least plan) workload.

I recall many hours in front of spreadsheets and 'war boards' in the late 2000s, moving pupils around, attaching interventions, solving a supercharged sudoku. Well, attempting to. It was fast-paced and a little exciting, and there was a genuine sense of this work helping children to have better life choices for the future. But it was not sustainable. And it was not really teaching; rather, solving the issue of passing exams. Or at least creating a narrative around the data that demonstrated *progress*.

When I lead Continuing Professional Development (CPD), I always start with two questions: Why did you want to be a teacher? And why did you want to teach your subject? And I always make the same observation when I take responses: never has anyone said because they were particularly passionate about Progress 8; or really enjoy creating intervention groups; or marking copious Pre-Public Examinations (PPEs) – (in order to create new intervention groups). Among other inspiring ideas, colleagues generally talk about subject passion and wanting to continue to study their chosen subjects. They talk about how they wanted to inspire young people to be interested in the world around them and to think, and to have a voice. The truth is, the extent of public accountability has warped the way curriculum, assessment and monitoring work together in school.

The spreadsheets and war boards of my yesteryears, the intervention groups and exam drilling were not 'teaching'. Certainly not what I would hope teaching is and should be. It was not leading in teaching either. Professor Becky Francis, rather encouragingly, commented in response to the 2023 EPI report on the widening attainment gap following COVID: 'If anything, today's findings reaffirm just how important great teaching and learning opportunities are for disadvantaged children and young people. For these pupils, every second spent in the classroom in front of a teacher matters'.[13] Because, of course, a great teacher understands that great assessment is integral to learning. If done well, assessment and learning should have a symbiotic relationship that allows all children to flourish and feel successful – this is the whole point of Assessment for Learning.

Tim Oates puts it well when he writes, 'Great assessment is accurate…[it] provides information that can be used to support teaching and learning, helping to shape future educational experiences'.[14] Whether the assessment is high stakes or low stakes, summative or formative, the assessment needs to be accurate, and it needs to be viewed as information that will prompt action. In other words, it can be used to shape teaching and improve the quality of education for all children. It is not about shifting children on a spreadsheet till the puzzle is solved. It is not about nudging enough children over the line to improve a collective school grade. It is about the experience of children as learners and shaping a curriculum which is challenging and enriching and leaves them wanting more.

Wood and Thomas explained, 'play is central to children's learning and development, providing opportunities for them to engage in exploration, problem solving, and negotiation, which supports their cognitive and social growth'.[15] Watching my own children learning to play an instrument or succeed in a sport, or even navigate their way through a soft-play area, I noticed how they were tireless in practising and rehearsing. Why? Because they *wanted* to do it. They wanted to get better; they enjoyed the praise when they succeeded, of course, and importantly, the intrinsic glow of personal success. But they also listened to advice on how to improve – they even made their own adjustments through trial and error to get better. They enjoyed the assessment part of the learning as much as the activity of learning itself. When they were very little, I watched them play with dolls and action figures, rehearsing conversations and social hierarchies. They were curious explorers, and they played to learn. Tirelessly.

Assessment needs to allow for play in learning. It also needs to reflect the full breadth of the curriculum, rather than focusing narrowly on what can be easily tested through exams. Prioritising assessments that form part of a monitoring cycle leaves little room for other types of assessment because they tend to be time-consuming, and also because the accountability around them at a school level positions them as the most valuable. Christine Counsell, co-founder and director of Opening Worlds Ltd, has called for assessments that promote deep learning and critical thinking, rather than simply testing pupils' ability to recall information with generic descriptors, 'seductive hierarchies of generic, skill-based descriptors ('describe', 'compare', 'analyse', 'evaluate') must go – once and for all'.[16] Mary Myatt shares this view, emphasising the need for assessments that challenge pupils to think deeply and apply their knowledge in a variety of contexts.[17]

Viewing assessment in this way is important for the future: integrating and balancing summative and formative assessment into curriculum planning; exploring technologies to support in assessing and monitoring; and aligning with creativity, problem-solving, and independent thinking – all essential skills for success. We want to make sure children have a meaningful and engaging learning experience. We want to bring play and joy in learning back to the classroom, minimising anxiety around making mistakes, because that is part of the learning process. School is more than just preparation for later; it is more than a set of exam results, and learning is more than a seven or five-year plan. 'Assessment should be a tool for learning, not a means of ranking and sorting children'.[18] Essentially, we need to separate assessment from public accountability and instead ensure it is fit for purpose by being fully integrated into learning. If we do not, we risk, at best, a situation whereby children's main concern lies in, 'Is it on the test?' when presented with learning opportunities. At worst, we alienate teachers and disengage children from learning completely.

Notes

1 Hunt E, Tuckett S, Robinson D and Babbini N, 'Social Mobility and Vulnerable Learners' *Education Policy Institute Annual Report 2023*, December 2023.
2 Hutchinson J, Reader M and Akhal A, 'Social Mobility and Vulnerable Learners ' *Education Policy Institute Annual Report 2020*, August 2020.
3 Oates T, 'What makes great assessment?' *Cambridge Assessment Network and Research*, 2017.

4 Oates T, 'National Curriculum: Tim Oates on Assessment,' *Cambridge Assessment Network and Research*, 2014.
5 Barton G, quoted in Roberts J, 'New GCSEs taking toll on pupils' mental health', *TES Magazine*, August 2018.
6 Barton G, quoted in 'ASCL leader calls for a more humane GCSE system' *Our News and Press Releases,* Association of Schools and College Leaders, August 2023.
7 Dorrell E, 'Covid has broken the social contract between parents and schools' *CapX*, September 2023.
8 Wyse D and Bradbury A, 'Evidence-led report on statutory assessment in primary schools in England' *The Independent Commission on Assessment in Primary Education* (ICAPE), November 2022.
9 Hutchinson J, Reader M and Akhal A, 'Social Mobility and Vulnerable Learners ' *Education Policy Institute Annual Report 2020*, August 2020.
10 Lucas B, 'Rethinking Assessment In Education: Part 1 The Case For Change' *CSE Leading Education Series*, 2021.
11 Lucas B, 'Rethinking Assessment In Education: Part 1 The Case For Change' *CSE Leading Education Series*, 2021.
12 Young M, *The Curriculum of the Future: From the 'New Sociology of Education' to a Critical Theory of Learning*, Routledge, 1998.
13 Francis B, responding to Hunt E, Tuckett S, Robinson D and Babbini. N, 'Social Mobility & Vulnerable Learners', *Education Policy Institute Annual Report 2023*, December 2023.
14 Oates T, 'What makes great assessment?' *Cambridge Assessment Network and Research*, 2017.
15 Wood E and Thomas JH, 'Play, Learning and the early Childhood Curriculum.' *Sage Publications*, 2023.
16 Counsell C, 'What a National Curriculum Can and Can't Do', *The Curriculum Conversation*, October 2024.
17 Myatt M, 'Thoughts on assessment.' www.marymyatt.com/blog, May 2021.
18 Peacock A, 'Assessment for Learning Without Limits', *UK Higher Education Humanities & Social Sciences Education*, June 2021.

Section 3
Essay 2

The role of public examination and qualifications

Ian Bauckham

Section 1: Introduction and context

In 2013, Professor Rob Coe gave his inaugural lecture at the University of Durham entitled: *Improving Education: A triumph of hope over experience*. In the lecture, and in subsequent articles, Professor Coe brought together a range of international measures of educational achievement, such as Programme for International Student Assessment (PISA), Progress in International Reading Literacy Study (PIRLS) and Trends in International Mathematics and Science Study (TIMSS), in England over the previous decade or two, and contrasts them with the pattern of rising GCSE and A-Level outcomes in England in the same period. The use of these international assessments to measure change over time is, Coe notes, problematic, but they are probably the best data available. The international indicators he plots are, at best, mixed: some do show rises, others fall, and others largely flatline. Meanwhile, from 1987 right through to 2012, the proportion of 16-year-olds who gained five grades at C and above rose inexorably year on year. In 1987, it was at 26.4%, and by 2012, it had climbed to 81.1%.

Faced with this data, Coe concludes:

Unfortunately, a clear and definitive answer to the question of whether standards have risen is not possible. The best I think we can say is that overall there probably has not been much change.[1]

It was in the context of growing public and political scepticism about continuous rises in grades in our national qualifications that the Office of Qualifications and Examinations Regulation (Ofqual) came into being in 2010. It is instructive to look back at the debates which accompanied the passage of the Bill.[2] On 23 February 2009, the then Liberal Democrat Education spokesman, David Laws, asked the then Secretary of State for Education, Ed Balls, in the House of Commons:

> The chair of the Ofqual committee spoke of the need for a clearer picture of what is meant by maintaining standards when the structure of qualifications changes. Can the right hon. Gentleman tell us what he means by maintaining standards in such circumstances?

To which the Secretary of State responded:

> I am not going to do that, because I will leave it to Ofqual. It is an independent regulator of standards, it is independent of Ministers and it reports directly to Parliament. It is clearly its job to ensure that standards are maintained across qualifications and over time. We have to get away from this ridiculous, damaging and draining debate about dumbing down, when, whenever standards go up and teachers and young people have worked hard, some politicians and commentators jump up and say, "This must be because standards have been dumbed down". That is not fair, and it is not right. Rather than my making such assurances about standards, it will be much better when Ofqual, the independent regulator, makes such assurances to the public and to families.[3]

What is fascinating to note is that there were at least two political motivations for the creation of Ofqual. One was to deal with the issue of ever-rising grades, which was beginning to be hard to interpret as reflecting ever-rising standards. The other, alluded to by Ed Balls, was the possibility that the newly created Ofqual might, in fact, confirm that those rising GCSE results were real, thereby silencing those who claimed the rising results were just evidence of dumbing down.

Around the time these debates were taking place, I had nothing to do with Ofqual. In 2009, I had been a secondary headteacher for five years, and a member of the Council of the Association of School and College Leaders (ASCL) for four. In those days, the elected members of ASCL Council met in person for debates and information sharing, which fed into the policymaking of the organisation. School accountability, through both the Department's performance tables and Ofsted inspections, was always high on the agenda. By then, Ofsted inspection outcomes were being significantly conditioned by published performance data, both raw (for example, percentages gaining five or more good GCSEs) and progress (value added and 'contextualised value added' (CVA), which weighted the pupil population for measures of disadvantage). As well as GCSEs, there were other ways to boost a school's scores, for example, by taking qualifications which, it was widely believed, yielded 'points' more easily than GCSEs. This was, of course, before 2014, when, following the Wolf Review, the range of qualifications that were allowed to 'count' for performance table purposes was restricted. Headteachers often avidly shared the latest intelligence on which qualifications were the most advantageous to take from the 'points' perspective.

I clearly remember at some point in that first decade of the twenty-first century listening to Steve Munby, who at the time led the government-funded National College for School Leadership (NCSL), explain the risks of high-stakes accountability for school leader behaviours. While accountability is good, he said, and the necessary counterbalance to school autonomy, if we turn up the accountability pressures on school leaders too fast without putting in place the right training and support to enable them to meet those expectations in ways that are beneficial to students, then we should not be surprised if school leaders resort to unintended and often perverse behaviours to meet them. That, I would contend, is what we were seeing play out in those discussions about which qualifications we could opt for to drive up our scores for accountability purposes. Some of those qualifications were certainly not worth the GCSE equivalency they claimed, and taking them may not always have been in the best interests of young people, yet many students were directed into them. As has often been described, the schools which felt most vulnerable to adverse inspection judgements or weak performance table data were often those serving the least advantaged communities. They were, therefore, sometimes the most susceptible to these pressures.

Summary

- For around 20 years, GCSE results rose year on year, but beyond that, the evidence of real improvement from other metrics is weak.

- Ofqual was established in 2010 to be an independent regulator of standards in qualifications.

- Strong accountability pressures, coupled with a greater diversity of 'points-bearing' qualifications, led to some schools over-weighting performance table outcomes in their choices of qualifications for students.

Section 2: Why trustworthy qualifications matter

Taking over the role of Chief Regulator of Qualifications in January 2024 prompted me to reflect on what qualifications are and why they matter. A good place to start is the Act which established Ofqual, the Apprenticeships, Skills, Children and Learning Act (2009). This sets out a range of statutory roles for Ofqual. Central to those are:

- to secure that qualifications give a reliable indication of knowledge, skills and understanding over time and between different awarding organisations

- to promote national assessments (for example, Key Stage 2 tests and other primary phase assessments), which give a reliable indication of achievement over time

- to promote the public's confidence both in qualifications taken in schools and colleges, and beyond, and in primary phase national assessments

The first two of these draw on the same basic idea. Qualifications must, so says the Act, *represent* the knowledge, skills or understanding of the holder, and do so in a way that is not only accurate within an age cohort but also consistent over time and between cohorts. That might sound obvious, but it is an idea which is not entirely uncontested. To say that qualifications must be 'representative' in this sense, in other words, representative of attainment as demonstrated at the time of assessment, excludes the possibility that qualifications, or the way in which they are graded, can legitimately be adapted so that they intentionally *compensate* their holders for variations in educational experience or social background.

The possibility of this latter approach became a serious question during the COVID-19 pandemic. There were many calls to award teacher or school-assessed grades, which were adjusted to take account of the differential impacts of COVID-19. After much reflection and debate, it was determined that, even if this were to be desirable (and there was certainly no consensus that it was), it would actually be impossible to achieve fairly, so many and varied were the shades of pandemic impact around the country, and actually even within schools. Moreover, if the principle of differentially compensating students for COVID-related disadvantage were to be accepted, what would the arguments be for not attempting to do likewise for a range of other disadvantages, such as family background, school quality, teacher absence and so on?

The concept that links together qualifications which accurately and consistently represent students' achievement on the one hand, and public confidence in qualifications and primary school assessments on the other, is the notion of *trustworthiness*. A qualification (or SATs result) can be trustworthy if it is believed to be both accurate (in other words, representative of the knowledge or skill demonstrated) and of comparable value from one year to the next. And when qualifications are seen as trustworthy, public confidence in them (and the public, of course, includes students, teachers, employers and universities, or courses) is built over time.

Qualifications cannot be trustworthy if their value is not held stable. It is interesting to compare qualifications to a currency. They draw their value and usability from a stable understanding of the educational 'goods' or achievements which underpin them. If that underlying educational achievement does not, in large picture terms, change, then a change in the value of qualifications that are supposed to be pegged to that underlying standard can be considered inflationary (or indeed deflationary, though that is much rarer because of our inbuilt optimism bias).

Of course, not all rises in qualification grades are inflationary. Inflation happens only when grade rises are unwarranted – in other words, not reflective of genuine rises in student achievement. I explained this point at a hearing of the House of Lords Education for 11-16 Year Olds Committee on 29 June 2023:

> I want to answer Lord Knight's question directly about what is wrong with grade inflation if things are getting better. If things are really getting better, I would not call it grade inflation. It is just grades rising. If grade inflation is happening when things are not getting better, the value or the currency of grades is being debased.[4]

The same hearing of the Lords Education for 11-16 Year Olds Committee raised a challenge related to the perception that, since the establishment of Ofqual, and the ending of (probably largely unwarranted) year-on-year rises in GCSE (and A-Level) results, a statistical model is used which predetermines the quantum of each grade in these qualifications. This is how the questioner put it:

> What is wrong with grade inflation if that is showing that things are getting better? Does it worry you if the Prime Minister says, 'It's terrible that a third of kids aren't getting to a certain grade', when you have to regulate on the basis that a bell curve is maintained and a certain number of people are always going to be at the wrong end of grade 4 and 5?

Let us consider the 'bell curve' point for a moment. It is sometimes thought that because qualification outcomes, plotted onto a graph, generally give a bell curve, that somehow, the outcomes are fixed into this shape. In fact, if the results of any curriculum-based tests like GCSE or A-Level did not show a bell curve, then there would be a good reason to suspect that the test was flawed. If results were clustered at the top end of the mark range, it would indicate that the test was probably too easy, and did not accurately show how much the highest performing students really knew: a large number have full marks, and some would probably have got still higher marks had the test been harder. And likewise, if the results were clustered at the lower end of the mark range, it would show that the test was probably too hard. In this scenario, many students would score zero, which means we have no information about the relative abilities of those students. A bell curve, therefore, simply shows that the test has been well designed for the cohort for whom it is intended; most students get marks in the central part of the range, and only very few get very high or very low marks. This gives us the best possible information about the relative achievement of the cohort that took the test.

So, back to the question of qualifications as a trustworthy currency: why does this matter? It matters for two important reasons. Firstly, as the currency of education, qualifications are portable, belong to their holders and are used to negotiate the employment and higher and further education market after education. They give objective, consistent information about the holder's abilities as demonstrated. They help ensure that selection for jobs and education places is fair, and they reduce cost and friction in the economy that would result if there were no evidence of prior attainment at the point of selection.

The second reason why it matters is because of the role of qualifications in shaping the work of schools and teachers. This is sometimes described (often pejoratively) as the 'backwash' effect of qualifications, the impact they have on curriculum, teaching and teacher behaviours. We will explore this further in the next section.

Summary

- The regulation of qualifications in England is designed to ensure they are *representative* of demonstrated student knowledge, skills or understanding, and *consistently representative* over time.
- Qualifications gain public confidence when they are a trustworthy currency which holds its value over time.
- Grade inflation happens when there are *unwarranted* rises in grades that are not reflective of genuine rises in underlying performance standards.
- A stable currency of qualifications matters because they open doors for students who hold them and reduce friction in the economy for those who use them.
- Qualifications may also have a 'backwash' effect on teaching in schools and colleges.

Section 3: Qualifications, curriculum and teaching

We turn now to consider in more depth the connection between the design of qualifications, including how they are assessed, and the curriculum, teaching, and, by extension, school leadership.

It is important to start by being clear about how 'general qualifications' (by which we mean GCSEs and AS and A-Levels) come into being. In England, all these qualifications must be linked to a content document which sets out what knowledge, skills and understanding must be demonstrated in that qualification. For example, the GCSE subject content document for history specifies that:

> GCSE specifications should include history:
> - from three eras: Medieval (500-1500), Early Modern (1450-1750) and Modern (1700-present day)
> - on three time scales: short (depth study), medium (period study) and long (thematic study)

- on three geographical contexts: a locality (the historic environment); British; and European and / or wider world settings[5]

While the National Curriculum sets out content for Key Stages 1–3, the curriculum for 14–16-year-olds is essentially shaped by the qualification they are taking, in other words, by their GCSE. GCSE specifications, which include both content and sample assessment materials, can only be accredited for use if they adequately assess the approved content, which is held by the Department for Education and, like the National Curriculum, is approved by ministers and therefore subject to democratic accountability.

Does this mean that the education of young people in Key Stage 4 (ages 14–16) must be shaped by the washback effect of their GCSE examinations? In my experience of school leadership, that is the wrong way to think about it. For school leaders and teachers, the focus should be first and foremost on what is to be taught, how best to teach it in a way that is both effective and engaging. This is what I would call the 'strong' approach to curriculum leadership. The 'weak' approach, by contrast, is to focus prematurely or excessively on the assessment methodology, for example, by multiple rehearsals of terminal assessment types from early on in the course, rather than on teaching the content well. It is important to remember that a desirable outcome (in this case, good performance at GCSE) is not the same thing as the means of its genesis (in this case, the means of attaining good GCSE outcomes is not primarily rehearsal of GCSE question types, but rather effective mastery of content through the most effective teaching possible).

What I have characterised here as the 'weak' approach to curriculum leadership is, when it occurs, shaped by the phenomenon remarked on by Steve Munby, quoted above: accountability pressures that we do not support teachers to respond to appropriately, through effective training to grow capacity and expertise.

What can school leaders do to make sure they are on the 'strong' side of curriculum leadership, keeping the focus on the effective teaching of content? My advice would be to focus strongly on investing in the professional development of the teaching workforce. And in so doing, ensure that the content of that professional development is grounded in good evidence on how learning happens and how teachers can make learning more effective. There is good emerging evidence about what well-designed professional development, which leads to better learning and stronger assessment outcomes, looks like. For example, Sam Sims *et al* at UCL conclude that good professional development provides insight, motivates teachers to goal-directed changes in practice, gives teachers new techniques and embeds those changes in practice.[6] The Education Endowment Foundation (EEF) has also published research-based guidance on professional development for school leaders.[7] A knowledgeable and confident teaching workforce is the most effective way to balance the scales and make sure that factors such as the assessment approach and the inevitable accountability pressures do not pull teaching out of shape.

Between 2020 and 2024, Ofqual led an important research project on the many and varied reforms which have happened to vocational and technical qualifications. One of the conclusions of the research is a set of reflections about the connection between qualification reform and reform in curriculum or pedagogy. Although the research is focused on vocational and technical qualifications, which we are not addressing in this chapter, this particular conclusion has implications across the board.

Describing what he calls 'anticipatory qualification design', the author Paul Newton, Ofqual's Research Chair and leader of this research project, writes:

> the most important lesson to learn from our historical research strand concerned the risk of conceptualising and operationalising qualification reform too narrowly. This is often associated with focusing too heavily on assessment implications, with insufficient attention to the wider education and training changes that are necessary for a reform to bed in, particularly the need to support teacher and trainer development from the outset. We argued that qualification reforms are best understood as education and training reforms that are initiated through changes to certification requirements.[8]

In spelling out in this way for policy makers and qualification designers the importance of holding together the assessment used to award qualifications, the curriculum we envisage qualification-takers learning, and the approach of teachers to teaching it, Newton gives important pointers also for school leaders and teachers. Avoid over-prioritising terminal assessment in your curriculum leadership and keep a balanced focus also on the content to be taught and the support for teachers, through professional development, to teach it well.

Summary

- In England, content for Key Stage 4 (ages 14–16) is shaped by the qualifications students take.

- 'Strong' curriculum leadership in schools keeps a strong focus on curriculum and teaching as students prepare for examined qualifications, rather than a premature concentration on assessment preparation.

- Improving qualifications outcomes in schools is best done through investment in high-quality teacher professional development.

- 'Anticipatory qualification design' should prompt school leaders and teachers to hold curriculum intent and planning, teaching and supporting teachers and terminal assessment in a healthy balance.

Section 4: Decisions and trade-offs

We turn, in this final section, to the challenges involved in improving qualifications and assessment. It is not necessary to look very hard to find those who are critical of any qualifications and assessment landscape, both at home and internationally. One of the things I have learnt as Chief Regulator is that in qualifications and assessment, there are many choices which can legitimately be made, but very few which are inconsequential. Every choice to do more of one thing, or less of another, will have an impact. In other words, assessment and qualifications decisions largely require understanding and accepting trade-offs.

The first example of this in action is on the subject of assessment burden, in other words, the volume of assessment, which we ask students to submit to in order to award a qualification. Because, as we have seen, GCSEs and A-Levels in England are based on externally defined subject content, when we design assessments for them in order to award the qualifications, we are assessing against that content. Let us imagine, for the sake of this illustration, that a GCSE content document has 100 bullet points of content. If we want to know with a high level of certainty how many of those bullet points of content every student has learnt, we would need to ask a series of several questions on each bullet. For the benefit of this example, we can say it would take 20 hours to accomplish under exam conditions. Now, very few of us would say that that volume of assessment is either desirable or necessary. The reasons for its undesirability are obvious. It is unnecessary because we do not need that degree of certainty in order to award a GCSE qualification, which can command sufficient confidence and be usable for the purposes intended. Therefore, we take the decision not to ask about all 100 bullet points, but to select, say, 20 areas to ask about, varying our selection each year. That might reduce the time needed for assessment from 20 hours to 4 hours. That is certainly more palatable in terms of examination volume, but we must also accept that it reduces the certainty the qualification grade carries. The student might just have 'got lucky' with the sample we chose that year for assessment and not have learnt much at all about the 80 bullet points we did not ask about that year. But we might also decide that that reduction in certainty is acceptable given the uses to which this qualification will be put. This is an example of a trade-off decision we make.

Let us take a second example. It is sometimes said that examinations are stressful for those taking them. Of course, we all know that to be true, though the extent to which we tolerate that stress, or indeed consider it to be 'desirable' stress, will vary. We might argue that we want to reduce the stress element by assessing some content by 'coursework' tasks rather than formal examinations. In so doing, while we might gain benefit by reducing exam stress, we expose our qualifications to higher risks of cheating, for example, through the use of artificial intelligence (AI), which is now readily available. This could mean that the qualification's claim to *represent* the actual knowledge, skill and understanding demonstrated by the student is weakened. Again, this represents a trade-off. We might accept some degree of weakening of that claim in order to reduce exam stress, or we might decide that our appetite for tolerating exam stress is stronger than for accepting compromises on the integrity of the qualification.

Summary

- The more one reflects on assessment questions, the more one sees that, while many changes and reforms are possible, the majority of them bring consequences and involve making trade-off decisions.

Notes

1. Coe R, *Improving Education: A triumph of hope over experience*, Durham University, 2013.
2. The Apprenticeships, Skills, Children and Learning Bill 2009 proposed a range of measures including the creation of the Office of Qualifications and Examinations Regulation (Ofqual).
3. 'Apprenticeships, Skills, Children and Learning Bill', *Hansard HC*, Volume 488, The Stationery Office 2009.
4. 'Education for 11-16 Year Olds Committee, Corrected oral evidence: Education for 11-16 year olds', House of Lords, 2023. committees.parliament.uk/oralevidence/13453/html/
5. *History GCSE subject content*, Department for Education, April 2014.
6. Sims S, Fletcher-Wood H, O'Mara-Eves A, Cottingham S, Stansfield C, Goodrich J, Van Herwegen J, Anders J, *Effective teacher professional development: new theory and a meta-analytic test*, CEPEO Working Paper No. 22-02, Centre for Education Policy and Equalising Opportunities, UCL, 2022.
7. Collin J and Smith E, *Effective Professional Development Guidance Report*, Education Endowment Fund, 2021.
8. Newton P, Curcin M, Clarke L and Brylka A, *Understanding Qualification Design Insights from the 2020 to 2024 CASLO qualification research programme*. Ofqual, November 2024.

Section 3
Essay 3

The school leader as emancipator

Michael Antram

Early in headship, I decided to move my office from the periphery of the school, where a predecessor had at some point ensured that staff and students were safely on the other side of a security door, to the centre of the school where I could be among the school community. Somehow, in the context of education, which is so much about people, this felt more appropriate. It was during the creation of my new office space that a sealed air duct was exposed, within which was found a forgotten letter from the early 1970s.

The letter was a plea from a mother for her son, and reads thus:

> William was told on Friday that he would not now be in the chorus for the Christmas show. If his voice was not suitable, and I do understand your point of view, surely this should have been noted at the start of rehearsals. He has worked extremely hard learning the songs with our help and has missed only one rehearsal. I do feel it was most unfortunate that he was not informed sooner that his voice was unsuitable, as it was the words and music that attracted him to the show in the first instance. And now to be told at this late stage he is to be an understudy is small consolation to a disappointed child.

From this letter, two things are noteworthy. The first is to observe, somewhat wryly, that in the 1970s, a parent was more likely to acknowledge that a school had a valid point of view than might now be the case in many schools. The second, and most important point, is that this mother who pleads for her son in his disappointment illustrates for me what can happen when quality outcomes are prioritised over the formation of the individual. William would now be in his sixties, and we will never know how many times he went to sing in the car, only to stop and remind himself that he could not sing. What his story illustrates for me is that, in the pursuit of quality outcomes, he, the person, came second. I am haunted, as a headteacher, by the thought of William because he reminds me in a small way that school outcomes, as currently measured, may well get a person somewhere, even somewhere very special, but it is the formation of the inner person that will determine *who* and *how* the individual is once they get there.

As we emerged from the COVID pandemic, I had hoped that we might have found the time and space to consider what education is or could be for. I am not sure that I have discerned the fruits of such a debate if it has happened. What I do know is that the country's young people are generally the least happy with life, and among the least happy with education of 27 countries participating in the latest Programme for International Student Assessment (PISA) study, according to *The Good Childhood Report*.[1] This is a picture of deterioration, representing a consistent fall in the emotional and mental wellbeing of significant numbers of young people in the UK since the report began in 2009/10, long before the global pandemic. What can we as school leaders offer to this situation? Prior to the report's introduction, we can trace the growing influence of a particular view of what education is for since the 1980s.[2] The movement of 'New Public Management', originating in the private sector, began to encroach upon the public sector with its attendant language of *performance, efficiency* and *outcomes*.[3] This, in turn, began to influence the professional identities of teachers and school leaders who now needed to focus on improving 'output' and to learn the skills and techniques that would make them efficient and effective as practitioners.[4] Education, which was now to serve economic ends at the service of the economy, was increasingly dominated by the language of performativity[5], and the collective preoccupation with the question 'what works?'

In those heady days as a deputy headteacher newly charged with leading teaching and learning, I was captivated by the thought of 'effect sizes'.[6] These were informed by meta-analyses of international studies, identifying and distilling the most effective teaching methods. With this new understanding I could lead teachers to develop their implementation of the science (note the loss of the concept of 'craft') of teaching, so that they could, through acquiring greater technical skill, leverage still greater outcomes from their students. Looking back, perhaps our increasing focus on how the brain works reduced opportunities for the deepening of our professional understanding of how the young *person* works. The relational may have become lost in pursuit of the technical.

The introduction of Progress 8 in 2016 as a measure of school performance, and, in time, *the* measure of school performance[7] increased for the nation's schools, a demand that they focus on progress from Key Stage 2 'starting points' to the outcomes of Key Stage 4 examinations. I had not, for some reason, made the connection between my own experience as a parent and what I was being asked to do as a professional. My own children had attended a school that was, in the then Ofsted parlance 'satisfactory' and in need of becoming 'good'. To do this, the school needed to improve its Key Stage 2 SATs outcomes in reading (together with punctuation and grammar) and Maths. The school drive, therefore, was to focus especially on those children who would get the school 'over the line' of accountability in order to satisfy the authorities. My own children were bored, as for quite some time creativity left the classroom, replaced by drill. We can imagine, then, what the professional focus and dialogue of school staff would need to be in order to achieve such 'progress'. Key Stage 2 'prior performance' (note the terminology) of each child in turn informs the subject targets in terms of academic outcomes at the end of Year 11. So it is that I have found myself as a secondary headteacher each September discussing with, for example, the Head of Art, the extent to which they have met the academic targets set for a 16-year-old, largely based on their competency in reading and maths on a hot late-spring's day when they were little.

There is a pull towards being a certain kind of headteacher exerted by the prevailing paradigm of performativity and the consequent expectations of government, governors and parents.[8] Within such a culture of high-stakes accountability, what is the school leader to do, and what are they called to be, given that academic performativity as a preoccupation does not seem to be lifting the spirits of the nation's young? Questions are being asked as to whether the knowledge-based curriculum that has dominated education in the past decade or more will continue to have currency as AI advances.[9] The school leaders of the future can, if they choose or are forced, continue the integration of the language of business and technology into education, talking of being 'the best' and the 'top' schools based on a narrow range of nationally preferred metrics. But school leaders, as emancipators, may need to be pushing for a different model of education if young people as individual human beings are to become once again the focus of all that we do in schools, rather than serving as means to performative economic ends.

I have felt the competitive pull of performance tables and the pressures of the gaze of accountability from Ofsted. But I am aware, sometimes, of what levers are pulled elsewhere for a school to rise through the performance ranks, and it is a game I do not want to play. I cannot deliver the open evening speech listing dazzling A-Level grades and sparkling progressions to 'top universities' when I feel that the horizon for schools needs to be reset to the longer term, at the fulness of the life well lived rather than the age of 21, when today's students will graduate and in turn become tomorrow's useful alumni, and school will just be a memory. There is a need for me, if I am to avoid becoming more cynical, and perhaps others who feel the same, to consider the sort of leader I need to become in order to free teachers once more to be creative practitioners, to free up space in the curriculum to support all children in their human formation, and to grow a school community that might one day hang oak boards honouring a broader definition of achievement.

Various models for leadership are offered beyond the 'new managerial' concept required for improving performativity.[10] In selecting an appropriate leadership approach, we need to consider what the context for leadership is and what the leader is being asked to do. Different contexts require different approaches,[11] and as I commented earlier, the context for education involves human beings at its centre.

Servant leadership is one such model that might serve school leaders well, given that it advocates the leader being at the service of others. The term implies a philanthropic intent, and if education is to be at the service of the young once more, it would seem like a good place to start. Servant leadership was developed as a model by Robert Greenleaf in 1970 and advocates the (business) leader placing themself at the service of their employees.[12] Through serving the needs of employees rather than seeing them as mere functionaries, the organisation enjoys many benefits, benefits that are intended to ripple outwards into society as a whole. The intention of this leadership approach in the context of employment is to grow employees who are happier and freer so that greater potential can be released within the organisation. The leadership approach promoted by servant leadership is the antithesis of a quest for personal power or an ego-driven pursuit of leading the best school in the area.

Having said that, it might be argued that the release of potential within the organisation is still serving the intention of securing better results produced by children. A leadership model that originated in the context of private-sector profit-driven organisations might retain some of its 'results driven' essence within the public sector. For this reason, in the wrong hands, servant leadership could become a cynical manipulation of people rather than a truly philanthropic disposition of a leader. In a society that might more easily reach for Downton Abbey or Bridgerton when seeking to understand servanthood, it may not accurately reflect the fullness and complexity of the demands made of the contemporary leadership role of headteacher, especially when performance tables continue to exist.

Perhaps a different model is called for? The post-pandemic, post-riots, post-truth context for our educational enterprise as school leaders serves as a backdrop to a confused educational landscape in the UK, wherein different multi-academy trusts, secular and faith-based, promote a conflicted educational *telos*. Schools have become increasingly used to providing the services internally that used to be provided externally. My colleagues pack carrier bags of food donated by the wider school community for those families who cannot provide enough food for their children. Schools divert scarce financial resources towards in-house mental health provision, because we struggle to comprehend what it must be like for a teenager in torment faced with waiting months for an initial assessment by an over-stretched external mental health professional. Standing in this space with its sociological and ethical confusion, school leaders feel the dilemma of whether to compete or to pursue something that feels more intuitively right in meeting the needs of the young people whom we serve.

Professor Gert Biesta, of Maynooth University, has long championed the need for us to reconsider the purpose of education and what constitutes a 'good' education.[13] He differentiates between 'education' and 'learning', preferring the more rounded, holistic and formative concept of *education*. Whilst views may differ regarding the content of education, we might unite around the ultimate pursuit of education for the individual, and hence for society as a life lived well. To this end, schools could become places of being and becoming, and not just doing. Biesta argues that educational priorities need to be refocused on the formation of the human person. Faced with a fragile and volatile world, He observes:

> I wish to remind us of three such challenges where I am absolutely sure that they will still be here 50 or even 100 years from now: the question of democracy, that is, of how to live together given that we are different and value our differences; the question of ecology, that is, how to manage to sustain our collective lives on a planet with limited capacity; and the question of care, that is, how we 'carry' others, particularly those who are not yet, or no longer able to carry themselves.[14]

Drawing on the writings of Meirieu,[15] Biesta asserts the educational 'duty to resist' those impositions upon education that draw it away from serving the interests of those who will form the (better?) society of tomorrow.

The duty to resist invites us as school leaders to be emancipatory and prophetic in our bid to cultivate the growth of the young towards adulthood, as education's gift to the future. Using what we know about the nation's young in working so closely with them, we cannot continue to do, uncritically, the same educational things. What is to be gained if results go up, but people go down? For Biesta, education needs to hold in balance three domains: qualification – the equipping of the young with knowledge and skills; socialisation – communication and living with others well; and formation into adulthood.[16] Recognising this and doing something about it may begin to offer something positive to the nation's young, who are among the most despondent in Europe, and so in need of happiness and hope. William's hurt, and the possible stunting of part of his formation, could have been prevented if performance became once more a joyful function, not just a value.

Notes

1 *The Good Childhood Report 2024*, The Children's Society, 2024.
2 See Goodson I, 'Context, curriculum and professional knowledge' in Robinson W, Freathy R and Doney J, (eds) *Politics, Professionals and Practitioners*, Routledge, 2017, p 48–56.
3 See Helgetun J and Menter I, 'From an age of measurement to an evidence era? Policy-making in teacher education in England', *Journal of Education Policy*, 37(1), 2022, pp 88–105.

4 See Crow G and Møller J, 'Professional identities of school leaders across international contexts: An introduction and rationale', *Educational Management, Administration & Leadership*, 45(5), 2017, pp 749–758.
5 For this argument see: Finn M, *The Gove legacy: education in Britain after the coalition*, Palgrave Macmillan, 2017.
6 The concept of 'effect size' was used in a meta-analysis of educational research undertaken by Professor John Hattie. See Hattie J and Yates GCR, *Visible learning and the science of how we learn,* Routledge, 2014.
7 See Prior L, Jerrim J, Thomson D and Leckiw G, 'A review and evaluation of secondary school accountability in England: Statistical strengths, weaknesses and challenges for 'Progress 8' raised by COVID-19', *Review of Education*, 9(3), 2021.
8 For an interesting discussion see Harris A, Campbell C and Jones M, 'A national discussion on education - so what for school leaders?', *School leadership and management*, 42(5), 2022, pp 433–437.
9 See Parris M, 'Will AI make bricklayers better-paid than barristers?' *The Spectator*, 28 September 2024.
10 See Gewirtz S and Ball S, 'From "welfarism" to "new managerialism": shifting discourses of school headship in the education marketplace', *Discourse*, 2000, 21(3), pp 253–268.
11 See Sivaruban S, 'A Critical Perspective of Leadership Theories', *Business Ethics and Leadership*, 5(1), 2021, pp 57–65.
12 For further information see Greenleaf RK and Spears LC (eds), *Servant leadership: a journey into the nature of legitimate power and greatness,* Paulist Press, 2002.
13 For examples of Biesta's thinking, see Biesta G, *Obstinate education: reconnecting school and society*, Brill, 2019. And Biesta G, *'Good education in an age of measurement: on the need to reconnect with the question of purpose in education'*, *Educational assessment, evaluation and accountability*, 21(1), 2008, pp 33–46.
14 Biesta G, and Matthes M, 'The duty to resist: Redefining the basics for today's schools', in Matthes M et al (eds) *Improving the Quality of Childhood in Europe*, Volume 7, Alliance for Childhood European Network Foundation, 2020, p 26.
15 Meirieu P, *Pédagogie: le devoir de resister*, ESF, 2008.
16 Discussed in Biesta G and Matthes M, 2020, in the work cited, p 23.

Section 3
Essay 4

Understanding, embedding and assessing complex competences such as Creative Thinking

Bill Lucas

That key dispositions or complex competences, such as creative thinking, collaborative problem-solving and communication, need to be at the heart of a contemporary curriculum is increasingly accepted across the world. Indeed, organisations like the Brookings Institution and the Center for Curriculum Redesign[1] track progress and have charted their formal inclusion in some 20 educational jurisdictions. In the case of creative thinking, there has been substantial research internationally,[2] a recent detailed examination of the research and practices in England[3] leading to a five-year funded programme, the Creativity Collaboratives, alongside more detailed exploration of pedagogies,[4] extensive exploration of assessment practices,[5] exploration of effective leadership for creative thinking and guidance for school leaders.[6] All of these developments were summarised by a recent global overview written by the author.[7]

So why, you might ask, if there is such substantial consensus about the importance of these dispositions and about how to do it, are schools in England still only dipping their curriculum and assessment toes into these exciting waters rather than diving in?

One immediate answer – and it is reinforced by the structure of this book – is that educators find it surprisingly difficult to think holistically about curriculum, pedagogy and assessment, preferring instead to think about them in separate silos. This is especially the case with assessment, which, at least in England, often gets reduced to considering the summative examinations taken by pupils at 16 or 18. Unless you look at the Higher or Extended Project Qualifications or at BTEC Nationals, complex competences are largely invisible.

An argument can then be made by those who do not wish to engage in the conversation that either (a) competences may be important, but we do not know how to assess them, or (b) if they are not going to be assessed, they cannot be a priority in an already overcrowded curriculum.

The recent Programme for International Student Assessment (PISA) Test of Creative Thinking[8] was a landmark moment for the status of one key disposition, creative thinking. Taken by some 140,000 15-year-olds across the world, the extensive new PISA data set reminds educators of the challenges faced by anyone trying to change a system predicated on individual subject disciplines and their largely content-based assessments. It also helpfully debunks some widely held myths about creativity – that it is vague, undermines scholarship, cannot be taught and cannot be assessed. On this last point, a global digital revolution is underway to make a reality of strengths-based assessment that puts complex competences such as creative thinking at the centre rather than on the margins.[9]

Understanding complex competences

A widely cited model of what a contemporary curriculum should contain[10] distinguishes between foundational literacies, competencies and character qualities (S3 Figure E4.1).

The italics in the figure description on the next page are mine. While I agree with its contents, the use of the phrase '21st Century Skills' is, I believe, deeply unhelpful, implying that we already know what will be needed in another 75 years and that these are already set in stone. This is patently silly and can so easily sound evangelical rather than research-led. In my own writing, I have summarised the state of play and made an argument for changing our language.[11]

And the language used by all those trying to reform the system presents its challenges. In S3 Figure E4.1, we have 'literacies' used in a way that is closer in meaning to applied knowledge or competence, and competencies (rather than complex competences or dispositions). Nevertheless, in numbers 7–16, in the second and third columns, are most of what many consider to be 'complex competences'.

There is another way of thinking about this, which seeks to distinguish between those that are about being a good person (prosocial) and those which help to make good learners (epistemic) (S3 Figure E4.2).

The words in the first column clearly relate to values, while those in the second speak specifically to attitudes to learning. Although in practice, these two categories

Understanding, embedding and assessing complex 151

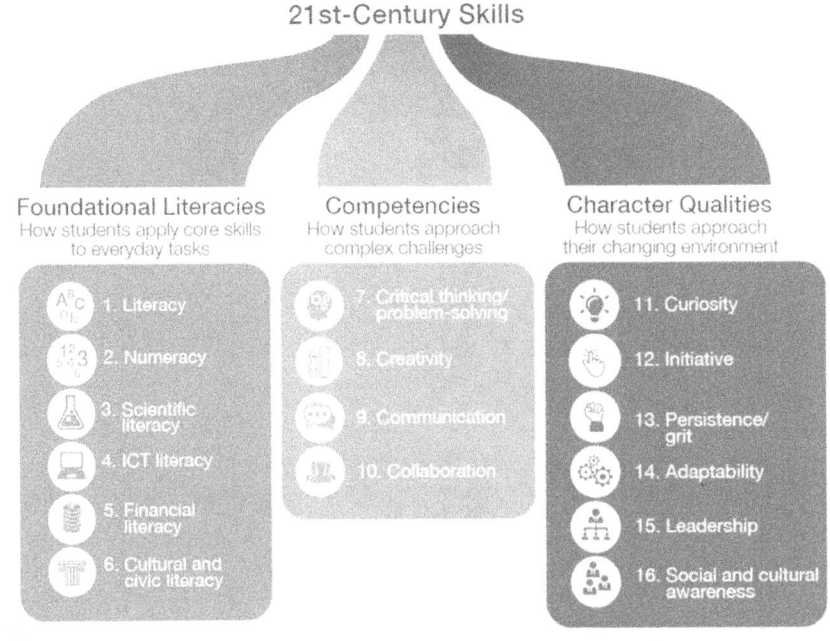

S3 Figure E4.1   *21st Century Skills*, World Economic Forum.[12]

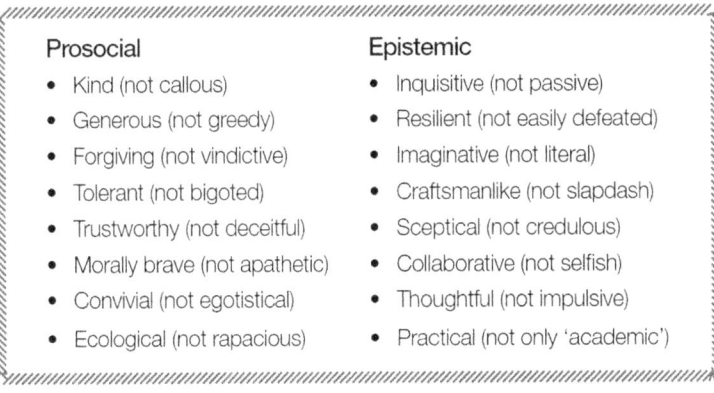

S3 Figure E4.2   Desired outcomes of education.[13]

are permeable. Being collaborative, for example, implies that you might also value and seek the contribution of others.

Nearly all schools have a vision and a set of values, and some also articulate the kinds of complex competences they seek to develop. At a global level, the Organisation for Economic Cooperation and Development (OECD) has been exploring the ways in which knowledge, skills and attitudes and values inter-relate. It usefully suggests that competencies (or complex competences in the language of

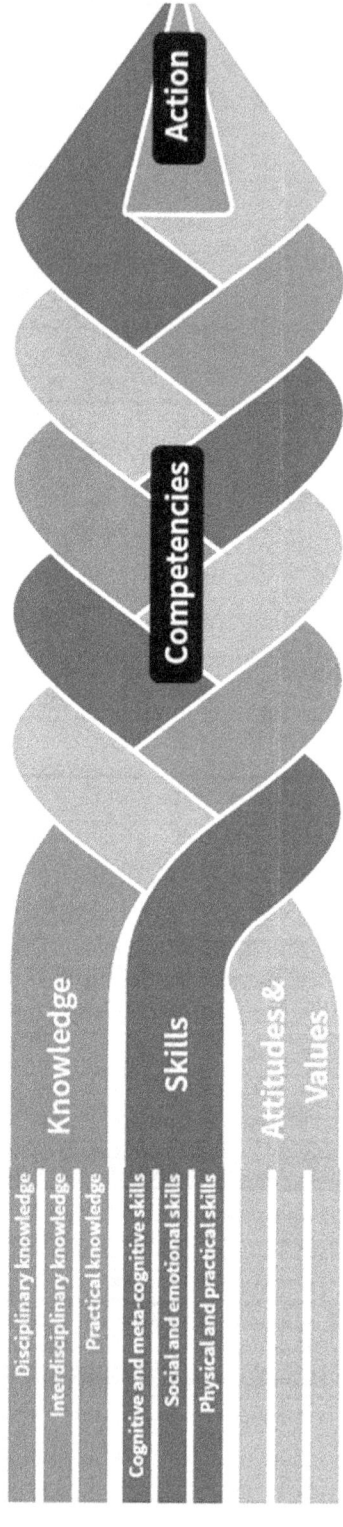

S3 Figure E4.3   OECD Education 2030 Framework.[14]

S3 Figure E4.4 Skillsbuilder Universal Framework 2.0.

this chapter) are the result of knowledge, skills and values as they are applied in the real world (S3 Figure E4.3).

Closer to home, Skillsbuilder[15], a global group of businesses, education institutions, and impact organisations, has developed, trialled and recently revised a very credible framework (S3 Figure E4.4) for complex competences (essential skills in their language).

In a similar vein, Guy Claxton and I have suggested seven competences we think that the evidence suggests are important – confidence, communication, collaboration, communication, creativity, commitment and craftsmanship.[16]

As we ponder what it means today to be 'well-educated' in this book, it is important that school leaders consider these contrasting views of what it is to be knowledgeable and skilful and then make the choices that they feel are right for their community. Whichever approach is chosen, a clear understanding of each competence needs to be articulated so that it can then be embedded in the life of a school systematically and intentionally.

Let us take Creative Thinking, a combination of Creativity and Critical Thinking, recently assessed by PISA[17], as an example. The PISA work emerged from our research at the University of Winchester[18] and an international implementation study[19]. The model of Creative Thinking developed with colleagues at the University of Winchester has five dimensions (S3 Figure E4.5).

The five dimensions – being imaginative, inquisitive, persistent, collaborative and disciplined – each have has three sub-elements. The model has now been used in more than 30 educational jurisdictions and, in each case, schools have tailored it to their own needs. So its adaptation by Thomas Tallis School in London is different from Rooty Hill High School in Sydney and different again from Kopernikus School in Frutillar, Chile.[20]

Embedding complex competences

Continuing the focus on creative thinking as one example of a complex competence from which lessons can be drawn, our own research has shown that the process of cultivating it requires teachers first to map key elements of the competence against key aspects of each subject and then to consider which pedagogy might be most suited to teaching both the knowledge and the skill components. We have called this 'split screen teaching', a process whereby teachers imagine a screen split into two 'worlds', the disciplinary subject matter of their lesson *and* the competence on which they are also focusing.[21] They then plan a curriculum accordingly. In a four-year, eleven-country study,[22] we found that schools which cultivated competences most effectively did so systematically and intentionally. Their assumptions were that almost any competence can be embedded in almost any subject; it is just a question of careful planning. A split-screen approach avoids a major difficulty: the perception that teaching complex competences involves doubling the workload.

Understanding, embedding and assessing complex **155**

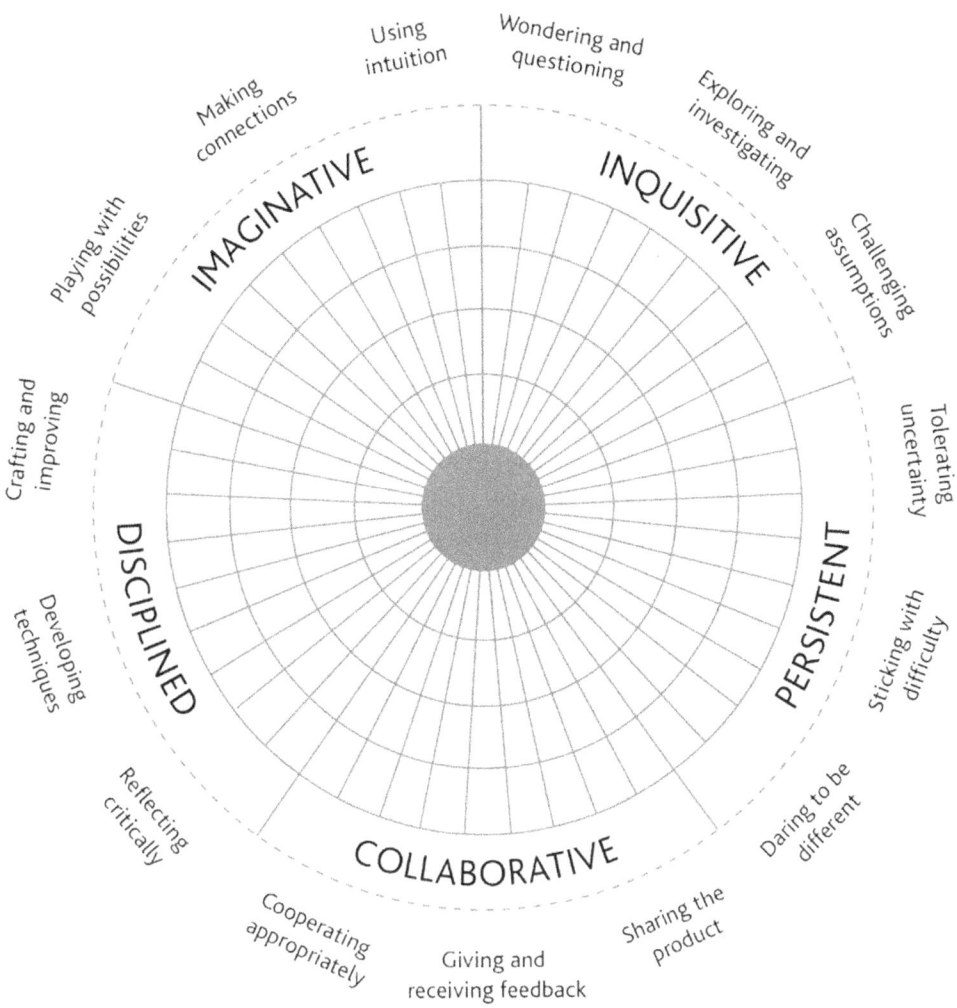

S3 Figure E4.5   The Centre for Real-World Learning's model of Creative Thinking.[23]

For it shows that, with careful planning, these can be woven into the fabric of the existing curriculum.

Some educational jurisdictions, Australia, Canada, Finland, Korea and Singapore, for example, organise their curricula by focusing not just on subject disciplines but also on competences. In Canada, where individual states determine what is done, policymakers in Alberta[24] have helpfully cross-mapped eight competences (competencies) – critical thinking, problem solving, managing information, creativity and innovation, communication, collaboration, cultural and global citizenship, personal growth and wellbeing – against each subject of the curriculum, showing where there are helpful overlaps. Alberta gets the balance just right between giving authoritative guidance and respecting local autonomy and innovation.

In England, the eight Creativity Collaboratives are providing a wealth of data as to how schools can best embed creative thinking in their schools,[25] with the majority using the Centre for Real-World Learning model and developing their own locally produced toolkits to support their teachers.

Assessing complex competences

Just over a decade ago, my colleagues and I were commissioned to develop a model of creativity specifically for schools and explore ways in which it could be assessed. At the first meeting of our teacher reference group, there was outright hostility to the idea that creativity could or should be assessed. Creativity, teachers suggested, is too close to what it is to be human to somehow be measured. Assessing it would kill creativity. There would be no point, as children were either born creative or not.

By the end of our research,[26] these concerns (in many cases myths) had evaporated. A shift of language from 'assessing' or 'measuring' to 'evidencing progress' helped. There was a realisation that the more you were able to tell whether how you were teaching was having a positive impact on pupils, the better and more precise the teaching became. And, most encouragingly, pupils found that the assessment process supported them in developing a deeper understanding of creativity and creative thinking.

The recent PISA test demonstrated unequivocally that it is possible to assess creative thinking summatively. This is important as a statement of creativity's importance and the rigour of its underpinning concepts. But it is not what matters in schools, where it is formative approaches that really count. Here, the point is to use feedback and other approaches from the broad field of assessment for learning to help pupils develop their creativity.

To evidence the development of pupils' creativity in schools, three things are required: a clear understanding of progression, a repertoire of assessment methods and a way of bringing all of this together so that students can gauge their achievements and teachers can moderate the evidence they have gathered.

In Australia, both nationally and in some States, learning continua or progression documents have been developed which enable teachers to see how their pupils are progressing over time.[27] In research carried out by the OECD,[28] the power of these kinds of documents, often taking the form of a clear descriptive rubric, was shown again and again.

In England, where creative thinking is largely absent from the curriculum, it would greatly help those seeking to embed complex competences if such progression 'maps' were available. To redress this, we recently undertook an exploratory study in English schools[29] and developed just such continua for three of the five dimensions of our model of creative thinking. S3 Table E4.1 is an example of one of these.

Teachers found the clarity of an overview like this helpful. For just as they have a mental model of what progress might look like in any of the subject disciplines they teach, so they have one they can refer to for a specific competence. One of

S3 Table E4.1 Progression framework for Being Imaginative developed by the author

	Starting point	Emerging	Developing	Deepening	Key indicators
1. Imaginative					
1.1 Generating ideas	Learners provide one or two simple/obvious ideas with strong support	Learners provide a small number of relatively obvious ideas with some support	Learners provide many ideas, some well-developed largely work on their own	Learners generate a large number of ideas relevant to the context, and work independently	**Number/agency**
1.2 Playing with possibilities	Learners provide a very limited range of ideas, all focusing on the same theme	Learner's ideas represent a small range of themes and show some exploration of the theme	Learners provide a range of ideas that are distinct from one another, and which show genuine exploration of the theme	Learners generate a wide range of alternative ideas and solutions, sometimes adapting existing ideas, sometimes integrating other perspectives	**Range/complexity**
1.3 Making connections	Learners present ideas that are very obvious or conventional, only containing concepts with which they are already familiar	Learners present ideas that are mostly obvious or conventional, containing a few concepts with which they are not already familiar	Learners present ideas which show some flexibility and willingness to go beyond their existing experiences, combining elements of a task to explore new combinations of ideas	Learners present ideas that show they can think flexibly, going beyond their existing experience or social context, combining elements of a task to allow for novel combinations of ideas	**Novel connections**

the challenges with creativity is that it is both a product (an artefact, essay, drama, presentation, image, exhibition and so on) and a process (of generating ideas, critiquing these, refining them, etc). The former is visible and often tangible; the latter is frequently invisible and fleeting.

In terms of assessment methods, it is important that teachers realise the usefulness of adopting a number of these simultaneously to enable them to get at both the pupils' perceptions and their own judgements. S3 Table E4.2 shows the kinds of methods which are helpful.

In work undertaken by the author in schools in Western Australia, it has become clear not only that, for many teachers, these are new or little-used methods. But, importantly, with effective professional learning, they can be learned.[30] Teachers both in Australia and in the exploratory study in England found that the most effective way of gathering evidence was in a portfolio, either hard copy or digital or both. Using examples of pupils' work alongside creative thinking progression documents provides the opportunity for teachers to find consensus in their evaluations and affords pupils the chance of learning from the various iterations of their work. In both countries, such portfolios are now beginning to provide data

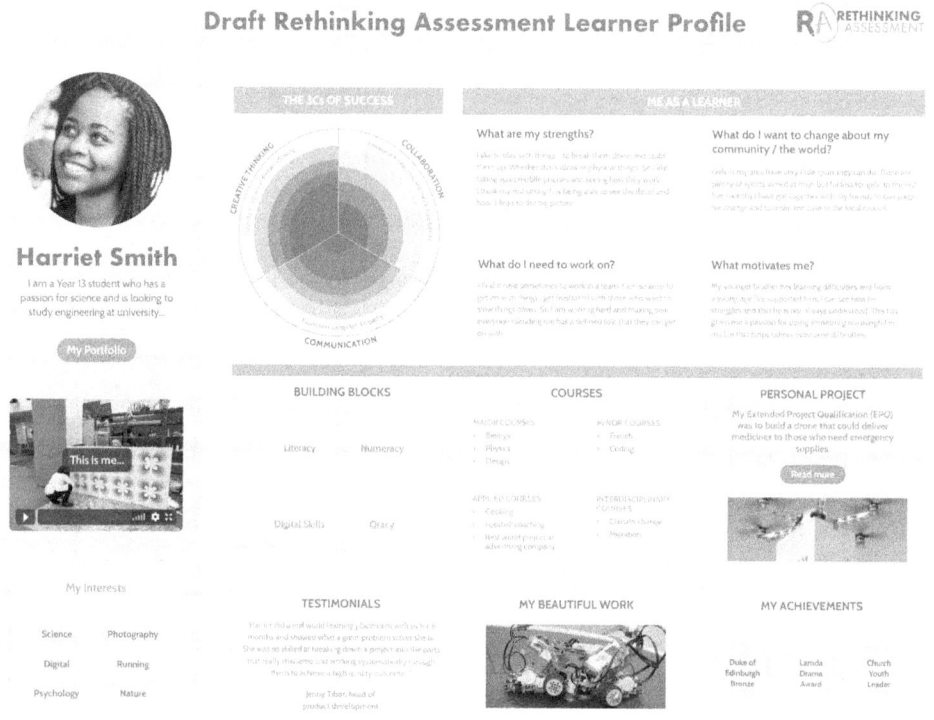

S3 Figure E4.6   Rethinking Assessment's prototype Digital Learner Profile.

S3 Table E4.2   Approaches to assessing creativity[31]

Pupil	Teacher	Real-world	Online
Real-time feedback Photographs Self-report questionnaires Logs/diaries/ journals Portfolios	Criterion-referenced Rating of products and processes Structured progress interviews Performance tasks Capstone projects	Expert reviews Gallery critique Authentic tests, eg displays/ presentations/ interviews/ podcasts/ films Exhibitions	Apps Digital badges E-portfolios

for a digital learner profile of the kind developed by Rethinking Assessment (S3 Figure E4.6).

A profile provides pupils with a visual map of their educational progress. We suggest that, as part of their educational journey in school (and outside), they will be gathering evidence of their growing capability in three complex competences – Creative Thinking, Collaboration and Communication. It may be that we want to move away from the neatness of three words beginning with the letter 'C' and rename Communication as Oracy, in the light of recent work.[32]

Putting it all together

To be well-educated at this moment in the history of the human race, it is important that school leaders and their staff blend curriculum, pedagogy and assessment, just as they interweave knowledge, skills and complex competences to ensure that all pupils can flourish in complex, fast-changing times.

This kind of system change will require brave leaders, individuals who are prepared to challenge the current overemphasis on testable knowledge rather than knowledge *and* demonstrable competence in a range of settings.[33]

Being well-educated requires us all to reach beyond the simple, often simplistic, binary alternatives as to what matters in schools. We need to grow learners who are passionately knowledgeable, skilled in many areas, and competently able to deploy their knowledge and skills in the real world.

Notes

1 Care E, Kim, H, Vista A and Anderson K, *Education system alignment for 21st century skills: Focus on assessment*, Brookings Institution, 2018. Fadel C, *Assessing countries' competencies: The 4D index, ranking of skills, character and meta-learning*, Centre for Strategic Education, 2021.

2 Vincent-Lancrin S et al, *Fostering Students' Creativity and Critical Thinking: What it Means in School*, OECD Publishing, 2019.

3 *The Durham Commission on Creativity and Education*, Arts Council England, 2019.

4. Lucas B and Spencer E, *Teaching Creative Thinking: Developing learners who generate ideas and can think critically*, Crown House Publishing, 2017. Cremin T and Chappell K, 'Creative pedagogies: a systematic review', *Research Papers in Education*, 36(3), 2019, pp 299–331.
5. Lucas B, *A Field Guide to assessing creative thinking in schools*, FORM-Rethinking Assessment, 2022.
6. Lucas B, Spencer E and Stoll E, *Creative leadership to develop creativity and creative thinking in English schools: A review of the evidence*. Mercers' Company, 2021.
7. Lucas B, *Creative thinking in schools across the world: A snapshot of progress in 2022*. Global Institute of Creative Thinking, 2022.
8. *PISA 2022 Results (Volume III): Creative minds, creative schools*, OECD, 2024.
9. Lucas B, *Rethinking Assessment in Education: the case for change*, Centre for Strategic Education, 2021.
10. *New Vision for Education: Unlocking the Potential of Technology*, World Economic Forum, 2015.
11. Lucas B, *Why we need to stop talking about twenty-first century skills*, Centre for Strategic Education, 2019.
12. *New Vision for Education: Unlocking the Potential of Technology*, World Economic Forum, 2015, p 3.
13. 'Desired outcomes of education' in Claxton G and Lucas B, *What kind of teaching for what kind of learning?* SSAT, 2013, p 9.
14. 'The Future of Education and Skills: OECD Education 2030 Framework', *Global Competence for a Changing World*, OECD, 2016, p 2.
15. Skillsbuilder Partnership, www.skillsbuilder.org.
16. Claxton G and Lucas B, *Educating Ruby: what our children really need to learn*, Crown House Publishing, 2015.
17. *PISA 2022 Results (Volume III): Creative minds, creative schools*, OECD, 2024.
18. Lucas B, Claxton G and Spencer E, *Progression in Student Creativity in School: First steps towards new forms of formative assessments*, OECD Education Working Papers 85, 2013. Lucas B, *A Five-Dimensional Model of Creativity and its Assessment in Schools*, Applied Measurement in Education, 29:4, 2016, pp 278–290.
19. Vincent-Lancrin S et al, *Fostering Students' Creativity and Critical Thinking: What it Means in School*, OECD Publishing, 2019.
20. 'Tallis Habits' Thomas Tallis School, www.thomastallisschool.com/tallis-habits. 'Rooty Hill High School aims to create effective learners for life', Rooty Hill High School, www.theconnection.org.au/wp-content/uploads/2023/07/Updated-TheConnection-CaseStudy-RootyHill-v2.pdf. 'Creativity Is Our Way of Doing and Thinking', Colegio Kopernikus, www.kopernikus.cl/copia-de-proyecto-educativo?lang=en
21. Lucas B and Spencer E, *Teaching Creative Thinking: Developing learners who generate ideas and can think critically*, Crown House Publishing, 2017.
22. Vincent-Lancrin S et al, *Fostering Students' Creativity and Critical Thinking: What it Means in School*, OECD Publishing, 2019.
23. 'The Centre for Real-World Learning's model of Creative Thinking', in Lucas B, Claxton G and Spencer E, *Progression in Student Creativity in School: First steps towards new forms of formative assessments*, OECD Education Working Papers 85, 2013.
24. 'Competencies in subjects', Alberta Education, www.education.alberta.ca/competencies/competencies-in-subjects/everyone/competencies-in-subjects/
25. 'Creativity Collaboratives', www.artscouncil.org.uk/developing-creativity-and-culture/children-and-young-people/creativity-collaboratives

26 Lucas B, Claxton G and Spencer E, *Progression in Student Creativity in School: First steps towards new forms of formative assessments*, OECD Education Working Papers 85, 2013.
27 'Critical and Creative Thinking' (Version 8.4), Australian Curriculum, www.australiancurriculum.edu.au/f-10-curriculum/general-capabilities/critical-and-creative-thinking/
28 Vincent-Lancrin S et al, *Fostering Students' Creativity and Critical Thinking: What it Means in School*, OECD Publishing, 2019.
29 Krystic S, *Putting Creative Thinking at the core of the English school curriculum: An exploratory study*. London: Australian Council for Educational Research UK, 2024.
30 Lucas B, *A Field Guide to assessing creative thinking in schools*, FORM-Rethinking Assessment, 2022.
31 'Approaches to assessing creativity', adapted from Lucas B and Spencer E, *Teaching Creative Thinking: Developing learners who generate ideas and can think critically*, Crown House Publishing, 2017, p160.
32 *We need to talk,* The Commission on the Future of Oracy Education in England, 2024.
33 Lucas B, 'Leadership for creative thinking in schools: How current research and innovation is putting creativity back into schools in England', *Impact Journal*, 2023, pp 26–29. Lucas B, Spencer E, Stoll L, Fisher-Naylor D, Richards N, James S and Milne K, *Creative Thinking in Schools: a leadership playbook*, Crown House Publishing, 2023.

Section 3
Essay 5

How do we know someone is well-educated?

Anna Trethewey

Capturing what it means to be well educated is a question many have struggled to answer. Policymakers want to establish that the public purse has been spent well. Practitioners want to demonstrate how they have added value. Parents and carers want reassurance that their child's time in education was well spent, and, of course, young people themselves want to demonstrate that they are able to progress to the next stage of their journey. Yet establishing whether someone is well educated or not is a fundamentally tricky question, and one that requires unpacking.

In this chapter, I will briefly talk about what is meant by being well educated and the limitations and benefits of the ways we try and measure that, before setting out how the current system could be improved.

What is it to be well educated?

Several significant Education Acts set out the mechanisms by which a universal education should be delivered, ranging from the Elementary Education Act of 1870 to the Education Reform Act of 1988. Those Acts have changed expectations of how – and, in the earlier Acts, even if children should be educated; yet by starting from the premise that education is an agreed right, there is little that sets out what 'well educated' means.

Given this lack of an agreed definition, in 2015, the Education Select Committee set out to establish the purpose of education. The Chair of the Committee at the time, Neil Carmichael, explained:

In this inquiry we want to ask the question, what is education for? What is the purpose of our educational system? Is it, for example, to prepare our young people for the world of work? Is it to ready our children for adulthood and provide them with the skills to lead fulfilling lives? Is it to provide them all with broad academic knowledge, based on a shared culture and values?[1]

In spite of its laudable aims and the wide range of evidence submitted, the enquiry arrived at no firm definition. As any experienced educator knows, attempts to answer this question often end similarly, as there are such different and, at times, apparently conflicting views. The answer is, of course, all of the above: a well-educated young person should have the tools and qualifications they need to navigate the world productively in whichever way they choose. And while there are some who would set up a false dichotomy between a progressive system that produces happy yet low-attaining students and a Gradgrindian system that produces miserable but highly attaining students, the reality is that delivering a good education and measuring it is much more complex than that. A well-educated young person has a rounded view of the world and is able to navigate it with the quiet self-assuredness of one who has the tools they need to adapt to an ever-evolving landscape. However, our curriculum and assessment fail to properly achieve those aims.

How do we know if the system has educated students well? What are the benefits and downsides of these measures?

Measurement and national standards, while well-intentioned and an integral part of the education landscape, can skew curriculum and assessment. Seeking to measure, or more accurately, assess how well-educated students are in the round is inherently difficult. We have different tools at our disposal that work as proxies, but they are markedly few, and all have their limitations. Some include: GCSE and A-Level exam results; performance in international rankings, such as Programme for International Student Assessment (PISA) and Progress in International Reading Literacy Study PIRLS; and destination measures. For a setting-wide snapshot, there are also Ofsted inspections. While an inspection report will not tell us anything about individual students, it will at least indicate how well leaders know and understand their setting and how effective the provision is at educating students well against the Ofsted framework.

We also use a raft of more subjective individual indicators, including certificates of participation, such as taking part in the Duke of Edinburgh programme or the National Citizenship Scheme, self-reported experiences, such as those that university personal statements are awash with, and of course, the presentation of the young person themselves. However, these are obviously not rigorous measures, so while they provide an indication that young people have received an education that goes beyond just academic study, they cannot and should not form part of any national accountability measure.

To consider what we mean by 'well educated' through the somewhat narrow lens of how well a student has achieved academically, it is important to consider what the assessment and examination system is designed to do and what it is not. As with any measure, exams are one of a range of tools we can use to consider whether a student is well educated, but they certainly will not tell us the answer in any totality. As Loic Menzies puts it in *Mapping the Way*:

> Data on educational attainment only provides a limited picture of what goes on in young people's lives… Improving outcomes for children and young people depends on piecing together a fuller picture of what is going on in and of school, drawing on a range of metrics and insights, both qualitative and quantitative.[2]

Yet before we move on to those wider metrics and insights, let us look for a moment at the value that system-level assessment, and as an extension, the value externally assessed exams bring.

The summative system-level assessment serves four main purposes:

1. Certifying student learning – measuring what students know and can do within the parameters of an exam series.

2. Gatekeeping access to future opportunities and triaging individuals.

3. Monitoring national education standards and showing policymakers where to intervene.

4. Monitoring school standards and ensuring the curriculum is covered.[3]

GCSE and A-Level exams provide a robust snapshot of student performance during a fixed period of time, alongside the performance of those also taking the same exams during the same period. As Sammy Wright puts it in *Exam Nation*, they provide evidence of competence but not proof.[4] So, although they do not demonstrate performance in the round, they do indicate a level of proficiency that gives an indication of how well educated a student is in a particular subject.

Furthermore, while it is somewhat instrumental to consider future earnings as a metric of success, if we agree that at least one premise of being 'well educated' is an increased likelihood of future progression to employment, it is worth considering what the data indicates. Government analysis of Longitudinal Educational Outcomes (LEO) data that matches income and employment records with attainment indicates that a one grade improvement in overall GCSE attainment is associated with an average increase in the present value of lifetime earnings of £8,500, implying an overall increase in discounted lifetime earnings of £96,000.[5]

This essentially confirms what we, as educators, assume and hope to be true: better academic performance broadly correlates with enhanced earnings over a lifetime. And this is certainly what I would tell my students when I taught English: get your GCSEs, particularly in English and maths, and it is a ticket to the next stage in education and a desirable job. So far, so good.

Yet, as Sammy Wright points out, because the nature of exams is to provide a 'developmental snapshot' of competence on a given day, they naturally favour those students who have the wider advantages and support network that set them up to succeed. Typically, those are children who: have parents and carers who provide a stable home learning environment and access to cultural opportunities; who are more likely to attend a school with other affluent peers; and who attend a school where the Ofsted grade is likely to be higher and teachers in more plentiful in supply.

Yet, as we know, the disadvantage gap is stubbornly pernicious, and it has increased in recent years, with the gap in GCSE English and maths widening in 2023 to its largest level since 2011.[6] While as educators, we tell students that the harder you work, the more likely you are to get that cluster of grades that take you onto the next stage, it would also be more honest to tell students who are disadvantaged that they will need to work harder to make the gains that their more advantaged peers are able to make more easily. So, while GCSE grades are a measure of proficiency, they are also a measure of advantage.

There are also some inherent tensions in the way in which exam performance is used. Because externally examined exams provide one of the most reliable measures we have in the system, they are used to ascertain system-level performance as well as to certify individual proficiency. When expressed as targets or used for accountability purposes, such as the expectation that 90% of students are entered for the EBacc, they distort how the system behaves. As we know, when a measure becomes a target, it ceases to become a good measure and instead drives system-distorting behaviour.

This is no surprise. Policymakers have few levers at their disposal to drive improvement, so adding in a new measure or expectation in the Ofsted framework is an intentional way to effect system-wide change. However, we now have a system that arguably prioritises particular measures to define success at the expense of practitioners being able to educate children well. Essentially, teachers gravitate towards teaching to the test at the expense of being able to educate students in the round, knowing one of the principal measures of their effectiveness balances on exam results. The time that teachers spend educating students well gets cut in order to achieve the kind of performance that will demonstrate they are a successful school.

The design of GCSEs and A-Levels creates further tension. They are intended to support progression to further academic study and denote students' understanding of a particular subject. However, employers tend to use performance at GCSE and A-Levels as a proxy for how well educated a student is in the round. As a student in the AQA Student Advisory Group put it, 'The whole point of GCSEs is to give you an idea of what you want to do at A Level – the whole system is streamlined to specialise to uni'[7]. For example, the GCSE history programme of study spans from 1066 to the present day. It is designed to indicate a level of academic proficiency and ability to progress to the next stage of academic study. A high grade in GCSE history indicates a level of academic attainment and ability to interrogate historical sources and bias, amongst other things, but it certainly does not indicate an ability to work as part of a team, problem solve or think critically, as some employers may assume. So while employers and parents assume a good clutch of grades at GCSE and A-Level indicates a readiness to enter the world, that may be absent unless a school or college has paid particular attention, as part of a wider curriculum, to equipping young people with the tools they need for the next step in their journey.

Teachers are similarly concerned that formal assessment is too narrowly focused on academic skills to the detriment of a wider range of skills. For example, according to a survey by the Edge Foundation, 92% of 1000 teachers indicated that they believed that the assessment system needs to recognise the full range of young people's strengths and skills, more than just written exams[8]. Teachers also worry about the impact of placing too much emphasis on exam results, with 91% believing that their students worry too much that exam results will determine their future, according to a Teacher Tapp survey for the NSPCC.[9] However, it is important to be cautious about the impact of exams on students' mental health and wellbeing. According to research by John Jerrim,[10] evidence indicates that mental health issues increase in line with age over proximity to exams, so there is not the sharp increase around GCSEs or A-Levels that we might expect if these issues were solely the fault of exams.

How could the assessment system be improved?

Given the issues above, it would be fair to ask why we have externally assessed exams at all, especially if they only serve to highlight disparities in the system and to skew teacher behaviour. Put simply, they are one of the fairest tools we have to understand student proficiency at a moment in time. And while a criticism of exams is that they simply indicate who has been more or less advantaged in their education, it would be deeply wrong to bend general qualifications to give dispensations to students who are less advantaged. To do so would introduce all sorts of unintended consequences into the system.

However, as I set out in this last section, there are ways in which policymakers could dial down the pressure that accountability measures bring and introduce a wider range of assessments in order to dial up the conditions that better support young people being educated well.

Before I explore those in full, though, a note on coursework and teacher-assessed grades. This is an area where great caution should be exercised. These methods tend to increase the likelihood of bias for those whom the odds are often already stacked against. For example, an Ofqual literature review[11] found that when teachers are asked to assess students' grades, there is evidence of bias against SEN students and more disadvantaged students. Indeed, during the pandemic, when centres had to assess grades in 2020, those with graduate parents were still 15 percentage points more likely to report having higher CAGs at A Level than their peers.[12]

Understandably, given the increase in teacher workload, coursework is also universally unpopular with teachers, particularly among science and maths teachers. Half of English teachers also oppose its reintroduction, according to a Teacher Tapp survey.[13] Similarly, teachers on AQA's curriculum and assessment advisory group, which includes teachers, school and college leaders, said that while they valued the premise of assessing students over time, they felt that coursework was 'problematic', particularly with the advent of artificial intelligence. As one said of coursework, 'I hated it as a teacher', with others agreeing they were happy when it went. They felt that it was hard to assess rigorously, and it really became a measure of which teachers had looked at the mark scheme and trained their pupils to match it.[14]

Nevertheless, that leaves plenty which is open to improvement: specification content, for example, the subject-level conditions the Government places on GCSEs and A Levels; and how those subjects are assessed. The Government is undertaking a significant review of the curriculum and assessment system, indicating that an evolutionary rather than revolutionary approach is the right way to tackle any reform. Ministers are right. If we are to help young people to be well educated in the round, we can reduce both the assessment burden and the amount of content in qualifications and thereby increase the time teachers can spend on things that fall outside what can or needs to be assessed. Updating the accountability measures on which schools are judged will also create more fertile conditions for children and young people to be well educated.

To start, there are certainly ways in which we could trim the average amount of time students spend in the exam hall, which is currently in the region of around 30 hours at the end of Year 11. Certain subjects lend themselves to increased practical, or non-examined assessment (NEA), such as GCSE Drama, Dance, and Design and Technology. NEA can be a drain on teacher time, but digital tools could help, providing opportunities for remote externally assessed NEA. Videos, easily taken on devices and uploaded securely, could be marked and moderated externally, decreasing the amount of time spent in an exam hall for subjects that lend themselves to practical assessment.

Similarly, there are subjects where the number of papers students have to sit could be reduced. For example, there is a high content burden for GCSE maths at foundation tier. This creates insufficient time to 'master' fundamental knowledge before building further, so students don't always grasp the basics before having to move on. Reducing the overall content at foundation would also allow for a reduction in the end-point assessment time – allowing two papers instead of three in our specification – without compromising validity. Something similar could be done at a higher level, trimming the content and cutting down from three to two papers – again, without compromising validity. We could also adopt more consistent mathematical methods across other subjects, including physics and geography, thereby streamlining the cognitive load for students working across disciplines.

In other subjects, the content is outdated, mechanistic, and, in the words of Professor Becky Francis, who is leading the current Curriculum and Assessment review, 'overprescribed and overstuffed'.[15] Examples of overstuffed subject-level conditions include GCSE History, where the specification covers 1,000 years. GCSE English Language is also due for an overhaul. It was highlighted by the Oracy Commission as not being 'fit for purpose'.[16] Students and teachers have told AQA that they have a sense of having to 'get through' the subject at GCSE, and this then puts students off studying it at A-Level. This is shown by the 39% decline in A-Level English Language entries between 2016 and 2021.

Those are just a few examples where content and the amount of assessment could be trimmed, and assessment methods updated to provide time for teachers to better educate students in the round. It could also be that parallel qualifications help. One such qualification is the Extended Project, which assesses the way students have tackled a task over the output they produce, and includes methods such as vivas and presentations. However, it should be noted that not all that students study is suited to being formally assessed and nor should it be. A streamlined set of more flexible qualifications could pave the way for not everything being distilled into a narrowly assessed metric.

The Government should also consider what changes to the accountability system could drive positive behaviours, with the first being the EBacc entry measure, which is the mix of perceived proto-academic subjects that the Conservative government actively steered young people towards. While the aim of supporting all students to have a strong academic grounding as a means of reducing educational inequality was laudable, the introduction of the measure has led to a significant reduction in the number of arts qualifications studied. For example, there has been a 42% decrease in the number of Arts GCSE entries since 2010, and 42% of schools no longer enter any pupils for Music GCSE.[17] These creative subjects often provide the potential for increased engagement for students who otherwise feel weighed down by a very heavy set of academic qualifications.

This was evident when I was teaching at a large comprehensive secondary school in Norwich: our Key Stage 4 timetable had core subject days, where English, maths and science were taught, and then options days, where the subjects students had chosen were taught. Attendance would peak on the options days and then decline for core days, particularly for disadvantaged and disaffected students, who simply voted with their feet. Re-emphasising the importance of creative subjects will increase the opportunities to build engagement and ultimately be well educated in the round.

The suggestions above address the assessment system as it stands today, but the potential for more radical change beckons this side of the horizon. Those more radical opportunities should be incrementally introduced, which may seem paradoxical but is actually imperative. At present, we are not adequately preparing students for the digital world in which they are entering. What if we were to widen the use of digital tools in the classroom and increase access to digital devices so that a gradual shift to digital exams was not such a leap? We already know that developments in AI mean that more students are using it as a study aid and, at times, for cheating. What if we assessed how well students were engaging with AI in some parts of the curriculum instead of completely forbidding it? And what if assessment were able to be more flexible, user-led and on demand? While this model poses logistical challenges given how schools are configured, we should prepare for all these possibilities and more.

This chapter has considered what we mean by well-educated, and how the assessment system does and does not create students who embody what it means to be just that. It has highlighted some of the drawbacks and tensions in the current system and suggested where we could better serve the students of today by preparing them for tomorrow. However, it has not suggested doing away with the prevailing model wholesale. The existing system has virtues of fairness and rigour that it would be ill-considered to do away with. However, given the ever-evolving world that students are stepping into, there are certainly ways we could better prepare students for their next steps.

Notes

1 'Purpose and quality of education in England inquiry launched', UK Parliament, 30 November 2015.
2 Menzies L, *Mapping the Way to Educational Equity*, Cambridge University Press and Assessment, November 2023, p 4.
3 Taken and adapted from Menzies L, Yates W and Huband-Thompson B, *Balancing act: Navigating the tensions in our school system. An evidence review on assessment, curriculum, wellbeing, and mental health,* IPPR, 2023.
4 Wright S, *Exam Nation: Why our obsession with grades fails to everyone – and a better way to think about school,* Vintage, 2024, p 65.
5 This is for students that took their GCSEs between 2001–2004. It is not necessarily directly applicable to one grade improvement today. Hodge, Little and Weldon, 'GCSE Attainment and Lifetime Earnings', Department for Education, June 2021.
6 *Annual Report 2024*, Education Policy Institute, 2024.
7 'AQA Submission to Curriculum and Assessment Review', December 2023.
8 Menzies L, Yates W and Huband-Thompson B, *Balancing act: Navigating the tensions in our school system. An evidence review on assessment, curriculum, wellbeing, and mental health,* IPPR, 2023.
9 'Large majority of secondary school teachers think students worry too much that exam results will determine their future', NSPCC News and Opinion, www.nspcc.org.uk. 12 August 2024.
10 Menzies L, Yates W and Huband-Thompson B, *Balancing act: Navigating the tensions in our school system. An evidence review on assessment, curriculum, wellbeing, and mental health,* IPPR, 2023.
11 'An evaluation of centre assessed grades from Summer 2020', Ofqual, 2 August 2021.

12 Anders, Macmillan, Sturgis and Wyeness, 'Pupils with graduate parents received an unfair advantage in their A Level results last year', LSE, 10 June 2021.
13 Menzies L, Yates W and Huband-Thompson B, *Balancing act: Navigating the tensions in our school system. An evidence review on assessment, curriculum, wellbeing, and mental health,* IPPR, 2023, p 15.
14 'AQA Submission to Curriculum and Assessment Review', December 2023.
15 Booth, Samantha, 'Becky Francis reveals "emerging themes" from review', *Schools Week*, 8 Nov 2024.
16 'We Need to Talk: the report of the Commission on the Future of Oracy Education in England', Oracy Commission, October 2024.
17 'Cultural Learning Alliance: Report Card 2024', Cultural Learning Alliance, 2024.

SECTION 4
Who benefits from education?

This section explores the role of education in the development of a fair and just society. Our judgements about the usefulness and efficacy of education are particular, so how well can we pursue or measure such an aim? Are the benefits of education understood and justly shared? When populist politicians talk about 'meritocracy', what does that mean?

Think

1. Should the state have a dominant view of educational success?
2. How do you know what your children and families want?
3. How powerful is conformity in your school? What does non-conformity tell you?
4. Where are young people's passions met in your school?
5. How do you feel about some parents being treated as deficits to be remedied?
6. From scratch, how would you design a fair system?
7. Is long-term thinking important in education?
8. Where do you find or see enemies of education?

Section 4
Essay 1

Creating joy: What educational success looks like

Richard Sheriff

Our challenges as education leaders have changed over the millennia as politics, science and economics have changed the world we live in. However, when defining educational success over 2,000 years ago in ancient Greece, as Aristotle was creating the language of learning, there would have been much in common with our views today. Although modern science had not yet arrived on the scene, he had a strong focus on reading and writing and saw real value in PE, music and drawing. Ofsted inspectors of that period would have also been asking lots of questions about citizenship and how our ancient Greek school leaders were ensuring the success and sustainability of the state. Perhaps not that much has changed. In the state education system, we always have to be mindful of our civic duty as well as our moral duty to the children we serve. The importance of 'educational success' was set out succinctly by Estelle Morris, the Secretary of State for Education, in the 2001 White Paper, 'Schools Achieving Success'.

> Success of our children at school is crucial to the economic health and social cohesion of the country as well as to their own life chances and personal fulfilment.[1]

Aristotle would have approved of the key elements in Morris's definition:

- Supporting economic prosperity for the state
- Supporting civic society
- Supporting personal fulfilment

Here, educational success from a modern governmental viewpoint is defined in a very similar way to in ancient Greece.

There is clearly more than one viewpoint to take when defining educational success. As a school leader, my response might be very different to that of the child, the state or the parent. I am sure there would be many words in common, but as school leaders, we have the challenging task of balancing the needs and wants of each of these parties in our quest to provide 'educational success'.

On starting as headteacher in a large comprehensive school, I asked the parents what they felt educational success looked like for their children. In a fairly affluent 'middle class' catchment in a school that, until 1973, selected only the brightest children, I was expecting a focus on examination standards. The overwhelming response was that parents wanted their children to feel safe and be happy. I am sure none of them wanted these outcomes at the expense of getting decent grades, but the emphasis was clear. One parent defined success as being: 'When my child comes home and is excited to go back the next day for more'. It is possible to be extremely well educated and be miserable at the same time; many recipients of a 'traditional' approach to education in high-performing state and public schools would attest to the brutality of the regime, but the excellence of the academic curriculum. To this day, parents with the means to do so decide, using their own definition of educational success, what environment, culture and curriculum their children will endure or enjoy. This may be through paying the fees for private education, cramming for the entrance exams or purchasing a house in the 'right' catchment area. Even for those parents with more limited resources, there is now often some choice in selecting which institution will provide 'educational success' as they see it for their child.

Most parents will want the common typic of educational success, for their child to be safe, happy and successful, whatever school door they walk through. Success will almost always be measured in terms of examination outcomes, and there can be little doubt that educational success is linked to longer-term health and happiness. It is equally true that we face a tidal wave of mental health issues within our communities, and often our curricula have become effectively planned, expertly implemented, but joyless. It might be worth remembering another piece of Aristotelian wisdom,

> Young persons will not, if they can help, endure anything which is not sweetened with pleasure.[2]

Educational success for parents in our post-pandemic, troubled world is much more entwined with emotional wellbeing and the ability of schools to meet the individual needs of their child.

We might, at this point, want to understand what children and young people think 'educational success' looks like. Having interviewed children whilst inspecting deeply troubled schools, I am only too aware that children have only a very limited view to share. Whatever the state of the school, children will often be incredibly loyal to their teachers; sadly, they have not had the opportunity to gain any perspective on their educational experience. Children's experience of being in school is one that we must listen to carefully, but we cannot rely on their view of what 'success' looks like for them or their school. As adults, we forget how little we knew as children about the wider world and the opportunities it offers. Part of educational success must be to equip our children with the knowledge and capability to make informed choices as they mature and change themselves. Too often, I find children who are capable of great things but who have set their aspirations too low, as they cannot even glimpse the possibilities that are out there.

So, what about school leaders? As the key agents in delivering whatever educational success looks like, their view is perhaps the most pertinent. Sadly, many of us leading schools have become rather limited in our answers to this question. Our inspectorate is too often seen as the only source for defining educational success. The 'high stakes' nature of our English system has resulted in a compliance culture that has certainly limited diversity. The Ofsted 'framework' defines educational success under four categories and provides clear criteria as to what warrants an 'outstanding' or 'requires improvement' judgement. It can be argued that the framework does away with the need for this generation of English school and college leaders to even consider the notion of what educational success looks like. The state has decided, and our job is to implement that view. Confident school leaders see the inspection framework as a starting point for defining educational success in their schools, not an end point. The school inspection framework could be compared to seatbelts in a vehicle; they keep the passengers safe, but they do not restrict or define the journey.

Diversity is not always a public good, and prior to inspection, school leaders, with the collusion of their governing bodies, could define or wander towards a notion of educational success that provided a meagre diet for the young people in their care. The laissez-faire approach to schooling in the 1960s and 70s in England, where regulation and oversight from LAs and school boards were weak, did not lead to widespread educational success for those in receipt of often ideologically driven methodologies and curricula. This was particularly true for underserved young people. Those with SEND, from lower income households and little 'social capital', fell further behind their peers who often attended the more 'traditional' Grammar and independent schools. The introduction of the 'seatbelts' of inspection to mandate the basic expectations of educational success was perhaps necessary and inevitable.

Government has also, in the past, encouraged diversity and choice rather than a singular view of what constitutes 'success'. The last Labour government introduced the concept of 'specialist schools' and asked every school to consider what they would like to specialise in, from a defined list. Specialisms in language learning, science, technology and performing arts allowed schools to develop differing offers to parents whilst still delivering the rest of the state-defined curriculum offer. Educational success was therefore redefined in each such school as they sought to demonstrate that their specialism formed a key component of that particular model. The mantra of the time was 'choice and diversity', school leaders and the system often had choices, but sadly, children still mostly just went to the school nearest to them or the one that had places or where their parents could afford to get them.

Despite these attempts to create a marketplace in the English school system by differentiating curriculum priorities, it might be argued that there has been little fundamental change in the consensus view of what educational success looks like, perhaps even over the last 2,500 years. One can also see how the aspirations for parents and the state align.

Educational Success	
The state	Parents
Economic prosperity	Successful
Civic responsibility	Safe
Personal fulfilment	Happy

The view taken by Aristotle that education had a fundamental part to play in creating and sustaining a civil society is still held today. It is also the reason that education remains a key aspect of government rather than being left to the marketplace. Politicians know the power of education to improve the economy, but also to keep public order and educate citizens on how we should live together.

The inspection framework and the notion of a 'national curriculum' are key tools to ensure the inclusion of content that the state sees as imperative to sustaining a civil society. The inclusion of 'Fundamental British Values' in the current framework is recognition of the fact that educational success is as much about strengthening civic sustainability as it is about academic mastery. Public education is a key tool that the state is able to utilise to define and influence public values. This is why each new Chief Inspector of Schools will be approached by ministers to include within the inspection framework new content that reflects the changing views of society and the electorate. Successful education from a state perspective needs to be inculcating into the recipients the values, attitudes and behaviours that our society deems as imperative to the wellbeing of the nation.

The impact of the pandemic on educational outcomes has been well publicised. What is only just being noticed is the impact of the absence of personal development education and socialisation within a structured school environment on the behaviours and wellbeing of children.

In school, children learn to communicate with their peers, explain their thoughts and ideas, appreciate the importance of compromise in relationships and their place within a community. We now find many children in our schools have a significant deficit in these skills and as a result often appear as highly 'dysregulated', unable to cope and disruptive to others. Their dysregulation is hardly surprising; they have not been educated on the 'regulations' that are woven into the experience of formal education. Educational success needs to be defined to include this fundamental learning that underpins a child's ability to thrive in society, and for our society to thrive.

As school leaders, we are accountable to parents, children and the state. Our job is to create the structures, systems and processes to deliver on each of their sometimes-conflicting expectations. The evidence from amazing schools across the country is that leaders are able to do this exceptionally well, most of the time. Great school leaders also know that educational success is more than just the outcome of a formula.

When you speak to young people and adults about their educational experience and how successful it was, the answers rarely involve pedagogical nuances and specialist curricula. Getting what you need from school and the examination system to get where you want to be is a vital factor, and one we must never forget. Social mobility is a dream without literacy, numeracy and the basic building blocks from the curriculum that support us to live our lives in a complex and ever-changing world. The ingredient that parents strive for without ever naming, that children enjoy but do not recognise, and that results depend upon, even though it is never on the syllabus, is joy.

This is what Aristotle recognised when he wrote of endurance only being possible with the 'sweetening of pleasure'. It is the joyful moments, activities and people who make educational success possible and transform the lives of the young people we serve. One can endure hard work learning a new language or mastering quadratic equations if the teacher smiles and welcomes you at the door. You feel able to try and fail at hard things if the response from your teachers is to encourage and congratulate you for attempting to fly higher. You want to come to school the next day if your day has been characterised by positive interactions with teachers and support staff who care about you and are willing for you to succeed. You keep coming in, even when you have a cold or a family crisis, because you know school offers joyful opportunities to socialise, play and learn with others.

Creating a joyful culture in a school is a great gift that a leader can give to young people and the colleagues who work so hard to create the success stories. As school leaders, we do have a recipe to follow that has been established over time and legislated for by the government of the day, but we have the power to combine these ingredients in a way that supports success for all.

The joy that great education brings to young people is hard to measure, but a vital component of the recipe that makes for educational success.

Notes

1 Forward to 'Schools Achieving Success'. White Paper, DFES Publications, 2001.
2 Aristotle. *Poetics*, VIII, vi.

Section 4
Essay 2

Who are schools failing?

Katherine Walsh

The view from the inside

As I look out of my window over our packed concourse, I see hundreds of children who are doing well. I see children who generally enjoy school and engage in powerful knowledge throughout their day and at home when they study independently. I see children who are developing their Tallis Habits. They are becoming increasingly inquisitive, collaborative, persistent, disciplined and imaginative. There are others exhibiting our character by showing their optimism, honesty, fairness, respect and kindness. These are many of our children. They conform and will do well in their GCSEs, then A-Levels. They will do incredibly well in some cases. We will celebrate their successes with the confidence that they have received a good education because their outcomes confirm this must have been the case.

As I look out of my window and see children flourishing, I also see others let down by the education system and not just those we are encouraged to focus upon, i.e. the disadvantaged, white, working-class boy. They are often grouped together, encouraging one another to wait before they go to class. Once in class, they may do everything they can to get out of the lesson or they may do everything they can to ensure they are not singled out and are left alone. They have just got to get through school. It is not for them. It is for people who are good at exams. People are good at writing, concentrating or doing what they are told. To be good in school means to conform. To do well in school means to be able to perform highly in tests and exams. If you see yourself as unable to do either, school can be a challenging place.

Conformity vs creativity?

Like many schools, we have an internal inclusion room with students who have misbehaved in a way which has affected the school community. We give them work to complete in silence. Some manage it. Many do not. We take the children who do not conform and expect them to observe rules in the most stringent of ways. They need to learn to do it not only because they must if they want to get decent GCSEs, but also not to affect the learning of other people. But this is often the only reason they get when asking why they need to learn anything in school. They need good exam results, and the reason they have to learn something is because 'it will be in your exam'. This is used as a strategy to get them to conform. Learn what we tell you. Do what we tell you. You will get better exam grades and a better life.

Children who do not conform face sanctions, yet some prosperous adults who do not conform often tell us how school does not matter and that conformity is a block to innovation. Social media is full of posts telling us about how you do not need A-Level knowledge after sixth form, while millionaires railing against the world order further entrench the idea that to be successful (at least monetarily) is to reject society's rules. Other voices purport to provide an alternative voice to 'wokerati' educationalists who do not listen to 'working people'. It is those who have not been served by the school system who are arguably the most likely to listen to those views, to sympathise with them and further perpetuate them, but the real economic differentials between those who have been successful in school and those who have not show that this is not the truth. The more time you spend in education, the healthier the life you lead and the more likely you are to have a successful career.[1] We need to combat the narrative being put forward to the next generation over social media with real facts. We need to show children why school is important to each and every one of them.

We know there is a necessity to accept adult authority within schools. There is no suggestion that anarchic behaviour should be encouraged in order to unleash a torrent of untapped creative thought, but there is a difference between encouraging engagement and independence through explanations of why this environment is important to a zero-tolerance approach. The shift to a knowledge-rich curriculum with teachers as experts is a valid aim, but has unfortunately sometimes led, via lethal mutation, to a diet of didactic lessons, often with an over-reliance on PowerPoint presentations and a lack of conversation in the classroom.[2] We need to get back to the notion of children experiencing what it feels like to be a scientist, historian or dancer as they move around the school with experts teaching them the knowledge needed to encapsulate those roles. No one would surely argue that they should simply be fed information telling them what they should know about science, history and dance while they listen and copy from the board, but those children who do this will get in less trouble than those who challenge it.

We talk about valuing creativity and innovation (whatever that means), but then we straight-jacket children to behave in a certain way in a classroom, and if they do not conform, they learn that unhelpful behaviour gets them out of it. It means they do not have to think hard. If we speak with these young people, they do not necessarily have the same aspirations as their teachers would like them to have: going on to university, wanting to learn more about the world or travelling but that does not mean they do not want to be successful or would not have ruled those out as options if they felt they were achievable. We make assumptions about what they should want out of life, without actually asking them or giving advice about how to make it happen.

This is not to endorse the Wilshawian 'poverty of expectation'[3] or to become one of Michael Gove's 'enemies of promise'.[4] Remembering the forgotten third is not about lowering our expectations, but it is about celebrating those who think and engage in all aspects of school. Helping children to feel proud of a range of recognised achievements to give them a sense of belonging and intrinsic motivation to make the world a better place. A desire to build on their learning so they can leave school in the best position for them. Not with shame because they have found reading hard, but pride in finding it hard, but keeping going. Not with hopelessness because they have not achieved the benchmark grade 4 in English GCSE or a top mark in a test, but a sense of accomplishment because they have been given the time to focus on hard thinking, which takes them outside of their everyday experience.

A well-rounded education is important: up to a point

As we know, education is not only about passing exams. It can test some of the knowledge which has been learnt, but it is not the crucial element. We know this, and every school year begins with a genuine desire to provide children with a strong education. But then, as exam season approaches, this valuable aim becomes overtaken by a necessity to ensure Year 11 get the best grades they can. In some cases, cover is redirected to KS3 lessons, trips are halted, and interventions are stepped up. GCSEs are dropped to ensure children get the best grades they can in the core subjects. Curriculums are stripped back so particular subjects are focused on from Year 9 or 8, or even Year 7. The unspoken fear among leaders to think about anything which is not related to accountability is mitigated by proclamations about the importance of improving life chances by moving children's grades. The assertion that we do not measure what we value but value what we can measure comes to fruition.[5] Are we really reducing educational success to the grades achieved by 16-year-olds in one set of exams? The children begin to think so, and this, again, feeds into their understanding of what it means to be good in school and to do well.

This also conversely results in those who choose not to conform facing this stranglehold. While leaders may fear trying new things in case they do not work and lead to a dip in results, some children who are conformist by nature may fear doing anything which could potentially jeopardise their chances of top grades. They might not choose to take advantage of opportunities at school because it will mean they are not in their lessons. They might not challenge or question in class because they have been taught that compliance will allow them to learn what they need for the exam. They might not question knowledge which has gone before because they have been told society values this particular viewpoint, as it has been chosen by the exam board as something which needs to be known about a particular subject. It appears this attitude may have been reinforced by the pandemic, with children increasingly used to feeling participation is unnecessary as a result of online learning.[6]

Focusing on the journey

But what if we could change this? By encouraging young people to engage in more, not less. Schools are encouraged to reject children interested in lots of different things and encourage them to focus on fewer to get better grades in those. Surely, encouraging children to be interested in many different things while they are developing is essential for building an engaged society. If we could start again, what could we make better? How could we develop a really strong education system which includes everyone? Could we shift the narrative from prizing outcomes to focusing on the journey in the classroom? The discussions, the experimentation, the thinking hard, and the learning become the achievement. Is this not what young adult life should be about: trying things out, grappling with difficult ideas rather than wholeheartedly accepting the authority of those who have gone before because, as is becoming increasingly apparent, those who have gone before having hardly set glowing examples for future generations?

This is not to say schools, in general, are not better than they have ever been. We have highly qualified teachers and an engaged educational community. Teachers, by their very nature, want to see things improve and pedagogical approaches rooted in cognitive research have provided vital information about how children learn. Teachers want this to happen and for the children to achieve everything of which they are able, and they are proud when they receive their GCSEs, knowing they have worked hard. But they are also proud when a child gives a thoughtful, imaginative answer. When a child in their class understands a concept, they have never really considered or become an expert in a new skill. They become disheartened when a child has engaged brilliantly but will never be as recognised as another who is able to express it better on paper in an exam.

Education should prepare us for adult life. It should challenge and give us knowledge about our own and other cultures. It should have practical applications, and while it does all these things, it will also have to change as society changes. Young people demand increasing personalisation, which reflects their passions, and this is recognised in educational research, but financial resources increasingly dictate a universal approach to classroom teaching. While at school, we should be opening opportunities for young people to decide what these passions could be and providing opportunities to experiment with experts in various subjects. We want to look out of the windows and see all children who are rightly proud of their achievements and who have all experienced success and been guided there by experts who are teaching them powerful knowledge. We also want them to have engaged in independent thought and challenging ideas so they can go out into the world and change it for the better. That way, everyone has something of which to be proud.

Notes

1 Mirza B et al, 'Effects of education on adult mortality: a global systematic review and meta-analysis', *The Lancet Public Health*, 9(3), 2024, e155 - e165.
2 O'Connor C et al. 'The silent and the vocal: Participation and learning in whole-class discussion', *Learning and Instruction*, 48, April 2017, pp 5–13.
3 Wilshaw M, *Unseen Children*. Church House, Westminster, 2013.
4 Gove M, *Teachers in Charge*. National College for Teaching and Leadership, 2013.
5 Biesta G, *Good education in an age of measurement: Ethics, politics, democracy.* Routledge, 2010.
6 Zhou J and Zhang Q, 'A Survey Study on U.S. College Students' Learning Experience in COVID-19', *Education Sciences*, 2021.

Section 4
Essay 3

Education for families who don't see the point

Daniel Talbot

Two stories about education

Why do some students and their families appear to opt out of the educational opportunities they are offered? Grappling with this question requires more than treating the symptoms of educational disenfranchisement. Interventions, extra maths and homework detentions become a laundry list of ways to deepen disaffection rather than confront it. What, then, can we make of why some students and their parents seem to move effortlessly through the school system while others simply do not?

Reflecting on the story we tell ourselves about what schools do and who they serve is a useful starting point. One story can be traced back to Matthew Arnold's invocation of an education representing 'the best that has been thought and said'.[1] A classical education, rooted in the great canons of the arts, sciences and humanities, serves to liberate students from the limitations of their own experience and community. The goal of education is the transmission of culture and knowledge, which will ensure the preservation of society over time. Patterns of underachievement amongst certain cohorts of students reflect a failure of those communities to equip young people with the necessary attitudes, dispositions and cultural capital to make the most of the educational opportunities they are afforded. Such a vision imagines education as the great liberator, a medicinal tonic to lift the pall of everyday experience.

In Story Two, far from being agents of social mobility, schools are the primary engines of social reproduction. The background inequalities that mark wider society find themselves replicated the moment children pass through the school gate. The curriculum, pedagogy and culture of schools serve as a sorting mechanism to entrench the class privilege of the already powerful. Support for such a view can be found in the long history of sociological research pointing to the denigration of working-class students and parents.[2] Academic ability is valorised to the detriment of practical knowledge and skills, working-class language is policed and sneered at as an aberration needing almost surgical correction by middle-class teachers. Parents and their communities are held responsible for cycles of underachievement, obfuscating the socio-economic and political root causes. What Story One sees as the best that has been thought and said is, in fact, little more than a 'cultural arbitrary'.[3]

A third story

The issue is not that the truth lies somewhere between these stories. Rather, it is more like the rabbit-duck illusion in which the same information can generate radically different perceptions. Understood this way, both stories contain truth, but social class will play a role in which story resonates. The task of school leaders is to build a school environment conscious of both. On the one hand, we must recognise that structured bodies of disciplinary knowledge have a language and logic that is often counterintuitive. In this sense, it is right that the curriculum is rooted in the powerful knowledge that inevitably, at times, rubs against the interests and knowledge students bring to school. At the same time, students should not be coerced into casting off their language, cultural experience and communities as if they were deviant distractions from educational success.

The pendulum swing of educational purpose in recent decades has leaned towards Story One. As it begins, inevitably, to swing back, we must be mindful of what a focus on a 'knowledge-rich' curriculum got right as well as where it went wrong. At the same time, the cavernous gap between disadvantaged students and their peers has been brought into sharp focus post-pandemic and is rightly gaining traction as one of, if not the most, urgent issues facing schools. What we need, then, is a renewed vision of how schools can promote social justice without abandoning their academic purpose. What would underlie such a vision, and how would it engage parents and students who have lost hope?

Psychological barriers: belonging, threat and bias

When trying to reach students and parents struggling to make the most of educational opportunities, school leaders would do well to keep in mind the following: Under-resourced students are offered less and make less use of what they are offered than their peers. Understanding some of the factors that lead to this provides a framework for building a more inclusive school culture. The barriers faced by under-resourced students are not just structural. Disparities in the provision of well-resourced schools and highly qualified teachers inevitably impact outcomes. Yet, there are also psychological barriers that disproportionately affect students and parents from already marginalised social positions. Understanding these processes and how they can be addressed is one way school leaders can bridge the gap between the two stories above.

Social identity threat and identity incompatibility are two such social-psychological processes that an increasing body of research has identified as salient in the educational achievement of students of lower socio-economic status.[4] The former describes the feeling that one's identity is denigrated, devalued or stereotyped based on membership of a particular group. The latter relates to the internalised belief that membership of a particular group is incompatible with success. The UK's historic and ongoing class stratification means that those from lower socio-economic groups predominantly suffer the adverse effects of these mechanisms. We are saturated with negative and pernicious depictions of working-class communities, which, along with concrete structural injustice, create the preconditions for internalised feelings of hopelessness when it comes to schooling. Being a member of such a marginalised group is to occupy a stigmatised identity, one that is perceived as incompatible with educational achievement and fulfilment.

What this means, in practice, is that under-resourced students and parents are less likely to take up opportunities nominally available to them in the belief that they are not for 'people like me'. At the same time, it can lead to students interpreting everyday setbacks and difficulties as confirmation that they have no future of educational success. For those experiencing identity incompatibility and social identity threat, a sharp word from a teacher or a bad day on a test is amplified by a context in which they are primed to believe they simply do not belong. Students and parents with a visible history of academic success can reframe such events as a part of the normal cut and thrust of schooling; this process of normalisation is not, however, distributed evenly across society and is in shorter supply for working-class students.

Compounding these problems is the issue of bias. Research has shown that low-income students are more likely to be placed in lower sets (even controlling for academic ability), are called on less in class discussion, and are more likely to have their work undergraded.[5] Under-resourced students then face a double bind in which negative internal psychological experiences are confirmed by the institutional biases of educators. All of this creates an environment of high threat and low belonging. However, whilst the above will strike educators as alarming, schools can intervene to disrupt some of these processes in subtle yet powerful ways.

Creating a culture of belonging for all

Addressing the above is far from straightforward. Not least because of the huge variation in the educational experiences and outcomes of students within any particular category. Social class, ethnicity and region all interact in highly complex ways, meaning there is no silver bullet that would substitute for a deep understanding of the communities schools serve. At the same time, this diversity reinforces the idea that students need to be treated as individuals rather than tokens of their demographic type. What is common to all contexts, however, is that schools need to actively intervene in the processes that lead to students and their families opting out.

A first part of this is trying to find out what the experiences of students and parents are actually like. This entails listening to them and their families rather than pathologising their perceived lack of engagement. Often, what will be uncovered is that parents receive a barrage of negativity and hectoring commands regarding their children. Given what we know about the psychological processes mentioned above, it is not surprising that this ends in a vicious cycle. What must be asked is: how can we build relationships with parents that short-circuit this unproductive one-way relay? How can we invite parents to contribute to issues affecting the school community in a spirit of collaboration rather than condescension?

Related to this, careful thinking is needed around how much responsibility for students' education is being outsourced to the home. Whilst students need to develop the dispositions required for independent study, this cannot be achieved by diktat alone. Under-resourced parents often struggle to navigate the demands of home learning amongst the plethora of other challenges they face. Much of this is likely to stem from their own negative experiences of schooling. A compassionate school needs to find ways of supporting and working with parents to meet these struggles rather than relying on punitive behavioural sanctions. This involves thinking hard about how homework and revision are explained to parents and students so that the level of threat is reduced.

Once schools feel confident, they understand their cohort, and it is then a collective effort to build a culture that actively fosters a sense of belonging for all students. One area of consideration is how visible the achievement of working-class students is. This is a conversation that reaches across all aspects of a school, from the diversity of its teaching body, through the attitudes teachers hold about certain groups and even the presentation of its marketing material. The role of alumni and older students cannot be overstated here. There is good evidence that hearing from students from similar backgrounds who have navigated education successfully can have a positive impact on students' outcomes by reducing feelings of incompatibility and lack of belonging. An approach to transition between phases of education should be rooted in an understanding of how daunting these can be for students who do not see themselves as potentially successful.

At the heart of such approaches needs to be a commitment to equity. Middle-class families hoover up opportunities as part and parcel of an educational arms race with credentialism as its aim. It is important to consider whether voluntaristic models of distributing opportunities, such as clubs, trips, interventions, etc, are viable under such conditions. Committing to equity would mean ring-fencing space for students from marginalised communities to build trust that a school is working for all students. Some families need more active encouragement to guarantee participation in what schools are trying to achieve, precisely because of the alienation they already feel.

Curricular Barriers: Building a relationship to knowledge

Michael Young draws a useful distinction between powerful knowledge (the hard-won outcomes of robust disciplinary, truth-seeking enquiry) and knowledge of the powerful (the knowledge powerful groups use to shore up positions of dominance in society).[6] Part of the job of curriculum makers is to ensure that what is taught in schools is rooted in the former and purged of the latter. Much of what passes for educational knowledge pays too little attention to prising these two apart. Yet to do so is of paramount importance in allowing students and parents, who may perceive education as a middle-class pursuit, to build a lifelong relationship with knowledge.

This endeavour is not helped by the current vogue for developing 'cultural capital', enshrined in the Ofsted inspection framework. It is no small irony that a term originally intended as a sociological critique of the elitism of educational knowledge has now become a central part of the assessment framework for schools. No wonder, then, that some families may feel sceptical that the school curriculum is designed for them and their children. Instead, we ought to interrogate whether the selection of knowledge in the curriculum harbours unhelpful cultural biases. Such discussion might consider whether varieties of spoken language, accent and dialect are recognised or diminished; whether the choice of exemplars in a field skews towards a narrow model of success; or whether the contribution of working-class artists and scientists is recognised. People adapt their ambitions to what they perceive as possible for them. The curriculum and pedagogy of a school set the tone for what different groups of students can imagine for their own future.

Dialogue or deficit?

Bridging the gap between Story One and Story Two is the central challenge in engaging all students and their families. Story One is right insofar as education has the power to transform students' lives. Story Two recognises that schools can often amplify rather than ameliorate the background inequalities of wider society. Understanding how a history of educational failure for certain communities manifests itself psychologically can provide a starting point for rethinking whether a school culture is built for those most vulnerable to rejecting it. At the same time, engaging in a nuanced way with the nature of educational knowledge can help ensure students are not alienated from the curriculum. Ultimately, a central part of a just education is allowing all students access to the conversations about the world they will inherit. But a conversation is only productive when participants are valued as contributors to a dialogue rather than seen as a deficit to be remedied. School leaders can create this environment and, as a matter of justice, they must.

Notes

1 Arnold M and Wilson JD, *Culture and anarchy*, 1932, p xii.
2 Ingram N, 'Working-class boys, educational success and the misrecognition of working-class culture', *British Journal of Sociology of Education*, 30(4), 2009, pp 421–434). Reay D, *Miseducation Inequality, Education and the Working Classes*, Policy Press, 2017.
3 Bourdieu P and Passeron JC, *Reproduction in education, society and culture*, 1990, p 8.
4 Easterbrook MJ and Hadden IR, 'Tackling Educational Inequalities with Social Psychology: Identities, Contexts, and Interventions', *Social Issues and Policy Review*, 15(1), 2021, pp 180–236.
5 Doyle L, Easterbrook MJ and Harris IR, 'Roles of socioeconomic status, ethnicity and teacher beliefs in academic grading', *British Journal of Educational Psychology*, 93(1), 2023, pp 91–112.
6 Muller J and Young M, 'Knowledge, power and powerful knowledge re-visited', *Curriculum Journal*, 30(2), 2019, pp 196–214.

Section 4
Essay 4

What is fairness in education?

Loic Menzies

Part 1: Introduction

It was one of those English 'summer' days when the sun refuses to come out. But over a thousand Teach First teachers had nonetheless gathered on the playing fields of Totteridge Academy in North London to celebrate the charity's twentieth anniversary. One marquee was playing the role of mini-Westminster for the day, hosting a series of discussions on education policy, and I was a panellist. The chair, Ndidi Okezie, was in despair. Ndidi is a relentlessly upbeat firecracker who believes that anything is possible if the will is there, but my fellow panellists and I were refusing to play ball.

The question being debated was, 'Will we ever have a fair education system?' and there was little optimism to be found. Everyone in the tent had seen the stats: a gaping attainment gap that had for a time shown tantalising-though-marginal signs of narrowing, despite vast investment – both in financial terms and in terms of teachers' blood, sweat and tears – before swooping back with a vengeance. And every day, the teachers assembled in that marquee – now muddy-footed and sheltering from an unseasonal downpour – watched their pupils swimming against a growing tide of poverty and deprivation.

At first, I had little solace to offer. My argument – which I want to expand on in this chapter – was that educational fairness is not just impossible; it does not even make sense as normally conceived. In fact, our thinking about this topic tends to be based on one of three conceptions of fairness, all three of which are 'chimaeras' – as Sammy Wright, a school head from Sunderland, puts it in his recent book, *Exam Nation*.[1] However, just as I did in that wet marquee, in the third part of this chapter, I want to turn to some of the greatest thinkers of the twentieth century for inspiration and argue that, if we change the way we think about educational fairness, then not only might we find the more optimistic answer Ndidi longed for, but we might also sharpen our educational discourse – and in the process find some practical lessons for both policy makers and those working in schools.

Part 2: The Chimaera

Equal outcomes

A decade ago, I researched and co-authored the Fair Education Alliance's 2014 'Report Card'.[2] I ploughed through reams of data, picking out the greatest inequalities in educational attainment and progress and painting those disparities in page after page of vivid maps. The report's premise was that fairness would have been achieved once gaps had closed and the maps turned green. It is an approach underpinned by the assumption that fairness means 'equal outcomes'. That is a useful-enough rule of thumb for monitoring the system. 'Closing the gap' is also convenient shorthand for what many of us in the education system are trying to do. However, the approach suffers from two main problems. Firstly, it does not really get to the heart of what anyone's trying to achieve, and secondly – much to Ndidi's horror, I have to admit – it is never going to happen.

Let us take the simplest and most obvious point here first: if all we cared about was equalising outcomes, it would be enough to just 'level-down' the achievements of the most advantaged until the gaps disappeared. Thus, to say 'the gap is closing' is not enough to tell us whether something good has happened. Indeed, even if disadvantaged pupils' attainment was falling, so long as it fell more slowly than that of advantaged pupils, gaps would still be closing. Increasing numbers of pupils might struggle to complete simple maths calculations or be unable to read basic health information, let alone access 'the best that has been thought and said' – yet we would still be pleased because the maps had turned green. That is why the phrase 'closing the gap' is, at best, shorthand. Most of us know we actually mean something different, hence why The Organisation for Economic Cooperation and Development (OECD) tends to refer to 'equity, excellence and inclusiveness' as a trifecta of policy goals.[3] All of this hints at an underlying understanding of 'fairness' that goes far beyond 'equalising outcomes'.

What really horrified the idealist contingent among those gathered on the playing fields of Totteridge was my claim that 'fairness as equal outcomes' is never going to happen – and that this might be a good thing. Variation is a feature of nature. Most measures reveal a distribution, so if you cut a population into different groups, the average for each will probably be different. I have conducted studies for the Social

Mobility Commission before, where we have carved up every subgroup of pupils and each intersection between them. We have then compared their averages and analysed the relationship between ethnicity, gender, socio-economic status and attainment at different stages of education.[4] It is a useful way of uncovering patterns (or 'demi-regularities'),[5] and of prompting questions as to what might be going on, but the chances of all the bars on the graph lining up to reveal a tidy, unblemished picture of equality are next to zero. Moreover, Ben Newmark and Tom Rees have sensitively and compellingly argued that there are plenty of disabled children – their own included – who will not, and cannot achieve *the same* outcomes as others.[6] To expect them to do so – and to wrap their value as humans up in those outcomes – is to deny whole swathes of the population the dignity to which they are entitled. Part of the beauty of humanity is its variation, and the path to fairness will never run through the blades of a homogeniser.

Just deserts

Famously, the term 'meritocracy' was first coined in 1958 by sociologist Michael Young,[7] who intended it as a description of a dystopian future, only for it to be recast as a longed-for utopia in popular discourse. The idea goes like this: if what you get flows from your talents or efforts, then you *deserve* what you get. Ideas of 'merit' often fuse those two ideas of 'talents' and 'efforts', but let us start with 'effort' before returning to 'talents' and 'potential', later.

The link between effort and fair deserts can be traced back to John Locke's theory of private property. In his *Two Treatises on Government*,[8] the seventeenth-century philosopher proposed that people had a natural right to that which they mixed their efforts with. So, if you found some unused land, worked on it and thereby turned it into valuable farmland, then you had a natural right to that land – in fact, you 'deserved' it. Similarly, as millions of parents have no doubt told their proud offspring, if you work hard to achieve an A*, 'you deserve' that result. From there springs a frequently-aired argument for assessment reform: how is it 'fair' that Amari, a child who works their socks off whilst living in an overcrowded flat and looking after their severely disabled parent, but who diligently completes their homework late into the night after working an evening job, 'deserves' to get a lower grade than the child who sails through life with the strongest of tail-winds? This, we are told, is unfair.

Once again, we are conflating what we actually care about with the shorthand for it: if Amari gets an A* because they 'deserve it', but they do not get the value that is linked to it – whether in terms of career opportunities, understanding of the world, or equal standing in society – then they still have not gotten their 'just deserts'. To insist that assessment reform is needed so that Amari gets what they deserve (in terms of grades) is a hollow cosmetic exercise unless those grades translate into a change in life circumstances. This is a case that the philosopher Elizabeth Anderson sets out particularly clearly in her appropriately named essay 'What's the Point of Equality?'[9] Anderson argues that everyone getting the resources they 'deserve' does not help unless these resources translate into dignity and equal standing in society. If we treat grades as a 'resource' and argue that educational (if not societal) fairness has been achieved once grades accurately reflect people's efforts, then even assuming effort *is* the basis of just deserts, we have still only achieved fairness on paper – in this case, a sheet of exam results. Perhaps Amari's hard work should translate into real rewards, rather than just grades on paper, but that is down to the fairness or unfairness of society and the labour market, rather than down to the education system. Recognising these points us towards the path of genuine fairness in education, which we return to in the third part of this chapter.

So maybe, just deserts are not only about outcomes but rather, about inputs. Perhaps what we are talking about is not Amari's A*, but the real (if intangible) 'quality of education' they 'deserve' to receive. As I will go on to argue, a focus on inputs is a more feasible way of thinking about system-level fairness than outcomes, but the idea of 'just deserts' based on effort still does not stack up – even when it comes to inputs. Take 'Billy', a second pupil, who also always completes his homework, but who spends far more time on it, always going the extra mile. Billy is a model student, always putting his hand up in class and staying behind to ask extra questions. Does he 'deserve' extra attention from the teacher? Should he also benefit from additional reward trips and enrichment activities? At this point, I feel tempted to say, 'Yes, that does sound fair, Billy is putting the effort and going above-and-beyond, surely he deserves it'. But the flip-side of that is the question: 'Who doesn't deserve extra support?' Perhaps Sasha? A pupil who does not put her hand up, who does not complete her homework and who does not listen when the teacher tells her to stop throwing paper balls at poor Billy, the class swot?

This is where big divergences in people's values and political standpoints come to the fore. Those on the right of politics will tend to be more comfortable with Billy jumping ahead of Sasha – and maybe even Amari. Meanwhile, those on the left will more likely start asking questions about what might be happening to Sasha.[10] Perhaps Sasha is actually living in similarly tricky circumstances to Amari and just happens to have given up a bit sooner. And what if things are actually considerably worse for Sasha than for Amari? Despite the challenges, Amari's family home is still a haven of love and mutual support, whereas Sasha faces an abusive and violent step-parent in a household that is constantly moving from one insecure tenancy to another. It is a stark contrast to Billy's experience with his parents, who follow up on what he has been doing every day at school, and who have always drummed into him that education and working hard should be his top priorities. How sure are we that Billy really deserves that end-of-term 'reward trip' and extra time with his teacher more than Sasha or Amari? On one hand, we risk simply rewarding Billy for being lucky, whilst on the other, it hardly seems fair for him to be deprived of attention and reward, just because he got lucky at home. His behaviour is still exemplary, and he has still done the hard work, and from the point of view of school culture, it is important for pupils to see desirable behaviours being rewarded.

The brightest spot on my colourful maps of achievement was always London. It turns out, the main reason why is that it is disproportionately home to ethnic minorities, amongst whom parents have distinctly pro-school attitudes and behaviours.[11] If maps of education so closely mirror parental attitudes that flow from cultural background, it is hard to picture how 'just deserts' can ever be the foundation of a fair education system.

The idea of 'just deserts' also requires us to make difficult moral judgments about who deserves what, and it is questionable whether the state – and public servants like teachers – should be making these decisions. As Anderson explains to those who argue that the state should not pick up the bill for bad choices:

> To determine whether a smoker who picked up the habit while a soldier shall get state-funded medical treatment for lung cancer, other people must judge whether he should have shown stronger resolve against smoking, given the social pressures he faced from peers and advertisers while serving in the army, the anxiety-reducing benefits of smoking in the highly stressful situation of combat, the opportunities he was offered to overcome his habit after the war…such a system requires the state to make grossly intrusive, moralizing judgments of individual's choices.[12]

Moreover, an approach to 'fairness' based on moralising ideas of 'just deserts' is even more problematic when children are involved, given children's limited agency.

We have not gotten very far with the idea of 'just deserts', so how about a different focus?

Potential maximisation

Why does the idea of grammar schools keep coming back again and again, like yet another remake or sequel in a zombie-movie franchise?[13] My theory is that it is partly down to a third idea about educational fairness: that of potential maximisation.

Former Conservative education secretary Edward Boyle recalls that during the 1970s, research demonstrated that pupils' abilities were more malleable than was previously realised. This convinced him and other policymakers that 'the pool of potential ability was deeper than we'd thought, and that the interplay between nature and nurture was more subtle than used to be accepted'.[14] That conclusion played a role in converting him to the case for comprehensive education and for expanding access to Higher Education, because deciding what education pupils should get, and whether they should leave school with CSEs or O-Levels based on their 'potential', no longer made sense. Returning to Michael Young's dystopic meritocracy, how can your talents determine what you 'merit' if those talents are fluid? The same can be said of 'potential': if what a child can achieve is malleable, how can you use an assessment of 'potential' to determine what education it is fair to give them?

The consequences of allowing apparent 'talents' and 'potential' to be deterministic (in terms of the education a pupil receives) are also worrying. Tailoring education to an apparent 'talent' can mean education fails to nurture underdeveloped skills, and that it no longer opens doors to the unfamiliar.[15] Both my parents hated maths, and unsurprisingly, I, therefore, showed no interest or aptitude for maths at school. Unfortunately, most adults around me just accepted that maths was not where my talents lay, so I was never pushed to address that gap. All sorts of doors closed to me as a result in later life, which, in retrospect, was not 'fair'. The fact that some perceived 'talents' open more doors than others exacerbates this problem. Indeed, as the Social Mobility Commission has argued, well-intentioned curriculum choice intended to provide flexibility and to adapt to a diversity of talents can result in disadvantaged pupils taking fewer academic subjects, and, therefore, being locked out of opportunities, entrenching inequalities.[16]

There is also a practical problem with 'fairness as potential maximisation' since it relies on the idea that 'potential' is somehow knowable. Not only is that unrealistic (as Boyle discovered back in the 1970s), but attempting to guess at it gives free rein to stereotypes and biases – the very opposite of fairness.

You cannot make education 'fair' by tailoring it to 'potential' because talents and aptitudes are malleable, shaped by upbringing and unknowable. Moreover, attempting to shape education this way can exacerbate inequality, entrench biases and increase the chances of some pupils ending up with far fewer doors open to them than others.

I have now set out three commonly held ideas about educational fairness and argued that all three are deeply flawed. This makes 'a fair education' – as normally conceived – not only infeasible, but in some cases, undesirable. It is no wonder Ndidi was beginning to despair as she pondered how to sum up the panellists' arguments that day at Totteridge. It was time for me to offer some hope, just as I intend to in the third part of this chapter.

Part 3: What might fairness *really* mean?

I believe that a fair education system would be one that distributes support to pupils in accordance with principles that individuals would agree to if they wanted to make sure education played its part in equipping them to write their own life story, so long as they chose those principles without knowing what circumstances they would be born into, or how easy they would find learning.

This approach has a number of advantages linked to the definition's three components. First, it engages with something people fundamentally care about as a goal – acquiring the capability to shape their own lives. Secondly, it emphasises a criterion that has been common to definitions of fairness throughout the ages: that of being unbiased, so that when making tough moral choices about who gets what, we are not skewed by our own circumstances and experiences. Thirdly, it recognises that education can only play 'a part' in the overall goal of giving people the capability to shape their lives. This definition does not (for now) state what the chosen principles would be, and it does not give classroom teachers or policymakers any easy answers regarding what they should do in a specific situation. However, it does provide a yardstick for debating and assessing what is and is not fair. Most importantly, it provides a standard which we can – and should – work towards; a standard which is both more meaningful and achievable than the three chimaeras rejected in the first section of this chapter.

Anyone familiar with twentieth-century philosophy or political theory will spot a lot that they recognise in my proposed definition of educational fairness. It draws significantly on ideas about 'distributive justice' and 'capabilities' elaborated by a series of philosophers, the most famous of whom are the Indian Economist and philosopher Amartya Sen, born in 1933, and the American political philosopher John Rawls, born in 1921. I have used their ideas as a jumping-off point, but rather than trying to summarise these thinkers' voluminous work (something I am not in the least qualified to do), I now want to use nuggets from their work as hooks on which to hang my argument for the three elements of my proposed definition.

The capability to write your own life story

When we say to our children and young people, 'You can be whoever you want to be', or, 'You can do whatever you want to do', we are not simply making a statement about their legal rights. We're talking about their actual ability 'to do' and 'to be' those things. Amartya Sen's concept of capabilities captures this by focusing on the freedom that comes from having the 'required means' of achieving that 'being or doing',[17] rather than just being allowed 'to do' or 'to be' something. A fair education should play its part in equipping everyone with the capability to do and be what they want. I will return to some of the limits or qualifications on that shortly.

Numerous frameworks have been proposed for capabilities, generally linking them to different 'functionings', which can range from the obvious, like 'having a good job' and 'being healthy', to the less obvious, like 'participating in democracy'. All of these require different conditions to make them possible. For example, the academic Caroline Sarojini Hart used the capabilities approach to structure a detailed, interview-based study of pupils' attitudes to higher education in Bradford.[18] She argues that focusing on simplistic metrics of equality in tangible outcomes – like participation in Higher Education – can hide very different sets of 'capabilities' in terms of pupils' real ability to pursue 'a good life' in the future.[19] In other words, being equipped with a university degree might be helpful in opening up some options, but it is not enough on its own. It is, therefore, unsurprising that there are significant differences in what people go on to be able to do, even if they have all gone to university.[20] A first advantage of focusing on capabilities is therefore that it encourages us to look beyond a narrow set of educational outcomes.

Using capabilities in our definition of fairness also means we can remain neutral about the value of different paths, except insofar as they open or close doors to future choices. In a fair education system, we should care about all children going on to enjoy lives 'of choice and opportunity', as Reach Academy Feltham puts it.[21] So, if a pupil develops the capability to become a Nobel-prize winner but prefers to live the rest of their life in the family home whittling teaspoons, then that is up to them. That said, choice in the future may require reduced choice at an earlier stage: returning to the question of flexibility and adapting to aptitudes, I would, therefore, argue that 'tracking' pupils onto different educational pathways is unfair, even if children choose their route 'freely' – since it closes down future choices. Childhood is a distinctive phase of life,[22] and although choice can be introduced gradually, if we are relying on education to endow us with capabilities, children cannot consent to having those capabilities curtailed too early. This is particularly important given the extent to which pupils' (and parents') 'choices' are socially determined. This raises questions about existing features of our education system, like the option of studying a single science, or dropping maths at 16, both of which close down future options (particularly for pupils from disadvantaged backgrounds) in potentially 'capability-limiting' ways. Of course, there may be a rationale for allowing such choices, particularly in specific individual cases, but the reasons need to be compelling. The bottom line is that what matters is whether options are being opened or closed down, rather than the inherent value of different paths, which we can all disagree about.

The third implication of a capabilities-based approach to educational fairness is that different people will need different support to develop a capability. In healthcare, we do not say that everyone should get the same package of hospital visits, CAT scans, checkups and physiotherapy.[23] We accept that people will need different packages of support to achieve healthiness. Similarly, a fair education system should give pupils different levels of – and types of – support, to make sure they are able to develop their capabilities. There is an overlap here with the common distinction between equality and equity, in which equality involves giving everyone the same support, whereas equity means giving people different levels of support to bring them up to the same level. However, a capabilities approach is slightly tighter in that the goal is to ensure everyone can achieve essential functionings, rather than achieving the same exact outcomes. So we might say that the capability to pursue a fulfilling life requires every child to develop a passion for an art or sport that provides meaning and joy in their life. A fair education system might, therefore, need to provide an enhanced programme of school-based enrichment activities for pupils whose families cannot afford such opportunities. But that is different to saying that every child should receive whatever support they need in order to achieve the same Grade 6 on the piano. In other words, a capabilities-based approach to educational fairness should accept that not everyone will end up with the same outcomes – or even the same option-set. If we accept a capabilities-based definition of fairness, the debate can, therefore, move on to what the essential functionings are and what counts as sufficient capabilities. According to Elizabeth Anderson, what matters is that citizens should have a right to 'a capability set sufficient to enable them to function as equals in society'.[24] Hence, the need to be able to access food does not mean we are all entitled to gourmet extravaganzas, but we are not capable of functioning as equals in society if we are reduced to eating pet food or rejected food from bins – even if this is enough to sustain us.[25]

The tricky thing is that in education, giving support to one person (to enhance their capabilities) often means not giving that support to someone else. That is true at a policy level, because if resources are channelled towards enhanced enrichment programmes for disadvantaged pupils, that can mean other schools no longer being resourced to provide extra maths tuition for their gifted and talented pupils. The same is true at a classroom level, where extra time explaining the equation for photosynthesis to Amari might mean less time helping Sasha work through the reasons why she is struggling to concentrate during period one on Monday. This leads to a tricky dilemma for our definition of fairness: the challenge of 'how much support to give to whom'. To address that challenge, let us turn to a device developed by another of the greatest philosophers of the late twentieth century, John Rawls.

The veil of ignorance

Amartya Sen was deeply influenced by John Rawls, recalling that, 'I had the privilege of having this wonderful person as a friend and a colleague – his kindness was astonishing, and his insightful comments, criticisms and suggestions have constantly enlightened me and radically influenced my own thinking'. Despite eventually concluding that many of Rawls' conclusions 'were seriously defective', Sen credited the American philosopher with providing a 'shaft of light' in moral and political philosophy.[26] A key point in common between the two of them was a belief that when evaluating questions of justice, the essence of fairness was to avoid bias, so that no one loads the dice in their own favour. In other words, a wealthy person should not be able to push for low taxes in their own interest, whilst someone who knows they will be destitute should not be able to demand that everyone's wealth be redistributed to them, just because it would suit them.

Rawls is responsible for introducing a famous thought-experiment known as the 'veil of ignorance', which embodies this principle. Behind the 'veil of ignorance', no one knows what circumstances they will be born into, what position they will come to occupy in society, nor what their personal idea of 'a good life' will come to be. Rawls claimed that any principles agreed in this 'original position' would be 'the result of a *fair* agreement or bargain' because no one has designed the principles 'to favour his [sic] particular condition'.[27]

Rawls' concept has clear applicability to fairness in education: if we know that we (or our children) are going to grow up in deprivation, with limited access to enriching activities, we might want a system that siphons resources towards schools serving disadvantaged communities to fund enrichment programmes. If we know that we (or our children) will find learning easy and have ready access to innumerable opportunities, we might prefer to see gold-plated gifted and talented programmes to develop 'excellence', or perhaps even the grammar schools that Boyle came to question back in the 1970s. Meanwhile, if we know that our notion of 'a good life' is wrapped up in professional success on the global stage, rather than loyalty to, and rootedness in community and family, then we will shape our view of how the education system should function on that basis. In each case, we are skewing the system on the basis of our own situation, and this is 'unfair'. In contrast, specifying that the system should follow principles that would be acceptable to and agreed by people in the original position provides an unbiased criterion for a 'fair education system'. If we remain true to the capabilities-based approach described earlier, this means our definition of 'fairness' is not about what outcomes (or 'functionings') people actually achieve, nor what people go on to choose to do with their lives, but about the principles on which the system runs. In other words, it is a 'procedural' notion of fairness based on the principles underpinning how benefits (like educational resources) are allocated. I would argue that this approach to fairness sharpens our thinking considerably compared to the three chimaeras rejected in the first part of the chapter. And, what I told the Teach-Firsters in the Totteridge tent was that there is no reason why our education system should not fall into line with 'fair' principles defined in this way.

What I have not done is specify what principles would be agreed behind the veil of ignorance, nor what this means for how educational resources are distributed. Rawls tries to do this by proposing two principles of justice, which I would roughly paraphrase as:

- Every person should be entitled to the greatest real freedoms possible, so long as these are compatible with everyone else having the same freedoms;

- Any social and economic inequalities should be arranged so that they are most beneficial to the least advantaged and in such a way that they are linked to positions which anyone can access.[28]

However, like Sen, I am not sure these specific principles have stood up to scrutiny over the years. Indeed, Sen's view is that the pursuit of justice depends much more on public reasoning and deliberation. A fair education system might therefore involve constantly weighing up how different options play out, how they affect different groups' capabilities, and whether this would be acceptable to us in 'the original position'. Meanwhile, Elizabeth Anderson argues that the demands made on behalf of some should not place an unreasonable burden on others, in terms of limiting their own capabilities.[29] One might, therefore, argue against taking the best teachers away from top sets to provide extra support to struggling pupils, since doing so might unacceptably limit the more advantaged pupils' future capabilities.

Others might claim that behind the veil of ignorance, the principle we would buy into is that education should be designed to stop any of our future selves from falling below a certain threshold. This is known as a 'a sufficientarian standard of justice'.[30] In other words, what matters is that education should ensure we cross (what we agree to be) a threshold of acceptable capabilities, so that we have 'enough' options from which to compose our life story. If pupils in top sets are already assured of meeting this 'sufficiency', the priority should be to bring others up to the bar. On the other hand, if the bottom sets are already over this threshold too, a sufficientarian might have no qualms about inequality beyond this point – potentially making extreme inequality acceptable.

Anderson counters that gross inequality undermines equal democratic standing in society.[31] What is 'sufficient' might therefore be relative, because too large a gap (as we call it in education) makes it impossible for people to stand shoulder-to-shoulder and participate with mutual respect in society. Indeed, for Anderson (like Sen before her), context specificity is important: what a person needs might differ depending on social conditions. As an example, she points out that what clothes someone requires depends on what they need within a particular geography and culture, in order to appear in public with adequate protection from the elements and without shame. Anderson also gives an educational argument, noting that in a country like the US, literacy in a single language (English) might be sufficient for equal democratic participation, whereas in others, more than one language might be required. Similarly, as societies become more educated, the level of education needed to function as an equal in society can shift. Once again, this does not in itself shift the proportion of people who *should* go to university (for example), but it does shift the proportion that should *be able to go* to university (if they so wish).

My own thinking on these questions is not developed enough at this stage to say what principles I think would (or could) be agreed to in the original position, but I believe that combining Sen's concept of capabilities and Rawls' veil does give us a standard to use in our deliberations.

Education's part in the puzzle

The final feature of my definition of a fair education system is that it explicitly recognises that education only plays 'a part' in the overall goal of giving people the capability to shape their lives.

In her Bradford study, Sarojini Hart identifies a series of 'conversion factors' like 'family/home', 'work', and 'leisure/social'. These depend on a young person's environmental context and have a significant effect on what pupils choose to, and are able to do. Education might, therefore, help someone from a disadvantaged group to secure the capability to write their own life story, but it will not necessarily fully 'compensate' for everything. As noted earlier, 'compensate' for everything, even if a capabilities-based approach does require us to respond to circumstances and give different support to different people if necessary, and the system should still respond to circumstances, though. Thus, even if it is systemic racism that curtails a young person from a Gypsy, Roma or Traveller (GRT) background's capabilities, a fair education system should still be structured to help that young person overcome adversity and should still challenge other pupils to be less prejudiced in future. But even if the education system were to do this adequately (which it does not at present), so long as society retains its prejudices, GRT young people's capabilities will still be constrained. Nonetheless, this is not wholly the fault of the education system and it is not enough, on its own, to make it 'unfair'.

Elizabeth Anderson draws an analogy to health to illustrate a similar point. She notes that 'the state can provide health care, but not health directly'.[32] I would argue that the state can go further than just providing health care, because other areas of policy (like welfare) shape poverty and, in turn, health. The point still stands though, that health depends on things beyond the control of those designing the health system – including a considerable degree of chance. The fairness *of the health system* should therefore be judged on its own merits.

Thus, although life might be 'unfair' because of the effects of chance, and the combined effects of innumerable circumstantial factors, the fairness of a particular *system* should be judged on the basis of what is within the system-designer's control. This view demands that we go far beyond the status quo and requires policymakers to look beyond the confines of single systems. However, it also provides the basis for a more realistic and readily achievable vision of *'educational fairness'* specifically.

Part 4: Conclusion

In this chapter, I have built on my previous work[33] to propose a new definition of educational fairness that combines three features: the capability to write one's life story; unbiased evaluation of the principles underpinning the system; and recognition that education can only go so far. This approach stands apart from perspectives that equate educational fairness to equal outcomes, just deserts, and 'potential' maximisation, and has six core implications, which I have set out over the course of this chapter:

1. Unless education equips young people with a range of attributes, beyond just the academic, their capabilities will be constrained.

2. A fair education system should be neutral about different educational paths, except insofar as choices open up or close down future choices.[34] The corollary of this is that early choices might sometimes need to be constrained to maximise future freedoms or capabilities.

3. Different pupils will need different levels of support, and it is fair to differentiate the inputs or resources we provide to them.

4. When evaluating the fairness of the education system, we should (at least attempt to) cloak ourselves in the veil of ignorance and free ourselves from the biases of our situation and preferences – particularly with regard to how easy or hard we find learning.

5. Fair allocations of support will vary between societies and evolve at different points in history (for example, with regard to whether all pupils should be supported *to be able to* go to university).

6. Education should attempt to mitigate for other sources of unfairness, but the education system's failure to compensate fully is not a mark of unfairness.

For the time being, I have stopped short of specifying either a set of 'essential functionings'; or an alternative to Rawls' 'principles'; or a specific distribution of educational support. Maybe one day I will get to that point in my thinking, but I am certainly a long way from doing so at this stage. However, I would like to hope that the arguments I have set out provide some increased clarity regarding what is and is not a relevant consideration. I am also by no means an expert in the work of the philosophers that I have touched on over the course of this chapter. Instead, I have simply used my (somewhat superficial) understanding of their work as a series of hooks on which to hang my thinking.

Sammy Wright argues that our chimaeric view of educational fairness is a serious problem, suggesting that

> the need for education to be fair is the great struggle of the modern system. [But] as teachers we know that we're losing that struggle.[35]

I share Sammy's concerns, hence my stark warning to the audience at Totteridge that educational fairness, as commonly understood, is both unfeasible and even undesirable. However, I still think that educational fairness *is* a valid and attainable goal – so long as we reshape the way we understand it.

Notes

1 Wright S, *Exam Nation: Why Our Obsession with Grades Fails Everyone – and a Better Way to Think About School*, The Bodley Head, 2024, p 240.
2 Gill K and Menzies L, *Will we ever have a fair education for all? The Fair Education Alliance report card 2014*. Fair Education Alliance, 2014.
3 Schleicher A, *Equity, Excellence and Inclusiveness in Education: Policy Lessons from Around the World*, International Summit on the Teaching Profession, OECD Publishing, 2014.

4. Shaw B, Menzies L, Bernardes E, Baars S, Nye P and Allen R, *Ethnicity, gender and social mobility*, Social Mobility Commission, 2016.
5. Pawson, R. (2024). *How to think like a realist: A methodology for social science*. Edward Elgar Publishing..
6. Newmark B and Rees T, *A good life: towards greater dignity for people with learning disability*, CST/Ambition Institute, 2022.
7. Young M, *The Rise of the Meritocracy, 1870–2033: An Essay on Education and Equality*, Thames and Hudson, 1958.
8. Locke J, *Two treatises of government*, Cambridge University Press, 1967.
9. Anderson E, 'What is the Point of Equality?', *Ethics*, 109(2),1999, pp 287–337.
10. Haidt J, *The righteous mind: Why good people are divided by politics and religion*, Vintage, 2012.
11. Menzies L, *The London Schools Effect revisited: A saga in many parts*, CfEY, 2021.
12. Anderson E, 'What is the Point of Equality?', *Ethics*, 109(2),1999, p 310.
13. Millar F, 'This zombie grammar school policy will only harm crisis-hit schools', *The Guardian*, 13 May 2018.
14. Kogan M, *The politics of education: Edward Boyle and Anthony Crosland in conversation with Maurice Kogan*, Penguin Books,1976, p 91.
15. Menzies L, Yates W and Huband-Thompson B, *Balancing act: Navigating the tensions in our school system. An evidence review on assessment, curriculum, wellbeing, and mental health*, IPPR, 2023, p 36.
16. *Cracking the code: how schools can improve social mobility*, The Social Mobility Commission, 2014.
17. Robeyns I and Byskov M, 'The Capability Approach' in Zalta E and Nodelman U (eds), *The Stanford Encyclopedia of Philosophy*, Summer 2023 edition.
18. Hart C, 'Education, inequality and social justice: A critical analysis applying the Sen-Bourdieu Analytical Framework', *Policy Futures in Education*, 17(5), 2019, pp 582–598.
19. Hart C, *Aspirations, education and social justice: applying Sen and Bourdieu*, Taylor & Francis, 2015.
20. Shaw B, Menzies L, Bernardes E, Baars S, Nye P and Allen R, *Ethnicity, gender and social mobility*, Social Mobility Commission, 2016.
21. 'Providing students with the skills, attributes, and academic qualifications to enjoy lives of choice and opportunity', Reach Academy Feltham website, 2024.
22. Arendt H, 'The Crisis in Education' (1954) in Arendt H, *Between Past and Future. Six Exercises in Political Thought*, Penguin, 1961.
23. Anderson E, 'Justifying the capabilities approach to justice' in Brighouse H and Robeyns I (eds), *Measuring Justice: Primary Goods and Capabilities*, Cambridge University Press, 2010, pp 93–94.
24. Anderson E, 'Justifying the capabilities approach to justice' in Brighouse H and Robeyns I (eds), *Measuring Justice: Primary Goods and Capabilities*, Cambridge University Press, 2010, p 83.
25. Anderson E, 'What is the Point of Equality?', *Ethics*,109(2),1999, p 320.
26. Sen A, *The idea of justice*, Penguin Books, 2009, pp 52–53.
27. Rawls J, *A Theory of Justice,* Harvard University Press, 1971, p 11. Emphasis added.
28. Rawls J, *A Theory of Justice,* Harvard University Press, 1971, p 266.
29. Anderson E, 'Justifying the capabilities approach to justice' in Brighouse H and Robeyns I (eds), *Measuring Justice: Primary Goods and Capabilities*, Cambridge University Press, 2010, p 97. Anderson E, 'What is the Point of Equality?', *Ethics*, 109(2),1999, pp 287–337.

30 Anderson E, 'Justifying the capabilities approach to justice' in Brighouse H and Robeyns I (eds), *Measuring Justice: Primary Goods and Capabilities*, Cambridge University Press, 2010, p 82.
31 Anderson E, 'What is the Point of Equality?', *Ethics*, 109(2), 1999, pp 287–337.
32 Anderson E, 'Justifying the capabilities approach to justice' in Brighouse H and Robeyns I (eds), *Measuring Justice: Primary Goods and Capabilities*, Cambridge University Press, 2010, pp 82 and 87.
33 Menzies L, *Mapping the Way to Educational Equity*, Cambridge University Press and Assessment, November 2023.
34 There may well be reasons for cultivating certain values, virtues or morals in the education system, but this would be for reasons other than fairness. Remember that fairness is only *one* of the things we might want from our education system.
35 Wright S, *Exam Nation: Why Our Obsession with Grades Fails Everyone – and a Better Way to Think About School*, The Bodley Head, 2024, p 74.

Section 4
Essay 5

The broader societal benefits of education

Neil Renton

Education has long been recognised as an institution that not only shapes individual development but also serves broader societal functions. This chapter will focus on the societal benefits of education through two distinct lenses: classical sociological theory and a contemporary view that takes a long-term approach. The first section explores how the founding fathers of sociology viewed education as a mechanism for social cohesion and economic functionality. These theorists offered a descriptive view of the role of education in the functioning of society. The second section offers an alternative approach that projects much further into the future. A contemporary ethical framework, proposed by philosopher William MacAskill[1], offers a unique insight into who may benefit from education now and in the future. By emphasising the long-term impact of current educational practices, I argue that educators and policymakers would be wise to adopt a far-sighted approach that not only addresses present needs but also maximises benefits for future generations. In doing this, education becomes a transformative tool for addressing existential risks and ensuring the long-term well-being of humanity.

Classical sociological perspectives on education

I have taught A-Level Sociology for a number of years and, as a headteacher, caught between roles when I walk through the classroom door, I think that the sociology of education has something to offer to our practical work in schools. It is interesting that the conceptual language of sociology has become common parlance for educationalists. The patterns of inequality across class, ethnicity and gender are now widely understood. Terms such as 'unintended consequences' and elements of labelling theory, such as 'the self-fulfilling prophecy', are all common concepts used in schools but were first framed by sociologists. However, the work of the founding fathers of sociology, such as Émile Durkheim and Karl Marx, laid a much grander framework for understanding the role of education. Each offers a distinct view of the functions and consequences of education, reflecting broader concerns about social order, power and economic structures. Their analyses allow you to consider the immediate effect of education and its broader role in society.

Émile Durkheim: Education and collective conscience

Émile Durkheim argued that education revolves around the transmission of norms and values in the regulation and integration of individuals into society. Durkheim's central view is that for any society to function effectively, there must be a 'collective conscience', a shared set of beliefs, values, and norms. Education, therefore, acts as a crucial mechanism through which collective sentiments are transmitted to the next generation. Assemblies, school symbols, traditions and rules play a key role in the socialisation process. Later sociologists talk about school being a 'focal socialisation agency' and schools being a 'bridge' between the family and adult society. The universalistic values of achievement are learnt, and education selects children into appropriate roles because it is based on meritocratic principles.[2]

For Durkheim, the education system was essential to the maintenance of social order. By teaching students discipline, respect for authority, and a sense of collective responsibility, education helped to ensure that individuals internalised the norms and values of society. Essentially, an approach that says education is vital for the smooth functioning of society. And who benefits from education? Both individuals and society.

However, Durkheim's theory has been criticised for simply being too positive about social cohesion and overlooking the ways in which education can perpetuate inequality and reinforce existing power dynamics.

Karl Marx: Education, ideology and preparation for work

Karl Marx viewed education as a tool for ideological control, serving the interests of the ruling class by sustaining capitalist relations of production. For Marx, education was not a neutral institution but rather a mechanism through which dominant ideologies were transmitted to the working class, ensuring that they accepted their subordinate position within the capitalist system. Schools, according to this approach, function to socialise students into the norms of the capitalist workforce, teaching them to be obedient, punctual, and disciplined – qualities essential for maintaining capitalism.

Bowles and Gintis focused on the link between school and work through the 'correspondence principle'.[3] The idea of a mirroring between education and work. They identified a number of examples of this through school and workplace hierarchies, motivation through external rewards (grades/pay) and the fragmentation of the day through a timetable, like tasks at work. For them, it was not the formal curriculum that prepared us for work but the 'hidden curriculum'. This hidden curriculum refers to the behaviours and attitudes learnt in schools, such as punctuality and accepting authority. Interestingly, the hidden curriculum also transmits the ideology of meritocracy. Bowles and Ginits argue that meritocracy represents an 'ideological myth' that encourages subservience and legitimises inequality – your own failure in education is caused by your own lack of talent and lack of effort, not, for example, inequality and poverty. Indeed, a 'long shadow' is cast where family background and social class have a lasting effect on your life trajectory, regardless of effort.

This analysis of education highlights its role in reproducing class inequality. The structure of education serves the interests of capital by producing a compliant and skilled labour force. From a Marxist perspective, education reinforces the status quo by obscuring the realities of class exploitation. It is interesting to see educationalists using the term 'cultural capital' in everyday language. The neo-Marxist concept of Pierre Bourdieu explains how non-financial assets, such as life knowledge, skills, education and cultural experiences, give advantages in social mobility and power.[4] Education benefits the privileged who have the cultural capital.

While Marx's analysis focuses on the immediate economic functions of education in preparation for work, it also critiques how education can shape consciousness in ways that perpetuate existing power relations. The dire statistics about the forgotten third[5] and the gap between disadvantaged and non-disadvantaged students indicate the need for a critical account of education. Whilst both approaches, one positive and one critical, provide valuable insights into the immediate social functions of education, they offer accounts that describe the impact of education on current society. They explain who benefits from education in the present. But what of the far-distant future?

Long-termism and education

Fifty years ago, a French-Canadian handyman, mechanic and plumber moved to Southern California. A craftsman, making climbing gear for his friends, starts a business that later enshrines his core beliefs long into the future. In 2018, Yvon Chouinard changed his now 3-billion-dollar company's business policy to state that, 'We're in business to save our planet'. Instead of going public to generate personal wealth, he decided 'to go purpose'. The Patagonia Purpose Trust was set up to protect the company's values. Each year, the money they make, after reinvesting in the business, is distributed through Holdfast Collective to fight the environmental crisis and defend nature. The approach of Patagonia is one of intentionality toward the future.

As educators, we influence the future – every day, our teachers have an influence that reaches into the far distance. Yet, our thinking in schools remains entirely short-term. We think of the school year in weeks and even days – 39 weeks of teaching or 195 days. We prepare students for end-of-year exams. Our school improvement plans exist in the short-term realm of a few years. If we set out a long-term vision, the maximum would be five or maybe even ten years. The issues schools face, through attendance, funding, workload, and recruitment crises, lock us entirely into short-term thinking. We focus on the present. Consider what impact we could have if we thought much more deeply about the long-term future and the lives of children not yet born? What decisions could we make now, as school leaders, that could benefit children in a hundred years or more?

MacAskill, in *What We Owe the Future: A Million Year View*, puts forward the idea that a clear moral priority of our time is to influence the long-term future.[6] Future lives count for no less than the present generation, and their future could be good or bad. MacAskill offers a compelling framework for understanding education's broader impact on future generations. And there are two practical implications of this through the curriculum and funding.

Long-termism and the curriculum

One of the key arguments of long-termism is that education can potentially mitigate existential risks such as climate change, technological stagnation, pandemics and the uncontrolled development of artificial intelligence. By integrating long-term thinking into educational systems, we can prepare future generations to address these global challenges in ways that minimise harm and maximise well-being.

For example, education can play a crucial role in fostering scientific literacy and critical thinking skills, essential for understanding and addressing complex issues like climate change and technological risks. Furthermore, education can promote ethical reflection on the societal implications of new technologies, encouraging students to think carefully about how innovations in fields such as artificial intelligence or biotechnology might affect future generations. By cultivating a sense of moral responsibility for the future, education can help to ensure that students are equipped to make decisions that prioritise the long-term well-being of humanity.

In addition to addressing existential risks, long-termist education can also foster innovation in areas that promote benefits in the far distant future. For instance, by encouraging creativity and problem-solving skills, education can contribute to the development of sustainable technologies and social systems that enhance the well-being of future generations. Placing greater emphasis on teaching ethical reasoning, teaching systems thinking, teaching about inclusion and giving students the capacity to navigate uncertainty also means they will teach their children the same. The future becomes brighter when what gets locked in benefits generation after generation.

Long-termism and funding

We have a persistent challenge about how we fund schools. Many issues come down to poor funding. There rarely seems to be enough money in the system to fund what needs to be done to tackle current issues in schools. But maybe we just have not been thinking about how we can fund schools for very long. Indeed, it was not until the 1880s that education became compulsory in England for children aged 5–10. We have only had 140 years to work out, as a state, how we fund education. And it seems we cannot fund the present properly, let alone think about the future.

One possible solution would be for every head teacher across the land to place the funding for one school child in a fund, every year, for the next 100 years, say. Remember, the ethical case for this – the volume of lives that do not yet exist outweighs those that currently do, and we are only using the funding of one student a year in the present. If I did this in my school of 2,100 students, that would be £5,043,084.62 by 2125. Imagine the collective impact of doing this. What would education look like in the future if there were no such thing as a funding crisis in schools or no such thing as a teacher recruitment crisis? Schools would have what they need.

Casting shadows far into the future

This essay has explored the broader societal benefits of education through the lenses of classical sociological theory and contemporary long-termist philosophy. Classical sociologists, such as Émile Durkheim and Karl Marx, emphasised education's role in maintaining social cohesion and reproducing the labour force. While these foundational perspectives provide valuable insights into education's immediate and structural impacts, they tend to overlook education's potential to shape the long-term future of society.

As educators, we would be wise to think about who education benefits in the future. A recent report by Tim Oates, *The COVID-19 pandemic may be a thing of the past – its impact in schools is not*, for example, challenges readers to think differently about the long-term impact of the pandemic. Oates argues:

> ..that the impact is differential in its form and effects as it slides through education – it is different within year cohorts and it is different between year cohorts.[7]

Indeed, there is a complex, sliding residual of the pandemic and 'it will require protracted, grinding effort'. But can we take this even further and cast a far-reaching shadow? Integrating long-termist principles into educational planning offers the potential to magnify the societal benefits of education far beyond the present moment. By rethinking educational practices through this lens, we ensure that education plays a central role in securing a prosperous and sustainable future for all – a very long-lasting benefit.

Notes

1 MacAskill W, *What We Owe the Future: A Million-Year View*, Oneworld Publications, 2023.
2 Parsons T, 'The school class as a social system' in Halsey A, Floud J, and Anderson C, *Education, Economy and Society*, The Free Press,1961.
3 Bowles S and Gintis H, *Schooling in Capitalist America*, Routledge and Kegan Paul, 1976.
4 Pierre Bourdieu outlines the concept of cultural capital in Bourdieu P, 'The Forms of Capital' in Halsey A, Lauder, Brown P and Wells A (eds), *Education: Culture, Economy and Society*' Oxford University Press, 1997, pp 241–258.
5 *The Forgotten Third*, The Association of School and College Leaders, 2019.
6 MacAskill W, *What We Owe the Future: A Million-Year View*, Oneworld Publications, 2023.
7 Oats T, *The COVID-19 pandemic may be a thing of the past – its impact in schools is not*, The Association of School and College Leaders, 2024.

Section 4
Essay 6

Is it possible to be overeducated?

Hugh Rayment-Pickard

Education is taken by many, perhaps most, people to be a 'natural good' that requires no further justification. To become 'educated' is a virtue, and like all virtues, it is hard to imagine there would be a limit to it, or that stopping learning would ever be a good thing. The idea that we should always be learning has become a modern truism, as John Dewey put it: 'The curious mind is constantly alert and exploring, seeking material for thought, as a vigorous and healthy body is on the *qui vive* for nutriment'.[1]

Dewey's idea of education as food for the mind or soul is rooted deep in Western consciousness. For Plato and his various philosophical successors, we are each on a personal educational journey, extending each day our understanding of ourselves and the world. Socrates, that inveterate questioner immortalised by Plato, famously declared that an 'unexamined life is not worth living' because the act of enquiry goes to the heart of what it means to be human.[2] Amongst all other creatures, it is only we humans who can embark on a quest for greater knowledge, so education is arguably the fulfilment of a uniquely human potential. If education is the gradual realisation of our true humanity, or as Dewey put it, if 'education is life itself', the idea of overeducation seems absurd because you surely cannot have too much of a good thing.

And yet, in recent years, the idea of 'overeducation' has gained increasing currency both among educational economists who ask whether schools and universities are producing people whose level of education is surplus to the requirements of the labour market and (in a not entirely discontiguous discourse) with those on the right of the culture wars who deeply resent what they see as the wealth and power of overeducated graduate elites who (allegedly) are out of touch with the concerns of ordinary people.

I will return to these arguments in a moment. First, I want briefly to note that the idea of 'overeducation' (although not that specific term) is already familiar within popular culture. Overeducated swots, brainiacs, clever clogs, eggheads and boffins have long been lampooned as people who are 'too clever for their own good'. We mock bespectacled, absent-minded, out-of-touch professorial types whose intellectual pursuits have paradoxically made them daft about the everyday business of living life. The stereotypical male academic is portrayed as physically frail and effeminate. The female academic stereotype – the 'bluestocking' – is naïve and socially awkward, yet to be awakened by a deeper knowledge of human affairs.

The underlying suggestion is that too much education may be bad for you and that formal learning is gained at the expense of common sense, character development and emotional intelligence. The further one climbs the ladder of learning, the deeper your head disappears into the clouds.

In the stock characterisation, high educational achievement is coupled with foolishness, allowing us to feel superior to those who have acquired greater knowledge. Professor John I.Q. Nerdelbaum Frink, the crazed Nobel genius in *The Simpsons*, provides 'solutions' for the townsfolk of Springfield, such as burger earmuffs. Professor Frink was modelled on an earlier movie egghead, Julius Kelp, played by Jerry Lewis in *The Nutty Professor* (1963). Kelp is an idiot-genius whose super-intelligence has made him chronically accident-prone and socially incompetent. He is portrayed as a lunatic who uses his intellect to invent a potion that turns him into Buddy Love, a charismatic womaniser.

The mad professor trope also appears in literary fiction. George Eliot's Edward Casaubon in *Middlemarch* has devoted his life to his *magnum opus*: *The Key to All Mythologies*, a pedantic and pointless academic project. Casaubon is depicted as vain, physically weak and sexually impotent:

> Mr. Casaubon had never had a strong bodily frame, and his soul was sensitive without being enthusiastic: it was too languid to thrill out of self-consciousness into passionate delight; it went on fluttering in the swampy ground where it was hatched, thinking of its wings and never flying.[3]

Eliot was also playing into a British suspicion of intellectuals. A certain anti-intellectualism is wired into the British mindset, which has traditionally prioritised common sense over book learning, fact over theory, and example over precept. Leonard Woolf once commented that 'no people has ever despised and distrusted the intellect and intellectuals more than the British'.[4]

Caricatures of the dotty professor seem harmless enough, but according to Richard Hofstadter in *Anti-Intellectualism in American Life*, they form the foundation of a more pernicious attack on intellectuals in public life. Hofstadter's landmark book argues that in an increasingly technological society, where expert knowledge is evermore in demand, ordinary citizens can feel disempowered and resentful: 'What used to be a jocular and usually benign ridicule of intellect and formal training has turned into a malign resentment of the intellectual in his capacity as expert. Once the intellectual was gently ridiculed because he was not needed; now he is fiercely resented because he is needed too much'.[5]

Hofstadter described anti-intellectualism as 'resentment of the life of the mind, and those who are considered to represent it; and a disposition to constantly minimise the value of that life'. Intellectuals are regarded as 'pretentious, conceited... and snobbish; and very likely immoral, dangerous, and subversive ... The plain sense of the common man is an altogether adequate substitute for, if not actually much superior to, formal knowledge and expertise'.[6]

Hofstadter's words from the 1960s now seem not only descriptive of his times but prophetic of ours. In 2016, Michael Gove mobilised the anti-intellectualism of the British public by declaring during the Brexit debates that people were fed up with hearing from 'experts'. It was a well-calculated political slogan, speaking directly to an audience of non-graduates who were resentful of a steadily growing and powerful university-educated class. Commentators from the Remain lobby reacted with scorn to Gove's comment, but they missed the point. Those who agreed with Gove recognised the need for technical expertise to address technical problems, but did not want expert opinion to be used as a trump card in political debate. They wanted, reasonably enough, for the views of ordinary, non-graduate citizens to be valued. For them, the reality of earning a living and paying one's way, particularly in challenging times, gives an economic perspective that is as valid, in its own way, as that of a professor of economics.

With the growth in university participation, graduates are no longer a closeted minority, as they were half a century earlier, but a colossal and powerful class within society. More than a third (33.8%) of adults in England and Wales and nearly half of the adult population of London (46.7%) are graduates. The UK university sector produces 28,000 PhDs every year. (2021 Census). Overall participation in higher education increased from 3.4% in 1950, to 8.4% in 1970, 19.3% in 1990 and 33% in 2000.[7]

The referendum result can be read as a successful attempt to wrest power from this new graduate elite. According to the Joseph Rowntree Foundation, 'educational inequality' was 'the strongest driver' of the Leave vote.[8] For all their learning, 'experts' were seen as remote from the lives of 'ordinary people', who, in any case, could exercise their own judgement about the merits of EU membership. And, in the eyes of the less-educated, it was perhaps precisely because of their education that 'expert' graduates had lost touch, immersed in a cerebral and cultural milieu that knew little, and perhaps cared less, about the fate of those who lacked their advantages.

Matthew Goodwin has described this graduate population as 'the epistemic class':

> For much of the last half century, the new elite, whose families often descend from the professional and managerial classes, benefitted far more than others from the shift toward a university-based meritocracy —a system which has increasingly whittled down the definition of 'success' to mean having a degree from the right university.
>
> Shaped by their privileged family backgrounds, their educational qualifications, and their much greater 'cultural capital' —gained from their more immersive experiences in the Oxbridge and Russell Group college system— the new elite hoovered up most of the gains from Britain's embrace of hyper-globalisation and a political economy which was rebuilt around them, which both demanded and rewarded their skills.
>
> They've benefitted culturally, too. After flooding into the creative, cultural, knowledge and public sector institutions, becoming a new 'epistemic class' which creates, filters and determines what is or what is not acceptable or desirable within the national conversation, the new elite watched the prevailing culture be completely reshaped around their far more socially liberal values, tastes, political priorities, and interests.[9]

We do not have to agree with Goodwin's thesis to recognise the tone of resentment that vibrates through his prose. For him, more education is not a 'natural good' at all, but is a cultural asset that can be, and has been, commandeered by the middle classes for their own advantage.

In the media, there are various voices echoing the view that graduates have perhaps been 'overeducated'. Employers often bemoan graduates who have higher-order knowledge but lack basic skills. There are tabloid myths about surplus-to-requirements graduates who will never get a decent job and are stacking shelves in Tesco or serving flat whites in coffee shops. In the pub or online, there are plenty of populist rants about the 'pointlessness' of school lessons that never teach us anything about 'life', and 'Mickey Mouse degrees' which allegedly lack academic credibility and have no relevance in the labour market.

Widespread though these attitudes may be, they are not anchored in reality: graduates are much more likely to be in employment than non-graduates. The government's graduate labour market statistics for 2023 show that 87.7% of working-age (16–64 years old) graduates were in employment in 2023, compared to 69.7% of non-graduates. If you learn more, you are also likely to earn more: graduate annual salaries are on average £6,500 higher than those of non-graduates.[10]

Irrespective of the facts, rhetoric about overeducation is being deployed cynically – playing to the cultural stereotypes of the out-of-touch academic, drawing on resentments created by very real economic and social inequalities and dragging education into the culture wars. Nigel Farage, for example, has denounced 'the poisoning of the minds of our young people' with 'woke' ideology and 'the march of the left through all our educational institutions'.[11]

***

The idea that education is a natural good has come under attack from another and unexpected quarter. There is also an academic critique of overeducation from within universities themselves, which regards too much university education as socially and economically corrosive. There is an obvious performative contradiction here, of course, in using learning to attack learning – as the philosopher David Hume put it wittily: reason is capable of offering invincible arguments against itself.[12] We may suspect, too, that those academics who question the value of university education are speaking about the education of *others* and not the university education they have themselves received.

Since the 1970s and Richard Freeman's *The Overeducated American* (1976), economists of education have tried to analyse the economic utility of education, particularly university education, asking what value is generated both for the individual recipient and wider society and whether the investment in university education can be justified by the economic returns. The individual economic benefits are connected with the social benefits, because the more graduates earn, the more they pay in tax and the less they draw in state-funded benefits. Furthermore, if graduates are, as has been argued[13], more likely to enjoy good physical and mental health, are more likely to vote and to make voluntary contributions to their communities, and less likely to end up in the criminal justice system, then the private benefits of education also have a powerful social value which (if we are so minded) can be monetised to make the economic benefits explicit.

Although our intuitive reaction might be that more education is always economically beneficial, there has been plenty of academic debate about 1) whether there are too many graduates and too few graduate jobs; 2) whether some graduates are overeducated for the jobs they are doing (so-called bumping down); and 3) whether graduate skills and knowledge are properly matched to the requirements of the labour market. Some conclude that, in the UK, there is indeed a problem with overeducation, and this should be addressed by controlling university admission numbers and promoting skills training as an alternative to academic study at school and university.

The editors of *Overeducation in Europe* (2003) are quick to say that 'the fact that part of the workforce is overeducated for their job is not an argument to restrict the inflow into higher education'[14] and that it merely suggests that universities could be more efficient in meeting labour market requirements. In fact, the opposite is true: once we view education simply in market terms, it is not only logical, but arguably morally necessary to control the oversupply of graduates. Once we treat education as a commodity like any other, then the whole shooting match is abandoned to a purely economic calculus.

One person who has, with great success, made the argument that we should reduce the number of university students is Euan Blair (son of New Labour Prime Minister Tony Blair), who has said that, for many young people, studying at university is a waste of time. He sees little value in the study of traditional academic subjects, preferring 'things ... learnt immediately in real life situations and ... applied learning', which 'has clear advantages over the academic approach practiced by universities'[15] (his spelling!). Ironically, Multiverse, the organisation Euan Blair set up to promote apprenticeships, has now applied successfully for powers to award its own degrees. *Tu quoque.*

One of the surprising aspects of the critique of overeducation is its virulence: One recent academic paper is titled: 'A knowledge curse: how knowledge can reduce human welfare'.[16] Another describes 'overeducation' as a 'disease':

> Overeducation causes a penalty to individuals in terms of earnings and employment opportunities and a waste of resources to the society at large in terms of state investment into education that do not bear its yields.[17]

This way of thinking about education is sometimes called Human Capital Theory,[18] in which education, training, skills and other experiences are seen entirely in economic terms.

On its own, Human Capital Theory is an impoverished and inadequate way of thinking about the value of education, because the Human Capital calculation of 'value' is restricted entirely to its utility in the labour market. Education also has a very obvious value *outside* the workplace, enriching lives and adding to human flourishing.

Human Capital Theory is also a crude tool for understanding the multi-dimensional choices that we make about education. When people choose to go to university, they are not only thinking in a narrow transactional way about their earnings potential. They will also be thinking about their intrinsic love of their subject, the joys of immersing themselves in learning, and the idea of becoming highly knowledgeable about that subject. For those young adults who are primarily looking for a degree that will pay a good earnings dividend, there are numerous online resources that will tell you, in precise economic terms, what jobs are available with that degree and what you are likely to earn.

As Amartya Sen has argued, a human capital analysis can explain what role education can play in promoting and sustaining economic growth, but it

> tells us nothing about why economic growth is sought in the first place. If, instead, the focus is, ultimately, on the expansion of human freedom to live the kind of lives that people have reason to value, then the role of economic growth in expanding these opportunities has to be integrated into that more foundational understanding of the process of development as the expansion of human capability to lead freer and more worthwhile lives.[19]

In other words, human beings have values, beliefs, aspirations, hopes, objectives and ambitions, which fall outside an economic calculus. Education concerns these things as much, if not more, than economic success.

The relationship between educational institutions and employers is also a dynamic one in which graduates are not only responding to the demands of the labour market but shaping them. Graduates are not simply units of human capital to be slotted into vacancies in a static employment market, but are innovators, inventors and entrepreneurs who develop the organisations that employ them. Graduates bring to employers the capabilities provided by their education and become creative agents in their places of work.

Euan Blair is, in fact, an excellent example of a graduate entrepreneur who has gone on to change the world of work. 8.7% of all Higher Education leavers in 2020 went on to set up businesses, 58% of those developed businesses in their university area of study and the majority of graduate entrepreneurs operate in 'knowledge-intensive' areas of work.[20] The caricature of the entrepreneur as someone who has been failed by the education system is very outdated. If you want to be an entrepreneur in a complex technological society, knowledge is essential.

The risks of an excess supply of graduates have been set out in even more apocalyptic terms by a much-celebrated contemporary philosopher of history called Peter Turchin. Turchin has an interesting background, starting out as a mathematician before turning his hand to history, which he believes can be analysed scientifically. The idea that history can be investigated empirically and that there are scientific laws that govern historical events is not new and can be dated back at least to the writings of Auguste Comte in the first half of the nineteenth century.[21] What is new, says Turchin, is the recent availability of vast quantities of historical data combined with the technology capable of analysing that data in search of patterns. And the patterns Turchin discerns are repeated cycles of growth and collapse in the social and political order. He traces these patterns back through prehistory to the present day, predicting that we are now in the midst of the collapse of the prevailing historical order, and one of the main causes of this impending disaster is overeducation.

There are several objections that can be made to Turchin's approach, not least the argument that the really interesting historical 'data', such as the thoughts, ideologies, beliefs and motivations of human actors, is never purely factual but is always the result of interpretation and can never form a 'dataset' for analysis. If we ignore the information that must be interpreted, the result is a very limited understanding of history, rather like trying to understand what it meant to be Margaret Thatcher by analysing the available empirical data on her life. But this is not the place to discuss Turchin's method in detail. What is relevant is Turchin's prediction that the overproduction of a graduate elite is a 'hidden force' pushing Western societies 'to the brink of collapse and beyond'.[22]

Turchin's overarching thesis is that societies collapse when there is something he calls 'elite overproduction', and as a consequence, there are too many 'elite aspirants' and too few positions of power. The frustrated aspirants coalesce into a 'counter-elite' who challenge and overthrow the ruling class. Under these circumstances, the corrosion of the norms and institutions of society can be dangerous and destructive.

> What determines whether we have a problem of elite overproduction is the balance of supply of youth with advanced degrees and the demand for them – the number of jobs that require their skills. By 2000, unfortunately, the number of degree holders was greatly outnumbering the positions for them.[23]

In Western nations who have, for the past 50 years, invested in the creation of a graduate workforce to overcome educational inequality and meet the challenges of modernity, there are now, says Turchin 'large swathes of degree holders, frustrated in their quest for elite positions' and that these are 'breeding grounds for counter-elites who dream of overthrowing the existing regime'.[24]

Turchin makes a very sweeping generalisation about the motivations of those going to university: that their primary aspiration is to join a controlling elite and that if this aspiration is frustrated, they will gather *en masse* and overthrow the established order. Turchin's thesis that revolution will come from the regiments of frustrated graduates does not apply at all in the case of the Brexit referendum, where it was the resentment of those who had not enjoyed the benefits of Higher Education which powered the Leave campaign. Graduates of all kinds overwhelmingly voted for the status quo.

It is also not obvious that Turchin is right about the dissatisfaction of graduates. A 2023 analysis by PwC showed that on 28 out of 35 undergraduate degrees evaluated, graduates enjoyed a 'wellbeing premium' of higher life-satisfaction than non-graduates and a greater sense of 'life worth'. The PwC report also says:

> Rarely do students pick undergraduate degrees based solely on future earnings. Instead, they pursue subjects on a mix of what they are passionate about and what is meaningful to them based on their personal experiences. This is why it is important to get a holistic view of the impact studying for a degree can have on individuals.[25]

Across the Atlantic, there is further evidence that graduates are not a frustrated elite. Forbes reported that,

> A college degree pays off better than any investment most of us will ever have the chance to make. And that's just the financial side of the equation. The more valuable rewards of a college education aren't found in actual bank accounts.[26]

For all his claims about 'data', Turchin's thesis ignores inconvenient data about the many benefits of higher education that are not related to earnings or positions of power. A university education allows for the development of intellectual potential, increasing human dignity and personal value.

Turchin may well be correct when he says that the United States is pulling itself apart culturally and politically, but the crisis is surely connected with deep-seated economic inequality and not a rising tide of the overeducated. Income and wealth inequality are greater in the United States than in almost any other developed nation.[27] Ironically, more education and not less may be part of the solution.

If we delve a little deeper into the assumptions behind the critique of overeducation, we are soon led to some nightmarish conclusions. An implicit premise of the overeducation theorists is that people should be educated only up to the level which is required for their particular line of work. If people have more education than is required by their job, we are told by The Chartered Institute of Personnel and Development (CIPD) that they become dissatisfied and this impacts 'performance and individual wellbeing, which, in turn, is linked to organisational productivity'.[28]

A second premise of the overeducation theorists is that the principal role of schools and universities is to provide appropriately educated employees to fill vacancies in the workplace. If the system works perfectly, it produces just the right number of square pegs for the square holes and the right number of round pegs for the round holes.

A logical remedy for the alleged dissatisfaction created by overeducation is to ensure that young people are 'well-matched' to their roles by steering *some of them* away from university, effectively bringing their level of education down to the bare requirements of their duties at work. The difficult question then is which young people should get the higher level of education and which the lower? Society would have to create a sorting system. The CIPD recommends, euphemistically, that this could be achieved by 'providing better careers advice and guidance to inform learner choice and action.'[29] In other words, career advisors will nudge certain students to 'choose' not to go to university, thereby ensuring that their future employers enjoy enhanced employee work performance and organisational productivity.

If we follow this logic a little further, we could apply it to earlier stages of education. If we accept the premises of the overeducation theorists, it would be very easy to argue that schools are overeducating huge numbers of young people all the time by teaching them about Queen Elizabeth I and the Tudors, teaching them about maths they will never need in 'real life' and knowledge about artists and artworks which are surplus to the demands of the workplace.

The fact is that overeducation is everywhere; we are all awash with economically non-productive knowledge and understanding. And it is wonderful. Dewey put his finger on it: education is life.

One very famous book that is often read by the 'overeducated' is Aldous Huxley's *Brave New World*, published in 1932, the year in which António Salazar became the fascist prime minister of Portugal, where he ruled for 36 years with the support of the PIDE, Portugal's secret police force. The title of the novel is taken from Shakespeare's *The Tempest*, in which the magus Prospero rules a remote island with his daughter and an enslaved servant called Caliban, who complains about his useless education: 'You taught me language, and my profit on't is I know how to curse. The red plague rid you for learning me your language'. Huxley's *Brave New World* depicts a future society which uses science to achieve maximum efficiency. Overeducation does not exist because every citizen is engineered and educated for a designated role in society. Alphas are taught well and occupy leadership roles. Betas are given technical skills. Gammas perform various service roles. Deltas are skilled with their hands. Epsilons are not taught to read or write, which is unnecessary for the performance of their menial duties. All the pegs sit neatly in the correctly-shaped holes. *Brave New World* is set in the year 2040.

Huxley's novel is a great example of the importance of 'powerful knowledge' to enable us to understand our world. Huxley was writing at the beginning of a decade of rising fascism in Europe: Mussolini, Salazar, Franco and Hitler. The novel is a nightmare vision of what state control could mean, an extreme metaphor for an extreme situation. Those whose education is correctly matched to their employment will probably never be taught about *Brave New World*, or *The Tempest* or study twentieth-century European history.

Overeducation is a concept that should be treated with maximum suspicion. The idea of the intrinsic value of education as a natural good is not invincible and has powerful enemies. There are, as we have seen, historic cultural prejudices against education, right-wing voices attacking 'experts' and intellectuals, and a toxic new academic critique of overeducation. It is important to keep explaining why schools must continue to teach subjects for their own sake, because this adventure into knowledge is indeed what makes us human.

Notes

1 Dewey J, *How We Think*, DC Heath, 1910, p 32.
2 Plato, *Apology*, 38a 5–6.
3 George Eliot, *Middlemarch*, Book III. Waiting for death, Chapter 29.
4 Cited in Hofstadter R, *Anti-Intellectualism in American Life*, Vintage, 1962, p 20.
5 Hofstadter R, *Anti-Intellectualism in American Life*, Vintage, 1962, p 34.
6 Hofstadter R, *Anti-Intellectualism in American Life*, Vintage, 1962, p 19.
7 'Education: Historical statistics', House of Commons Library, 2012.
8 Goodwin M and Heath O, *The Brexit vote explained: poverty, low skills and lack of opportunities*, Joseph Rowntree Foundation, 2016.
9 Goodwin M, 'Rise of the New Elite: How Britain's new ruling class lost touch with the country', Matt Goodwin's Substack, 5 April 2023.
10 'Graduate labour market statistics 2023', Department of Education, 27 June 2024.
11 'Farage SLAMS woke education system', Nigel Farage's YouTube channel, 3 Sept 2024.
12 Hume D, *Dialogues Concerning Natural Religion*, 1779.
13 For example, Balloo et al, 'Differences in mental health inequalities based on university attendance: Intersectional multilevel analyses of individual heterogeneity and

discriminatory accuracy', *SSM - Population Health*, 19, September 2022. *Labour market value of higher and further education qualifications: a summary report*, The Social Mobility Commission, 2023.
14 Buchel F, de Grip A and Mertens A (eds) *Overeducation in Europe: Current Issues in Theory and Policy*, Edward Elgar, 2003. p 9.
15 Blair E, 'An apprenticeship alternative to university' in Goodhart, D (ed), *The Training We Need Now: Essays on technical training, lifelong learning and apprenticeships*, Policy Exchange, 2020.
16 Basu K and Weibull J, 'A knowledge curse: how knowledge can reduce human welfare', *Royal Society Open Science*, 11(8), 2024.
17 Caroleo F and Pastore F, 'Overeducation: A Disease of the School-to-Work Transition System', in Coppola G and O'Higgins N (eds), *Youth and the Crisis: Unemployment, Education and Health in Europe*, Routledge, 2016, pp 36–56.
18 Becker G, *Human Capital*, Columbia University Press, 1964.
19 Sen A, 'Human Capital and Human Capability', *World Development*, 25(12), 1997.
20 Velez J, Rodriguez M and Rodriguez O, *An insight report into the UK's Graduate Entrepreneurs*, National Centre for Universities and Business, 2022.
21 Burns R and Rayment-Pickard H, *Philosophies of History from Enlightenment to Postmodernity*, Blackwell, 2000. See chapter on 'Positivism'.
22 Turchin P, *End Times: Elites, Counter Elites and the Path of Political Disintegration*, Penguin, 2024.
23 Turchin P, *End Times: Elites, Counter Elites and the Path of Political Disintegration*, Penguin, 2024, p 89.
24 Turchin P, *End Times: Elites, Counter Elites and the Path of Political Disintegration*, Penguin, 2024, p 221.
25 'Does studying and undergraduate degree make you wealthier and happier?', PwC, 2023.
26 Newton D, 'There's Even More Evidence That A College Degree Is Worth It', Forbes, May 2024. See also deCourcy K and Gould E, *Class of 2024: Young college graduates have experienced a rapid economic recovery*, Economic Policy Institute, May 2024.
27 'The U.S. Inequality Debate', Council for Foreign Relations, April 2022.
28 Crowley L, 'What is the scale and impact of graduate overqualification in the UK?', Chartered Institute of Personnel and Development, 2022.
29 Crowley L, 'What is the scale and impact of graduate overqualification in the UK?', Chartered Institute of Personnel and Development, 2022.

SECTION 5
What is an educated society?

Our book began with a question about good education and ends with a question about society. What do we want from education? How clearly do we express this? What kind of people do we want to be forming the citizens of tomorrow?

Think

1. What is your dream of an educated society?
2. Is national identity a useful concept?
3. How do you use Fundamental British Values?
4. Are perverse incentives inevitable?
5. Where do you find thoughtful, evidenced expertise?
6. How is the curriculum a window or a mirror?
7. Who is othered or absent from your curriculum or your school experience?
8. What is the critical social role of teachers?

Section 5
Essay 1

Education as a means to foster a nation with a shared culture, tradition and values

Dominic Robson

Introduction

Schools are custodians of national culture, tradition and values. As Headteacher of a school founded during Henry VIII's reign, I bear responsibility for preserving a legacy that extends across five centuries. Yet, it is equally crucial that education reflects and addresses today's global challenges. Nelson Mandela's words above my desk remind me daily: 'Education is the most powerful weapon which you can use to change the world'.

It is not always easy to balance tradition with change. But it is a very important challenge that we, as headteachers, are uniquely placed to tackle, for the benefit of all of our students.

This essay explores the role of education as both a custodian of a shared culture and a changemaker, emphasising the need to foster a nation united by shared values and inclusivity.

I will discuss:

1. The historical role of education in fostering a shared culture
2. The relationship between modern education and national identity
3. Education's role in fostering tradition and values
4. The challenges in using education to foster a shared culture and values
5. The future of education in fostering shared values and traditions.

The historical role of education in fostering a shared culture

Throughout history, education has played a role in fostering a shared culture. In Ancient Greece, for example, Athenian education taught rhetoric, philosophy and civic duty. Through studying texts like Homer's *The Iliad* and *The Odyssey* and engaging in public discourse in the democratic assembly, citizens developed a common identity based on intellectual inquiry and a commitment to the 'polis', the city-state. In ancient China, education promoted Confucian ideals. By teaching moral conduct, respect for authority and social roles, this system fostered societal harmony and stability.

In medieval times, the Christian church dominated education in Europe, controlling schools and universities. Monasteries and cathedral schools taught religious doctrine, Latin and classical texts, instilling Christian values and promoting societal order. The Church's influence fostered a shared Christian identity across Europe. At the same time, madrasas were key educational institutions in the Islamic world. They taught religious studies, including the Quran, Hadith and Islamic jurisprudence, while also covering philosophy, science and mathematics. Madrasas promoted a unified Islamic culture and scholarly tradition, emphasising faith, law and ethics, which helped maintain social cohesion across the Islamic empire.

Later, in the colonial era, education often promoted European culture and values, creating a shared identity aligned with colonial powers. Post-colonial education systems shifted focus to indigenous languages, histories and values, fostering national identity and unity while reclaiming cultural heritage and resisting colonial legacies.

In the United Kingdom, there have been a number of government laws introduced since 1870 to develop a national state education system. A key policy aim has been to foster a nation with a shared culture, tradition and values as it faced challenges, such as illiteracy, or developing a more equitable country.

The relationship between modern education and national identity

The origin of the UK's modern education system can be traced back to 1988 and the National Curriculum introduced by the Conservative government under Margaret

Thatcher. The establishment of the National Curriculum was to standardise education, including British history and values, ensuring cohesion across the country. In July 1997, amidst concerns about diminishing democratic engagement from young people and worries about social decline, the incoming Labour Government, taking inspiration from countries like France, which have a long-standing historic commitment to teach civics, pledged in the white paper, *Excellence in Schools,* to strengthen education for citizenship and the teaching of democracy. What could be done to promote 'British values', such as tolerance, democracy, the rule of law and individual liberty? An Advisory Group on citizenship was established, which was headed up by the political theorist, Professor Sir Bernard Crick. Consequently, citizenship education became compulsory for children in UK secondary schools from 2002, with an optional GCSE available in the subject, underscoring an active commitment to fostering an inclusive national identity.

In the early 2000s, the UK government became increasingly aware that the country was not as united or cohesive as it would have liked. Between May and July 2001, a series of riots involving clashes between men of white and South Asian background broke out in parts of northern England: in Oldham, Burnley and Bradford. This unrest, and the later 7/7 bombings of 2005, led some commentators to conclude that 'multiculturalism' had failed. Much thought was given to how citizenship education might address that perceived failure.

In 2011, the Prevent Strategy was created. This is a government counter-terrorism policy that aims to protect people from radicalisation and extremism. This requires schools and other public bodies to help prevent people from being drawn into terrorism. There was a new emphasis on schools enabling students to challenge extremist views and providing a safe place for students to discuss issues.

Teaching citizenship is, of course, an important vehicle to address all of the above matters. However, there is so much more that all schools can and should do, beyond citizenship lessons, to promote social cohesion. For any school leader, this starts with our values and extends beyond 'respect and tolerance' towards a more fulsome 'respect for the inherent worth and autonomy of every person'.[1] At Bishop Vesey's Grammar School, we are committed to being 'a warm, outward-looking and supportive community, celebrating and promoting diversity and equality, actively anti-discrimination'. These values are central to our school vision of developing 'students of excellent character, responsible global citizens, who will make the world a better place through their kindness, thoughtfulness, confidence and resilience'.

Education's role in fostering tradition and values

Schools are custodians of culture, teaching traditional practices, customs and history. At Bishop Vesey's Grammar School, our history curriculum teaches British history with a focus on the Middle Ages, the Tudor and Stuart eras, the Industrial Revolution and both World Wars. This allows students to understand the evolution of British society, government and legal systems. Cultural capital is further developed by studying Shakespeare in English and introducing British classical composers in music. Outside of lessons, traditional events like the Year 7 procession to the annual service at the local Holy Trinity Parish Church, which houses the tomb of our Founder, Bishop John Vesey (1462–1554), foster an enduring connection to our school's legacy. At the service, we listen to readings and prayers and sing music from the different faiths and secular traditions, which form part of our school community. It is a brilliant way of outlining to our new Year 7 the key values, which are central to being a Veseyan. Just a few weeks later, on Remembrance Day, the whole school gathers together, as it has for over 100 years, to remember, with great reverence, the many Veseyans who died in war, and all the other lives touched by conflict across the world. We remember our history and reflect through poems and prayers from the different faith traditions, on our collective and individual responsibilities to make the world a better place. These ceremonies serve as reminders of shared responsibilities and collective memory, encouraging students to reflect on the values of community and remembrance.

At the same time, Bishop Vesey's Grammar School is inclusive, reflective of the diversity of our school community. For example, our Key Stage 3 history curriculum has been adapted so it now includes a study of the Mali Empire, the Kingdom of Benin, Disability in Medieval England and Life in India before the Raj. Meanwhile, in English, pupils hear from a range of author voices. Outside of the taught curriculum, we have sought to ensure we appreciate the range of cultures celebrated across our school community. In October, for example, we celebrate Diwali. The Main School corridor is transformed with beautiful garlands. The dining hall echoes to the sound of Diwali karaoke. Pupils compete in the House Rangoli competition and enjoy eating mouth-watering samosas. Meanwhile, our astro facility hosts a vibrant cricket carnival. In February and June, we celebrate the LGBT experience through student and staff-led assemblies marking LGBT+ History Month and Pride Month. Our librarian has ensured we have a library, well-stocked with texts touching upon the LGBT+ experience. We have been delighted to welcome LGBT+ alumni and authors to visit our school and inspire current pupils. A new addition to our calendar in March 2024 was a community iftar, a fast-breaking evening meal of Muslims in Ramadan. This was complemented by excellent pupil-led assemblies during Ramadan.

All these events foster inclusivity and empathy, inviting students to see themselves as part of a vibrant, respectful community. A recent letter from a pupil beautifully captures how such initiatives impact our students.

Dear Mr Robson,
I wanted to take a moment to express my deepest gratitude for facilitating the community iftar event last Thursday. The event was not only a wonderful opportunity to break the fast together, after a long, hard day, but also a powerful reminder of the beautiful sense of brotherhood and unity that exists within the Vesey community.

I truly enjoyed Thursday's event. The discussions during the iftar were not only enlightening from the speeches but it was heart-warming to witness individuals from diverse backgrounds coming together, sharing their stories, and fostering a sense of community and fellowship.

In a world often marked by division and discord, events like these serve as beacons of hope and solidarity. They remind us of the importance of empathy, compassion, and coming together as one community, regardless of our differences.

It is through initiatives like this that we can continue to nurture a culture of inclusivity and mutual respect within our school and beyond.

The challenges in using education to foster a shared culture and values

In today's diverse and often divided world, fostering shared values in schools presents complex challenges. Our school community has been impacted by the fractious nature of Middle Eastern politics. There is a legitimate concern that some pupils might feel marginalised by these events. It has not always been easy to chart a response. However, at Bishop Vesey's Grammar School, we try to acknowledge the pain and suffering felt by everyone impacted by war, while reminding pupils of all the things that we share in common. Ensuring school is a non-political space, where everyone feels valued, is paramount.

There are also times when there are tensions over values. Situations like discussing LGBT+ inclusivity illustrate the need to approach differences with empathy and openness. On one Open Morning, a prospective parent asked one of our pupil tour guides if the school was pro-LGBT. I was very proud of the pupil's response that the school was welcoming of everyone. On another occasion, I was asked by a pupil to remove a Stonewall poster on the basis that it was upsetting his fellow Muslims. I did not accede to this request. However, there was positive pupil acknowledgement of my efforts in explaining my reasoning, even if they did not agree with my actual decision.

The future of education in fostering shared values and traditions

As society continues to evolve, how will education systems adapt? Looking ahead, schools will need to balance the preservation of tradition with the inclusivity that reflects modern values. Technology and artificial intelligence will require that education highlight our common humanity and interdependence. We need to celebrate what makes us individual, authentic and distinctive and, at the same time, our ability to work as a collective in a harmonious way for a greater good, fostering a global culture rooted in mutual respect and ethical responsibility.

From ancient Greece, through the Middle Ages to the 19th Century and today, education has fostered a shared culture, tradition and values. Leadership of culture, tradition and values is not without its challenges. However, here, at Bishop Vesey's Grammar School, honouring tradition while embracing inclusivity ensures that each generation upholds the values that bind societies. As education adapts to societal change, it must continue to unite us, fostering both shared values and a deep respect for each person's unique worth.

Note

1 Education (Values of Citizenship) Bill, 2024.

Section 5 Essay 2

Is there an education utopia?

Hugh Rayment-Pickard

The idea of 'the future' is wired into the circuitry of educational thinking – whether in the design of a curriculum (literally 'a course' with a future goal), in the wording of a school's aspirations, or the ambitions of a national education system. Education always takes place for the sake of the future, and inevitably, educationists are motivated to ask what kind of future that will be, could be, and should be. As Zongyi Deng has put it, 'The curriculum is future-oriented in the sense that it aims at the formation of autonomous and responsible individuals who can thrive and flourish in the present and future world'.[1]

School prospectuses often reach beyond the aim of providing a good education for individual pupils and speak about the contribution their school will make to 'the future' in general. One well-known independent school hopes its pupils will 'solve problems that are not yet problems, using technology that has not yet been invented'. Another state school says it is 'preparing the next generation of leaders for our country'. A third wants its pupils 'to know that they can be a hope for humanity'. Not all schools are this explicit, but deep down every school believes that if it does its job properly, the world will be a better place.

At the national level, politicians and policymakers invariably see education as a means by which we will secure an ideal future. The architects of the 1944 Education Act not only wanted to create a fair education system but saw education in the service of 'a society where the advantages and privileges, which hitherto have been enjoyed only by the few, shall be far more widely shared by the men [sic] and youth of the nation as a whole'.[2]

At the 1963 Labour Party Annual Conference in Scarborough, soon-to-be Prime Minister Harold Wilson cranked the utopian rhetoric of the 1944 Act a notch higher. Wilson famously said we were entering a new age of scientific progress fuelled by 'the white heat of technology'. This scientific revolution would – through a modernised system of education – 'make it physically possible, for the first time in human history, to conquer poverty and disease, to move towards universal literacy, and to achieve for the whole people better living standards than those enjoyed by tiny, privileged classes in previous epochs'. Visions of the future do not come much bolder than that.

Three decades later, Tony Blair put education at the centre of an entire government programme of social and economic improvement that would usher in what he called a new 'Age of Achievement' where everyone would share in the success and wealth of the country: 'An Age of Achievement is within our grasp – but it depends on an ethic of education. That is why I said that my three priorities for government would be education, education and education'.[3] In the build-up to the 1997 general election, Blair said (without any apparent irony) that the Labour Party was preparing 'for the thousand years' of the coming millennium.[4]

For more than 80 years, utopian ideals have been a persistent and powerful feature of public discourse about education in the United Kingdom. This may seem strange when the post-war period has also been haunted by a series of dystopian spectres: the annihilation of the planet by nuclear weapons; environmental catastrophe; asteroid collisions; genetic engineering; the prospect of 'Pathogen X' (a pandemic even more devastating than COVID); and, most recently, Artificial Intelligence. These threats are also not hallucinations, but material dangers with possibly world-catastrophic consequences. The utopian mindset clearly goes very deep into our collective psyche and can flourish, even in an age of dystopian anxiety.

Take the example of Greta Thunberg. On 23 September 2019, at 10 am Eastern Daylight Time, the 16-year-old Thunberg addressed world leaders gathered at The Headquarters of The United Nations in New York City. 'You are failing us', she said, her voice taut with emotion. 'The eyes of all future generations are upon you. And if you choose to fail us, I say: We will never forgive you. We will not let you get away with this. Right here, right now is where we draw the line. The world is waking up. And change is coming'. Thunberg accused her audience of peddling a false utopia, 'a fairytale' of endless economic growth. In reality, she said, we are driving headlong towards 'mass extinction'. Ours is a blinkered generation, she argued, which has been educated about the catastrophe of climate change but refuses to act on this knowledge. Environmental disaster is a symptom of an even deeper crisis: 'an extreme system built on the exploitation of people and the planet… A system defined by colonialism, imperialism, oppression and genocide by the so-called global North to accumulate wealth that still shapes our current world order'.

Within this doom-laden vision, there does not appear to be much room for utopianism. What is more, a key element of Thunberg's analysis is that the education system itself has failed to change public consciousness about the dangers of climate change.

> What is the point of learning facts within the school system when the most important facts given by the finest science of that same school system clearly mean nothing to our politicians and our society.[5]

But Thunberg is a 'curious mix of pessimism (we're doomed if we don't act) and optimism (we can avert catastrophe if we do)'.[6] As well as berating world leaders about impending catastrophe, Thunberg mobilised a movement of four million utopian child activists called Fridays for Future (FFF), with the twin goals of 'overcoming the climate crisis' and building 'a society that lives in harmony with its fellow beings and its environment'. Thunberg simultaneously holds two very different visions in her gaze: on the one hand, the nightmare of environmental disaster, and on the other, the dream of a Marxian anti-capitalist paradise. Thunberg believes that a bright future is still possible, but to achieve this, the world needs to 'listen to the science' and be educated (or re-educated) about the reality of climate change.

The resilience of utopian thinking and the role of education can partly be explained by its long evolution within the history of Western ideas: from Plato's ideal city state ruled by an educated elite, to Francis Fukuyama's argument that in highly educated liberal democracies we have reached the 'end of history', which although not utopia, was at least the best form of human government he could think of.

Ideas about the role of education in the creation of an ideal future can be traced back through the intellectual history of Europe to the late Renaissance and early Enlightenment period, when the question of how humans could create their own brilliant future, free from ignorance and oppression, became a central preoccupation of philosophers and scientists.

Renaissance humanist thinkers like Petrarch and Ficino had already placed a huge emphasis on the importance of learning. Petrarch, for example, scoured Europe searching for books, particularly ancient texts, to amass the largest private collection of classical literature in existence. 'Lost' knowledge from the classical period was flowing into Europe from Islamic scholars. But the Renaissance approach to education was essentially retrospective, looking back to the wisdom of the past and trying to integrate it into a total system of knowledge, incorporating Christianity and classical thought alongside pseudo-sciences such as astrology and alchemy.

As the Renaissance flows into the emerging age of Enlightenment, education becomes increasingly concerned with *historical advancement* rather than knitting together the learning of the past. Thomas More, writing in the sixteenth century, sets out a plan for education as the means to create a perfect future state: an island called Utopia. A century later, Francis Bacon imagined another ideal island called Bensalem, with a college dedicated to 'the knowledge of causes and secret motions of things, and the enlarging of the bounds of human empire, to the effecting of all things possible'.[7]

Both More and Bacon imagine Christian utopias where learning is (in Bacon's words) 'dedicated to the study of the works and creatures of God'. But More and Bacon also look forward to exciting new values that will shape the nascent modern period. More stressed the importance of equality of educational opportunity for all citizens, and economic equality so that every person 'lives in plenty'. Unlike his Renaissance forebears, Bacon believed in 'the advancement of learning' through observation, experimentation and inductive reasoning. In a famous engraving on the frontispiece to *Novum Organum*, Bacon imagines 'the ship of learning' sailing out to explore the world beyond the current limits of knowledge.

Among the diverse thinkers gathered under the banner of 'the enlightenment', the French mathematician Nicolas de Condorcet most clearly expressed the utopian ideals of education, which have shaped the modern period. Condorcet was a contributor to Denis Diderot's *Encyclopedia*, an attempt to capture the most valuable human knowledge – scientific, artistic and artisanal – in a single work of reference. It ran to 28 volumes and over 70,000 articles with an ambition to the kind of total knowledge that we now associate with Wikipedia. By assembling all serious knowledge in a unified work, the authors of the Encyclopedia (the so-called philosophes) hoped to provide a resource for the intellectual and social improvement of humankind.

The Encyclopedia was not just a summary of learning; it was also a platform for the continuing advancement of knowledge, which would lead us upwards and onwards to a better human future. In his *Plan of a University or of a Public Education in All Sciences*, Diderot linked education with civilisation – education not only leads to a better understanding of the world, it creates better people: 'To educate a nation is to civilise it. To stifle its knowledge is to push it back to a primitive barbarian condition. Greece was barbaric; it educated itself and flourished'.[8]

Condorcet had been a leading figure at the outset of the French Revolution, working on the agenda for social reform and drawing up a blueprint for a new education system. But having fallen out with the Jacobins, Condorcet went into hiding and, in these very difficult circumstances, wrote what is arguably the world's most influential exercise in utopian thinking: the *Sketch for a Historical Picture of the Progress of the Human Spirit* (1794). For Condorcet, education was the means by which the human species could advance towards a more perfect future. The more we expand human knowledge, the better we can solve social problems, develop new life-saving technologies, perfect our political systems and create a peaceful world order.

Condorcet's utopia was a properly *human* paradise in which humanity had used reason and ingenuity to solve all of its own problems: not only would poverty be eradicated, but the curse of 'excessive wealth' would be abolished. Diseases would be cured and the human lifespan would 'inevitably be extended'. There would also be international harmony with 'the destruction of inequality among nations; the progress of equality within each people; and the real betterment of humankind'.[9]

Education provided the road by which humanity would reach this paradise. By 'education', Condorcet was not thinking of a narrow 'education system' but a universal human spirit of educational endeavour in which knowledge would grow, fuelled by new discoveries in the arts and sciences. There would be access to education for all citizens regardless of gender or class, and learning would be a lifelong project.[10]

In all the essential ways, and 200 years before their time, Condorcet had prefigured the egalitarian principles of the 1944 Act and the utopian optimism of Wilson and Blair. Condorcet also restated the belief already held, for example, by Bacon and Locke that 'we are born with faculties and powers capable of almost anything'.[11] The only limit on learning, argued Condorcet, would be if human beings had reached 'perfection', which was for him a theoretical possibility. 'Learning without limits' is now a familiar education mantra and indeed the name of a UK education trust. This idea, however modern it might seem, is straight out of the early Enlightenment philosophy of education. It is because the utopian idea of limitless human potential for learning is so deeply embedded in our historical consciousness that it seems today to be obviously natural and right.

Condorcet believed that the progress to an ideal future was an inevitable consequence of the growth of human reason. There were certainly many political, social and cultural barriers to be overcome – tyranny, ignorance and superstition – but he believed that the principles of equality and the power of reason would necessarily succeed. For one key thinker, however, the path to a utopian world would not be incremental growth. Fifty years after Condorcet's death, Karl Marx set out a picture of another necessary ideal future – communism – but the means of getting there would require a vast social and economic revolution.

For Marx, progress towards a communist utopia will only be possible once the workers have thrown off 'false consciousness', so that they can see the stark reality of their oppression.

Although Marx believed that the education system provided by the ruling class was part of the dominant bourgeoise state apparatus or 'superstructure' that sustains capitalism, he realised that the revolutionary power of education could not be totally suppressed: 'The bourgeoisie itself supplies the proletariat with its own elements of political and general education, in other words it furnishes the proletariat with weapons for fighting the bourgeoisie'.[12] In addition, the workers can begin to shrug off false consciousness by examining and critiquing their own circumstances.

The world that the workers will inherit on the far side of revolution is not sketched out very fully. 'The germ of the education of the future', writes Marx in *Capital*, is an education that 'will combine productive labour with instruction and gymnastics, not only as one of the methods of adding to the efficiency of production, but as the only method of producing fully developed human beings'.[13] The means to reach a final stage, communism, may be very different from Condorcet's progress of science and reason, but Marx's utopia is very similar: a peaceful state of equality and human fulfilment.

However, Marx brings to the fore another important dimension of the Enlightenment vision: the liberating power of education. The French Enlightenment thinkers had seen rationality as an instrument of freedom that would open up the possibility of a fair and free society. It was Immanuel Kant, however, who properly theorised the idea of freedom. Freedom is crucial to scientific and intellectual enquiry, and according to Kant, the central principle of enlightenment progress: 'Nothing is required for this enlightenment, however, except freedom; and the freedom in question is the least harmful of all, namely, the freedom to use reason publicly in all matters'.[14]

The theme of education-as-liberation reappears in such different places as the contemporary social mobility agenda, where the individual freedom of children to realise their ambitions is taken as an absolute value, AS Neill's vision of unfettered personal development, and Paulo Freire's critical pedagogy, where education should enable 'the oppressed' to overcome their subjugation. In each case, education is the key that unlocks liberation, even if liberation is conceived in different ways. If Kant were alive today to adjudicate in a conversation about social mobility, education and liberation, he might point out that true freedom is not a license to act as we want, because must also submit to 'duties' and that one of those duties is the preservation of freedom for all people since it would be irrational to assert one's own freedom and not defend the freedom of all others.

Although the heady historical optimism of the Enlightenment was arrested in its tracks by the slaughter of the First World War and then the Holocaust, the importance of education for the future became, if anything, more crucial than it had been before: progressive educational reforms took place in the UK after both World Wars. The 1918 Act raised the school leaving age and abolished fees in state elementary schools. The more famous 1944 Act opened up schooling to the working classes. In 1948, Article 26 of The Universal Declaration of Human Rights (1948) asserted the right to free education for all. Naïve utopianism was shattered by the barbarism of the World Wars, but education remained a source of hope in a world that was seeking to find a positive future – 'a land fit for heroes' – on the far side of horror.

Even for such a staunch critic of utopian thinking as Theodore Adorno, education remained, if not the key to a positive future, then at least the way in which we can prevent another disastrous one. In *The Dialectic of Enlightenment* (with Max Horkheimer), Adorno had argued that enlightenment progress was a myth and that reason, far from being a means of liberation as Kant had believed, had become an 'instrumental' force of oppression. But for Adorno, education, in the form of self-critical reflection, is our best protection against another Auschwitz; in fact, *the primary function* of education is to prevent another Auschwitz.[15]

What Adorno had in mind was not just school education, but 'the general enlightenment' of the populace 'that provides an intellectual, cultural, and social climate in which a recurrence [of the Third Reich] would no longer be possible, a climate, therefore, in which the motives that led to the horror would become relatively conscious'. He imagined educational programmes on television, and 'mobile educational groups and convoys of volunteers' who would provide 'supplementary instruction' for people in remote rural areas. Reflecting critically on history and psychology will give us, he argued, the power to resist nationalism and fascism, the ability to understand the roots of persecution and the motivations and psychology of persecutors. Adorno was one of the most pessimistic of German post-war thinkers, famously declaring that it was 'impossible' to write poetry after Auschwitz, but he clung to a subtle and minimal utopia: 'education and enlightenment can still manage a little something'.

For other thinkers, the carnage of the World Wars taught a different lesson: that utopian thinking itself is highly dangerous and that all designs for the future should be treated with extreme care. Adolf Hitler had, after all, been a utopian, as had Stalin. Karl Popper makes this case most powerfully:

> The Utopian attempt to realize an ideal state, using a blueprint of society as a whole, is one which demands a strong centralized rule of a few, and which is therefore likely to lead to a dictatorship.[16]

Although utopias may be toxic, Popper still believes in human progress. But we must step forward with caution: all progress should be a patient, incremental process of 'social engineering' (meant in a positive sense), grasping proximate opportunities, making small adjustments, learning from our mistakes and solving problems.

A key task for Popper is to stop the education system from being captured by ideologues: the main risks to education are indoctrination and state control: 'too much state control in educational matters is a fatal danger to freedom, since it must lead to indoctrination'.[17] Within a free education system, Popper's educational proposals are very functional, focusing on the development of the critical skills to identify errors and the independence of thought.[18]

For another thinker, Ivan Illich, Adorno's re-education remedy was not nearly radical enough. It was not sufficient merely to change what is taught in schools; schools themselves needed to be abolished in order to make way for new utopian possibilities. For Illich, schools in all their forms are oppressive institutions that stifle the critical faculties that Adorno saw as vital for the future.[19] Ironically, Illich's solution to oppressive education systems is *more education*, but of a very different kind. New networks – 'learning webs' – would allow for a radically personalised and self-directed education.

Despite his damning critique of 'schooling', Illich was an optimist: 'the mood … is propitious for a major change of direction in search of a hopeful future', he declared at the end of *Deschooling Society*. But what of historical pessimists, who reject all utopian ideas? What role does education play in their ideas of the future? Anti-utopians often take a cyclical view of history, and that is certainly true of Nietzsche, Spengler, Toynbee and more recently John Gray. Human history is stuck in deadly cycles of failure. Civilisations, no matter how great, sooner or later collapse from internal contradictions. Grand designs for social improvement are sabotaged by the perversity of human nature, what Kant called 'the crooked timber of mankind out of which no straight thing can be made'.

For the philosopher John Gray, all ideas of progress are a kind of Prozac to deaden the grim reality that humanity has advanced technologically but can never overcome its 'natural tendency to animosity and destruction'.[20] We lack the moral capacity to use technology for good and end up abusing science for personal profit or to attack our enemies more ferociously.

And yet, even within the grim logic of Gray's pessimism, education has an optimistic role to play. On the grand scale, humanity may be stuck in a doom loop, but our individual lives have meaning. Gray is a secular mystic: the point of life is to appreciate the world around us. Instead of clinging to deluded dreams of a better future, we should learn a kind of contemplation and be grateful for what we have in the here and now.

The value of learning and the development of critical faculties is implicit in everything that John Gray writes. Education may not be able to cure our destructive nature, but it can certainly restrain it and ameliorate its negative effects. Education can hope to lead us to the least of the possible evils. There is also a performative contradiction at the heart of Gray's work as a philosopher: there may be no point to human history, but there is presumably a point to philosophy. At the very least, Gray's writings assume that what he writes is worth reading. A world educated by his ideas is presumably better than a world of ignorance.

The resilience and durability of utopianism are one of the defining features of the way we think about education. Wherever we turn in the history of ideas, educational philosophy is fused into the thinking of an ideal future, because education is the means by which we get there.

Our modern utopianism has a history that goes back at least 500 years, and our belief in the power of education to create an ideal future burns as brightly now as it ever has, despite the many spectres of dystopia. But we, utopian educators, are perhaps acting not only out of habit and tradition. Perhaps there is a universal *moral imperative* to envisage a perfect future, and perhaps this imperative is all the more vital in an age hemmed in by the possibility of catastrophe. Paulo Freire argued exactly this case: educators *must* be guided by 'dreams and utopias … I can't respect the teacher', he said, 'who doesn't dream of a certain kind of society that he would like to live in, and would like the new generation to live in'.[21]

Notes

1 Deng Z, 'Powerful knowledge, educational potential and knowledge-rich curriculum: pushing the boundaries', *Journal of Curriculum Studies*, 54, 2022.
2 *Education After the War* ('The Green Book') 1941.
3 Blair T, 'The agenda for a generation', Ruskin College lecture, December 1996.
4 White, M, 'Blair spells out his "Age of Achievement" for Britain', *The Guardian*, 2 October 1996.
5 Thunberg G, *No one is too small to make a difference*, Penguin, 2019.
6 Interview with Greta Thunberg, *The Guardian*, 25 Sep 2021.
7 Bacon F, *New Atlantis*, 1627.
8 Diderot, 'Plan d'une université ou d'une éducation publique dans toutes les sciences', 1774, cited in Maury L, 'Diderot et l'éducation du people', *Bibnum*, June, 2013.
9 Condorcet N, *Sketch for a Historical Picture of the Progress of the Human Spirit*, Hyperion, 1990.
10 Condorcet N, 'Report on Public Instruction', 1792.
11 Locke J, *Some Thoughts Concerning Education & Of the Conduct of the Understanding*, Hackett Classics, 1996.
12 Marx K and Engels F, *The Communist Manifesto*, 1848.
13 Marx K, *Capital*, Vol 1, Section 9.
14 Kant I, *Foundations of the Metaphysics of Morals'* and *'What is Enlightenment?* Liberal Arts Press, 1959.
15 Adorno T, 'Education after Auschwitz', in *Critical Models: Interventions, and Catchwords*, Columbia University Press,1998.
16 Popper K, *The Open Society and Its Enemies Volume One: The Spell of Plato*, Routledge, 2014.
17 Popper K, *The Open Society and Its Enemies Volume One: The Spell of Plato*, Routledge, 2014, p 111.
18 See, Chitpin S, *Popper's Approach to Education: A Cornerstone of Teaching and Learning*, Routledge, 2016.
19 Illich I, *Deschooling Society*, Marion Boyars,1971.
20 Gray J, 'The truth about evil', *The Guardian*, 14 October 2014.
21 Freire P, speech given at the Association for Supervision and Curriculum Development (ASCD) Annual Conference in New Orleans,1996. Cited in 'Paulo Freire Invokes Dreams and Utopia', *Educational Leadership*, ASCD, Vol 38 (3), May1996.

Section 5
Essay 3

A vision for a better world?

Carolyn Roberts

My grandfather was born in 1899 and used to say there was nothing sadder than a young conservative. He was certain that it was the youth's job to envision a better world and try their hardest to keep it before them as they grew, voting accordingly. After basic education, he worked in the Tyne shipyards, but night school enabled him to become an engineer in the Merchant Navy and the emerging Teesside chemical industry. He fulfilled education's ambitions as formulated between 1904 and 1926:

> The purpose of the Public Elementary School is to form and strengthen the character and to develop the intelligence of the children entrusted to it...... assisting both girls and boys according to their different needs to fit themselves practically as well as intellectually for the work of life.[1]

The 'Code' of Public Elementary Schools, as rehearsed in the many editions of *The Handbook of Suggestions for Teachers*, was far-reaching. It sought to give children – most of whom would have finished school by 13 – 'habits in observation and clear reasoning', arousing in them, 'a living interest in the ideals and achievements' of humanity, giving them 'power over language as an instrument of thought and expression', and developing in them 'a taste for good reading and thoughtful study' as well as physical and basic scientific education.

It is in the matter of 'conduct', however, that the highest ideals are described. Children should develop 'habits of industry, self-control and courageous perseverance in the face of difficulties'. Schools and their teachers are expected to model how 'to reverence what is noble, to be ready for self-sacrifice, and to strive their utmost after purity and truth'. They should 'foster a strong sense of duty' and instil 'consideration and respect for others', 'unselfishness', 'good manners', 'fair play' and 'loyalty'. In all this, schools should work with the home.

> ....to enable the children not merely to reach their full development as individuals, but also to become upright and useful members of the community in which they live, and worthy sons and daughters of the country to which they belong.

The Code also goes beyond the obvious in its exhortation of teachers and their leaders: outcomes are not enough. Children should leave with a 'due degree of proficiency' in their subjects, but teaching and the other activities of the school are only valuable in their contribution towards the general purpose, hence its reiteration at the start of the *Handbook*. Teachers should never allow 'the real end of their work to become obscured'. They must keep the 'inspiration which a strong sense of purpose affords'.

Further, teachers should note that the education they offer should never be sacrificed for easy metrics: 'the balance of the curriculum should not be interfered with by examination requirements'.

> Again, the examiner's aim should not be so much to find out whether definite lessons can be reproduced, as whether the scholar possesses the power of applying his knowledge to the solution of fresh problems.

Little about the structure of state schooling before the 1944 Act (and much of it afterwards) sounds acceptable to modern ears. Education stopped in early adolescence, and children were packed off young to menial jobs. Girls and boys were treated differently for generations, and 'the number of individual children who show promise of exceptional capacity' (such as my grandmother) and were then sent to secondary grammar schools was necessarily few. Teacher training was patchy and the language of SEND chilling: the 1926 handbook contains descriptions of schooling 'merely dull and backward', as opposed to 'defective' or 'imbecile' children, who need to be dealt with otherwise. Yet, there is a vision of a better world which adults educated properly under the Code might generate by their personal development, and a visionary focus on children as valued citizen works-in-progress, no matter their background.

In 1938, the *Consultative Committee on Secondary Education with Special Reference to Grammar Schools and Technical High Schools*[2] appeared (the 'Spens Report'). It is a fascinating document built on a deep concern for developing scholarship, practical and technical ability, and an independent intellectual hinterland in each child in darkening times.

The Committee, in its turn, looks back half a century to the 1895 Royal Commission (the Bryce Report)[3] on secondary education, agonising about the interrelationship of technical and classical education in mass public schooling.

> All education has aspects of the technical in that principles need to be applied to perform or produce something, interpret a literature or a science, make a picture or a book, practise a plastic or a manual art, convince a jury or persuade a senate, translate or annotate an author, dye wool, weave cloth, design or construct a machine, navigate a ship, or command an army. Secondary education, therefore, as inclusive of technical, may be described as education conducted in view of the special life that has to be lived with the express purpose of forming a person fit to live it.[4]

The 1938 report builds further. Creative activities spring 'from the deepest needs of human nature' and must be central to a liberal curriculum. This, in its turn, develops free human beings, encourages initiative and responsibility from the earliest years and exalts public service above self-advancement. Teachers develop this in the way they run schools, not just in their classrooms, particularly capitalising on the 'classless society' to be found in day schools.

A deep concern for the future of humanity bursts through regularly.

> Democracy is now challenged, and the duty of citizenship in a democracy renders it essential that all should be taught to understand and to think to the best of their ability.......it is not too much to say that all teaching should contribute to this end. On the extent to which the youth of this country can be fitted to fulfil later their duties, and to take advantage of their opportunities, as citizens of a democratic state may well turn the whole future of democracy, and that not only in this island.

Therefore, children should be trained to think and reason for themselves so they may judge the mass suggestions they will meet as adults. While schools provide the means for the state to ensure good aspects of the nation's life pass from generation to generation, even that contains danger. Forgive the lengthy quotation.

> ...observing, as one cannot now fail to do, how completely and exclusively the State may occupy that field – turning the schools and the teachers into mere instruments of its policies, vehicles for the dissemination of the ideas it approves, and means for excluding from the minds of the young all ideas of which it disapproves – then we feel bound to assert our faith in the English compromise between State regulation and freedom of teaching, and to express the hope that circumstances will never arise to endanger its continuance. For where the schools lose their freedom, the freedom of the individual citizen is in peril.

At the individual level, good intentions and unselfishness are not enough. Social problems demand self-sacrifice and intellectual effort. Children should also discover the important influences of other peoples and civilisations, and how international co-operation increases global health and wealth.

Is it a utopian vision that shines through the 465 pages of this remarkable document? A vision of a new society made up of intellectually striving, liberally educated, independently thinking free citizens with scholarly, practical and creative skills, unselfish, self-sacrificing, committed to a classless society, democracy and global cooperation? We could do worse than learn from it.

Despite the pressing need to defend democracy, the vision of public education for a better society continued during the Second World War. There was greater criticism of the social and educational predominance of the independent, direct grant and public schools. Sir Fred Clarke of the London Institute of Education argued in *Education and Social Change* (1940).[5]

> We can hardly continue to contemplate an England where the mass of the people coming on by one educational path are to be governed for the most part by a minority advancing along a quite separate and more favoured path. There is no honest defence, no democratic defence, indeed no genuine aristocratic defence, for the continuance of their present position. To continue it against all the forces that are coming into play will both intensify social conflict and weaken the power of Britain to co-operate with the other free peoples of the world, even with those in the British Commonwealth itself.

Churchill himself joined the debate rather more cautiously, declaring in a speech at Harrow School in December 1940, that

> when the war is won ... it must be one of our aims to work to establish a state of society where the advantage and privileges which hitherto have been enjoyed only by the few should be more widely shared by the many and the youth of the nation as a whole.[6]

Yet, while the tripartite post-war system was gestating, there was pressure for a more radical solution.

> I am utterly opposed to the idea of segregating adolescents in different types of schools. (Or even, for that matter, of segregating them on the score of ability in different classes in the same school.) All such segregation results inevitably in lack of mutual understanding, narrowness of outlook, and the formation of castes. A true democracy must be a community, united by a common purpose, bound by a common interest, and inspired by a common ethos. These ideals cannot be realised if from an early age children are segregated into mutually exclusive categories. All should be members of the one school, which should provide adequately for diversity of individual aptitudes and interests, yet unite all as members of a single community.[7]

These 'multilateral' schools were discussed at the Board of Education in 1942. Inspector and Civil Servant Graham Savage argued that:

we ought to make progress in the direction of the evolution of a classless society. If we do not reformers will, sooner or later, try to force such a form of society by revolution, with the inevitable result that a new arrangement of classes separated by hatreds may emerge. Whilst it is true in some degree that our system of education must be a reflection of the order of society in which it is set, it is wise in planning reforms to look ahead and to plan education a little in advance of the existing state of society, and our ideas on education should be informed by sociological ideals.[8]

Comprehensive schools as a counter-revolutionary policy: by 1947, London councils at least had a plan.

The Committee laid the groundwork for the 1944 Education Act, by which time the global threat to democracy was being routed and a new world order was potentially appearing. The Act was the mechanism by which the hopes and dreams of the earlier groups might have been established; it resulted in the tripartite system, which failed to unite the different strands, approaches, and classes, and may well be laid at the feet of economics. The Spens Report looked at the establishment of 'multilateral' (comprehensive) schools, but, given existing buildings and teachers, could not recommend it. Perhaps this was the best education to be got under the circumstances, for the money?

Therefore, in 1944, a Minister for Education was proposed 'whose duty it shall be to promote the education of the people of England and Wales and the progressive development of institutions devoted to that purpose'. It set up local education authorities charged to provide sufficient schools for full-time primary and secondary education for all from the ages of 5 to 15. Children without clothes suitable for school should be provided with them; dirty children should be washed, milk and a nutritious midday meal provided, for which most parents would pay. Adequate facilities for full- and part-time Further Education for those over compulsory school age, including organised cultural training and recreational leisure-time activities, should also appear.

General education provision should also include:

> adequate facilities for recreation and social and physical training, and for that purpose a local education authority, with the approval of the Minister, may establish maintain and manage, or assist the establishment, maintenance, and management of camps, holiday classes, playing fields, play centres, and other places (including playgrounds, gymnasiums, and swimming baths not appropriated to any school or college)… and may organise games, expeditions and other activities for such persons, and may defray or contribute towards the expenses thereof.[9]

Therefore, by the end of the War, state education should provide for all and make adaptations for those in the most need. In the secondary sector, this generally meant grammar, technical, modern and special schools. The different schools would enable all children to thrive intellectually and economically and be able to play their part in the new world. The vision – an educated populace driving economic recovery.

Twenty years later, Government decreed that it would end this selection and separatism in secondary education. They declared themselves firmly for comprehensive schools, which would be communities in which pupils of all abilities, interests and backgrounds could mix together, gaining stimulus from contact and learning tolerance and understanding in the process.

> This House, conscious of the need to raise educational standards at all levels, and regretting that the realisation of this objective is impeded by the separation of children into different types of secondary schools, notes with approval the efforts of local authorities to reorganise secondary education on comprehensive lines which will preserve all that is valuable in grammar school education for those children who now receive it and make it available to more children; recognises that the method and timing of such reorganisation should vary to meet local needs; and believes that the time is now ripe for a declaration of national policy.[10]

Schools need buildings, however, and as in 1944, buildings got in the way.

> If it were possible to design a new pattern of secondary education without regard to existing buildings, the all-through comprehensive school would in many respects provide the simplest and best solution. There are therefore strong arguments for its adoption wherever circumstances permit.
>
> In practice, however, circumstances will usually not permit, since the great majority of post-war schools and of those now being built are designed as separate secondary schools and are too small to be used as all-through comprehensive schools.

It would take time, but the evolution of separate schools into a comprehensive system must be carefully planned. Building on 'the spontaneous and exciting progress' of some councils, change was possible, popular and widely accepted.

Despite such radical dreams, when Labour Prime Minister James Callaghan made a speech at Ruskin College, Oxford in 1976, it allegedly began a 'Great Debate' about public education. Arguing that education was too important to the nation to be left to teachers and the universities and that the 'secret garden' should be thrown open to national debate, Callaghan quoted RH Tawney: 'What a wise parent would wish for their children, so the state must wish for all its children.'[11]

What should constitute that wish? Education – by now largely in comprehensive schools – should equip children to the best of their ability for a lively and constructive place in society, fitting them to do a job of work. Upon basic literacy and numeracy, an understanding of how to live and work together, respect for others and respect for the individual would be built, knowledge, skills and reasoning ability so they develop lively inquiring minds and an appetite for lifelong learning.

Education should mitigate the disadvantages of poor home conditions or 'physical or mental handicap' (to use the language of the time). In a modern world demanding more of individuals, with fewer jobs for the unskilled, this vision is necessarily more ambitious and complex: 'We demand more from our schools than did our grandparents'.

One of the demands was a better education for those with the newly coined 'special educational needs'. Baroness Warnock's 1978 report[12] radically changed expectations of education for the most vulnerable children, beginning with a general vision for education:

> We hold that education has certain long-term goals, that it has a general point or purpose, which can be definitely, though generally, stated. The goals are twofold, different from each other, but by no means incompatible. They are, first, to enlarge a child's knowledge, experience and imaginative understanding, and thus his awareness of moral values and capacity for enjoyment; and secondly, to enable him to enter the world after formal education is over as an active participant in society and a responsible contributor to it, capable of achieving as much independence as possible. The educational needs of every child are determined in relation to these goals. We are fully aware that for some children the first of these goals can be approached only by minute, though for them highly significant steps, while the second may never be achieved. But this does not entail that for these children the goals are different. The purpose of education for all children is the same; the goals are the same. But the help that individual children need in progressing towards them will be different. Whereas for some the road they have to travel towards the goals is smooth and easy, for others it is fraught with obstacles. For some the obstacles are so daunting that, even with the greatest possible help, they will not get very far. Nevertheless, for them too, progress will be possible, and their educational needs will be fulfilled, as they gradually overcome one obstacle after another on the way.

Despite significant changes of government, Warnock and the Ruskin speech foreshadowed the Education Reform Act (ERA) of 1988.[13] The ERA provided for the National Curriculum and issued new instructions on religious education, collective worship, admissions, local management of schools, grant-maintained schools, city technology colleges, changes in further and higher education, the establishment of curriculum and assessment councils and the abolition of the Inner London Education Authority (ILEA).

Vilified for its lugubrious bureaucracy and prosaically described as 'designed to equip learners with the personal, learning and thinking skills they will need to succeed in education, life and work', the National Curriculum itself had visionary aims:

> Education influences and reflects the values of society, and the kind of society we want to be.

and values:

> Education should reflect the enduring values that contribute to personal development and equality of opportunity for all, a healthy and just democracy, a productive economy, and sustainable development.

The values include:

- **the self**: each person is unique and capable of spiritual, moral, intellectual and physical growth and development
- **relationships:** valuing others for themselves, not only for what they have or what they can do
- **diversity in society:** valuing truth, freedom, justice, human rights, the rule of law and collective effort; families of different kinds; the contributions of a diverse range of people, cultures and heritages.
- **the environment**: the basis of life and a source of wonder and inspiration requiring protection.

The National Curriculum was adapted and expanded by different governments for the next quarter of a century, incorporating solutions to every moral panic from citizenship to sex, as politics required. Compliance was monitored by the subsequently (and similarly frequently reorganised) inspectorate Ofsted, established in 1992 as a part of PM John Major's aim to make public service more accountable.

The first HMCI (Her/His Majesty's Chief Inspector) was Stewart Sutherland, a philosopher personally committed to a conception of education as crucial for a fulfilling and socially cohesive life. Ofsted, however, has never been prone to abstraction in its public pronouncements, perhaps apart from January 2019's Inspection Update.[14] This introduced the concept of 'Cultural Capital' to schools, thus:

> The essential knowledge that pupils need to be educated citizens, introducing them to the best that has been thought and said, and helping to engender an appreciation of human creativity and achievement.

Bourdieu defined cultural capital as what helps a person successfully to participate in society. Introducing the concept could have been a genuine forward step for a national understanding of the purpose of education and schools, in line with the visions of 1926 and 1938. However, Ofsted's definition is explained by reference to Matthew Arnold.

> Culture being a pursuit of our total perfection by means of getting to know, on all the matters which most concern us, the best which has been thought and said in the world.[15]

Under the prevailing political circumstances, however, this version of cultural capital was combined with the insights of American educator ED Hirsch[16]. Hirsch wrote on a different continent for a different purpose, righteously lamenting the fissiparous nature of school curriculum across the USA's multiple legislations. He hoped for a common core which would enable citizens of a diverse society to be able to understand one another and thus continue to strive for a better nation together.

One of Hirsch's books included a fascinating list of the words, ideas, technical terms, sayings and quotations used regularly in US national discourse and therefore required for his vision of active citizenship for a better nation. Experimenting with this is a diverting classroom activity, but lists have a limiting allure. These snapshots of Hirsch and Arnold, combined with Ofsted's simplified inspection processes to the detriment of both. 'Cultural Capital' in the current context is more likely to conjure a checklist of learnt technical terms jammed into an overloaded assessment specification evaluated by terminal examination. Had the concept stayed truer to Bourdieu in the context of a clear national conception of the purpose, rather than the content, of learning, it could have been a real vision for a better world.

Policymakers, in 1926, warned teachers to be wary of examiners' limited vision. In 1938, any alleged conflict between the technical and the classical was theoretically resolved, and a clear warning given about any over-interference by the State. In 1944, the disproportionate influence of the minority privately educated over the majority state educated was thought to be receding, and by 1965, the vision of comprehensive schools successfully serving all was clearly the future's path. Policymakers, for over a hundred years, have tried to describe and conceptualise schools as crucial to a better world.

It is interesting, therefore, that a combination of developments in English schooling in the twenty-first century has led to an oddly prosaic, anti-intellectual realisation of what schools might achieve for society. Right and proper policies, such as the establishment and development of a National Curriculum, a reliable inspectorate, scrutiny of student outcomes, accountable deliverance of public service, and a focus on school leadership methods could be said to have led to the denigration of education itself as an academic discipline and a deep preference for the easily measured and publicised. The lingering perverse incentives of a well-meaning accountability system seem to have led to a focus on performativity in place of thoughtful, considered expertise evaluated in the long term. It is no wonder that, at the time of writing, the teaching profession is yearning for a clear vision for education from an incoming Labour government after 14 years of Conservative rule. Whether they have the courage of their twentieth-century predecessors remains to be seen. Can the discussion of an educational utopia be revived?

Notes

1. Symonds A, *Handbook of Suggestions for the consideration of teachers and others concerned in the work of public elementary schools*, Fourth Impression, HM Stationery Office, 1927.
2. 'The Spens Report', *Secondary Education with Special Reference to Grammar Schools and Technical High Schools*, HM Stationery Office, 1938.
3. 'The Bryce Report', *Report of the Royal Commission on Secondary Education*, HM Stationery Office, 1895.
4. 'The Bryce Report', *Report of the Royal Commission on Secondary Education*, HM Stationery Office, 1895, p 60.
5. Clarke F, *Education and Social Change: An English interpretation*, Sheldon Press, 1940.
6. Churchill W, speech at Harrow School, 1940.
7. Dent H, *A New Order In English Education*, University of London Press, 1942.
8. Taken from a 1942 briefing memorandum by Graham Savage cited in Simon B, *Education and the Social Order 1940–1990*, Lawrence & Wishart, 1991, p 49.
9. Education Act 1944, Chapter 53, HM Stationery Office.
10. 'The organisation of secondary education', Department of Education and Science Circular 10/65, 1965.
11. Callaghan J, 'A rational debate based on the facts', a speech at Ruskin College Oxford, 18 October 1976.
12. 'The Warnock Report', *Special Educational Needs: Report of the Committee of Enquiry into the Education of Handicapped Children and Young People*, 1978.
13. Education Reform Act, HM Stationery Office, 1988.
14. 'School Inspection Update Special Edition', Ofsted, January 2019.
15. Arnold M, Preface to *Culture and Anarchy*, 1869.
16. Hirsch ED, *The Schools We Need and Why We Don't Have Them*, Random House, 1999.

Section 5 Essay 4

An educated society as a community of individual talents

Lucy Hyams

This above all: to thine own self be true,
And it must follow, as the night the day,
Thou canst not then be false to any man.
    Hamlet, Act 1, Scene 3.

These lines, spoken by Polonius to his son Laertes, capture the essence of authenticity, self-awareness, and integrity – qualities that an enriched, educated individual would ideally embody. The advice to 'be true' to oneself suggests that by understanding and respecting one's own unique talents and values, one will act ethically and responsibly towards others. This idea aligns well with the aim of an educated society: to cultivate individuals who are confident in their own identity and, as a result, contribute positively to collective well-being. In order to understand how schools are able to cultivate such individuals, it is necessary to explore the power of the curriculum, the responsibility of those who wield it and how to ensnare a range of individual talents in systems that are increasingly under strain.

An educated society is a community where knowledge, critical thinking and lifelong learning are valued and accessible to everyone. In such a society, individuals are empowered to develop their talents and skills, enabling them to make meaningful contributions to their communities and beyond. This model values the unique strengths and skills of each individual. This diversity in expertise – from science and technology to arts and humanities – enriches society as a whole. It allows for a broad range of ideas, perspectives, and problem-solving approaches, which is essential for innovation and resilience. The concept of the 'broad and balanced' curriculum is not without its contentions, but in order to nurture the individual and provide opportunities for individual talent to thrive, a curriculum must recognise and harness individual talents for the benefit of the community as a whole. Amartya Sen suggests that 'human capabilities are not merely the ability to do things but also the freedom to choose what to do.'[1] In order to give the young people we encounter this freedom of choice, there must be breadth of choice and balance of options.

Colin Richards proposes that a problem with the concept of 'breadth' is that 'it is indeterminate, a matter of judgement and context.'[2] To be 'broad' in terms of scope and coverage, both in the range of subjects offered and in the curriculum content within *and across* subject areas, is a useful starting point. Additionally, to judge whether a school curriculum can be 'balanced' is to understand that the concept itself is bound up with issues surrounding what it means to 'diversify' or indeed to 'decolonise' existing curriculum models to create access and remove barriers. Phil Beadle makes some compelling arguments in *The Fascist Painting- What is Cultural Capital?* which highlights the tightrope school leaders walk between 'establishment' ideals and the execution of these ideals in contexts across the UK, in sometimes contradictory ways. Namely, the inherent inconsistencies within the concept of 'cultural capital' and the necessary power structures that surround it which suggests that 'what culture is, and who has access to it, is profoundly and intensely political,[3]' so to be 'broad and balanced' in many ways is dependent on the quality and dynamics of the 'scale' being used to measure. Ultimately, how does a system under the considerable strain we find ourselves, ensure no individual talent slips through the net?

For Christine Counsell, 'curriculum is all about power. Decisions about what knowledge to teach are an exercise of power and therefore a weighty ethical responsibility',[4] for example, promoting literature and histories and successes in a range of fields by underrepresented communities, could help to challenge traditional ideas held by the immediate community and broaden students' perspectives and therefore widen the options for these students as they enter society. These decisions are not without inherent bias. Workplace ethnicity data displays a disparity; school workplace ethnicity figures in 2023 display that white British people made up 92.5% of headteachers, 90.8% of deputy headteachers and 87.8% of assistant headteachers[5] whilst only 65.4% of pupils were from a white British background: there is a clear disconnect between the make-up of school leadership teams and the communities they serve. This raises questions regarding recruitment and suggests that within curriculums and curriculum delivery (amongst other socio-economic factors), there is space as yet unused to reach underrepresented marginalised groups in order to open the teaching profession (for starters). Allen et al. show us that 'ethnic minority applicants to teacher training have grown, and may now be slightly over-represented, but they have a lower average acceptance rate, worse employment outcomes after training, and higher dropout from the profession',[6] this analysis is from a 2016 study, but the trends seem consistent with the 2023 report data above and point to the fact that this disparity has implications for curriculum content. In short, coverage will need to work harder to reach pupils of an ethnic minority background who are more likely to never be taught by a teacher of their own ethnic background. To revisit Sen: 'Education is a crucial means of reducing poverty and inequality and lays the foundation for sustained economic growth. An educated society is one in which each individual can contribute their talents and abilities to the community'.[7]

In light of this, researchers like Grant and Zwier argue that it is important for teachers to have an 'intersectionally-aware teacher identity'[8] and argue that addressing biases is vital to ensuring at least a reasonable understanding of, and appreciation for, all people. By addressing unconscious biases and diversifying the curriculum, education can create a culture of belonging where each individual is celebrated for who they are and can start to expose the power dynamics of representation for pupils. But before schools undertake the loaded task of diversifying their curriculums, or indeed decolonising the curriculum, there has to be groundwork done in so far as personal reflection for unconscious bias across educational institutions as a whole and for practitioners individually, where this is done there can be honest reflections of what needs to be readdressed within curriculum content to 'balance' the disparity and to diversify what manifests as individual talent. Sharp and Aston's key findings in a January 2024 evidence review of 'Ethnic Diversity in the Teaching Workforce' suggest that 'an anti-racist school culture is a key enabler of progression' and a necessary step in ensuring that the system is not inadvertently reproducing damaging narratives and perspectives that restrict students on the grounds of their ethnic or socio- economic backgrounds. The concept of the 'individual' needs to be more in line with Jacques Lacan's concept of the 'subject' as fragmented and constituted by language offers insight into multiple identity profiles, 'I think where I am not, therefore I am where I do not think'.[9] This enigmatic statement captures the Lacanian idea that identity is never singular or entirely self-contained. For Lacan, the self is dispersed across various roles and spaces, constructed in relation to the 'Other'. An unpicking of 'what' or 'who' is othered or absent within existing curriculum content might be a starting point.

I work as an Assistant Headteacher in a girls' secondary school in East London, and my subject area is English (Hamlet as an opener may have shown my hand here). The ethnicity of our pupils is 88% Asian/Asian British, whilst our leadership team is 75% white/white British. We are in the process of diversifying our curriculum towards a model of inclusivity and are expanding the curriculum by incorporating contributions, voices and stories from marginalised groups, and interrogating historically dominant narratives. We are acutely aware of the fact that this is a journey: beginning with curriculum audits, becoming sensitive to our unconscious biases and moving away from representation that could be deemed tokenistic. In the case of my own setting, our ethnicity data works against the trend in that 58% of our teaching body is Asian/Asian British, meaning that our students are statistically more likely to be taught by someone of their own ethnic background than in other London Boroughs. Professional Learning for staff this academic year is in response to this data and in order to reflect on our curriculum offerings, it is necessary to reflect on Emily Style's call in her 1988 paper 'for curriculum to function both as window and as mirror, in order to reflect and reveal most accurately both a multicultural world and the student'.[10] In our case, this is true of teaching staff and the work we are doing to unpick unconscious bias to expose and question the dominant narratives at the foundation of our own curriculum and community. When we also consider that the economic benefits of education are far greater for women, we need to ensure that our curriculum does its utmost to create a window whereby our students can visualise themselves in society in a way that celebrates their individual talent.

In *Tradition and the Individual Talent*, TS Eliot contends that true creativity requires a balance between individual expression and a respect for tradition. He describes this as 'a continual self-sacrifice, a continual extinction of personality'[11] – a process through which the artist both innovates and contributes to a shared cultural legacy. This idea aligns closely with the ethics of an educated society, where individual talents are nurtured not only for personal fulfilment but for the enrichment of the whole community. Such a society celebrates each individual's strengths while fostering a sense of responsibility toward collective knowledge and heritage. By cultivating diverse talents, supporting multiple perspectives and honouring both tradition and innovation, an educated society becomes a community of individuals who, in embracing their distinct identities, contribute to a resilient, inclusive future. For Piaget, as for Eliot: 'the principal goal of education is to create [people] who are capable of doing new things, not simply of repeating what other generations have done'.[12] This vision underscores the responsibility of educators to craft curricula that reflect diverse voices, ensuring that each learner's potential contributes to the societal tapestry, reinforcing that education is as much about fostering self-discovery as it is about sustaining collective growth.

Notes

1 Sen A, *The Idea of Justice*, Harvard University Press, 2009.
2 Richards C, 'Broad? Balanced? Curriculum?' *Impact Magazine*, Chartered College of Teaching, May 2019.
3 Beadle P, *The Fascist Painting: What is Cultural Capital?*, John Catt Educational, 2020, p 11.
4 Counsel C, 'Taking curriculum seriously', *Impact Magazine*, Chartered College of Teaching, September 2018.
5 School teacher workforce ethnicity facts and figures, Department for Education, 6 July 2023.

6 Allen R, Bibby D, Parameshwaran M et al., *Linking ITT and workforce data: initial teacher training performance profiles and School Workforce Census*, NCTL/DfE, 2016.
7 Sharp C and Aston K, *Ethnic diversity in the teaching workforce: evidence review*, NFER, 2024.
8 Grant C and Zwier E, 'Intersectionality and Pupil Outcomes: Sharpening the Struggle against Racism, Sexism, Classism, Ableism, Heterosexism, Nationalism, and Linguistic, Religious, and Geographical Discrimination in Teaching and Learning', *Multicultural Perspectives,* 13(4), 2011, pp 181–188.
9 Lacan J, *Écrits: A Selection,* Sheridan A (tr), WW Norton & Company, 1977.
10 Style E, *Curriculum as a Window and a Mirror. Listening for All Voices,* Oak Knoll School monograph, Summit, 1988.
11 Eliot TS, 'Tradition and the Individual Talent', *The Norton Anthology of Theory and Criticism*, Leitch V, et al. (eds), WW Norton, 2010, pp. 956–961.
12 Piaget J, *The Origins of Intelligence in Children,* International Universities Press, 1952.

Section 5
Essay 5

Does society still value teachers?

Alison Peacock

We have to learn to 'love the ones we are with'. For wider society to value teachers, we need to start by ensuring that, as teachers, we value ourselves, our colleagues and our wider profession. Only through belief that our profession is important will we ensure that others see us in this way.

Researchers Müller and Cook at the Chartered College of Teaching published a review of professionalism, which suggests that there are three domains at play when reviewing the qualities and standards required in pursuit of professional status.[1] These domains are the cognitive domain, the ethical domain and the legal and social domain, illustrated in S5 Figure E5.1:

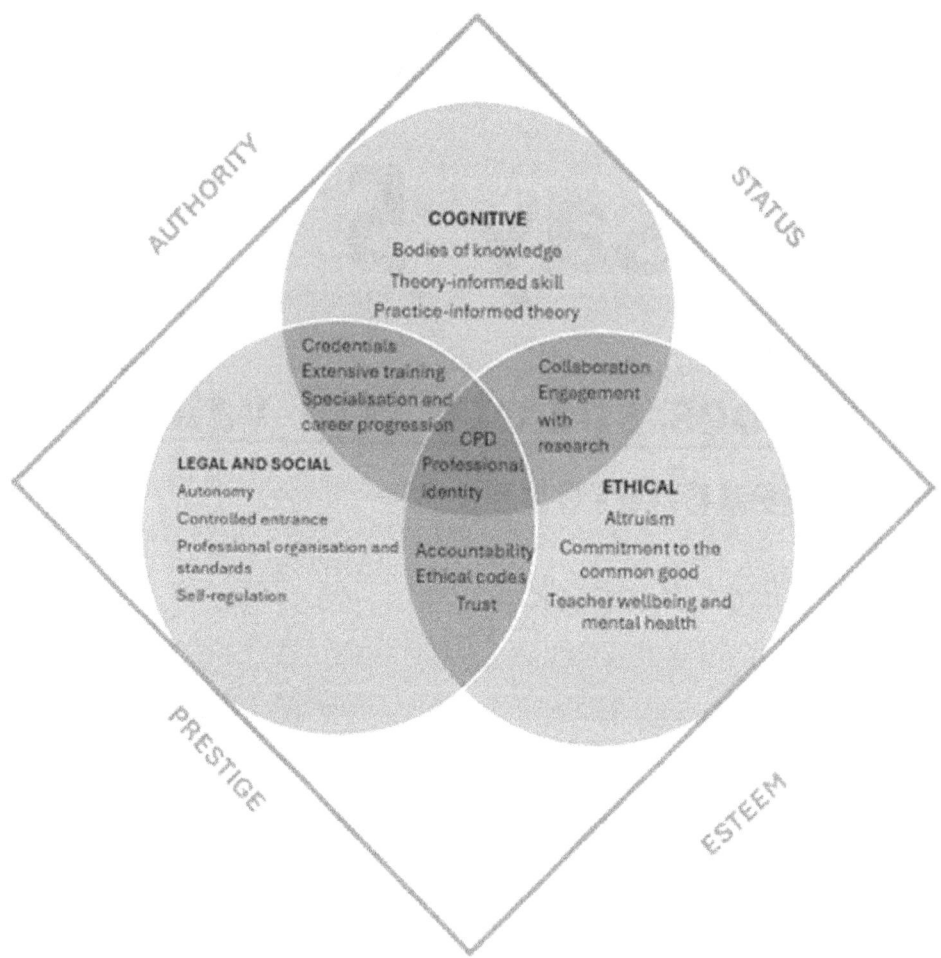

Cognitive domain

The cognitive domain builds status, authority, esteem and prestige through required breadth of educational theoretical knowledge, combined with phronesis – the ability to transfer that theory into practice in the classroom. Accreditation that recognises progress in gaining knowledge and experience is an important factor, as is specialisation. If we draw comparisons with the medical world, we should not expect the specific complex learning needs of children to be diagnosed and supported by an unqualified generalist. When parents or carers visit school to hear about the progress of their child, there is an expectation of encountering the teacher as a professional who can provide an analysis of what the child has achieved and needs to focus on next. Teachers who gain respect within education and across broader society are those who have the intellectual capacity to hold theoretical and practical knowledge about their pupils, but do so with an ethical, altruistic stance.

Ethical domain

The ethical domain intersects with cognition in the realm of collaboration and through engagement with research. Understanding what has already been studied in relation to the teacher's subject discipline or phase of teaching is an important part of building professional skill and enacting that skill through commitment to the common good. The Education Endowment Foundation (EEF) was created by Michael Gove (former Secretary of State for Education) to bring what he envisaged as rigour to the educational research world. Through randomised control trials, the EEF seeks to provide evidence of impact to advise the system where to invest resources. Where the EEF provides evidence of large-scale intervention, the Chartered College provides a conduit for research to inform everyday practice. Increasingly, schools and colleges are appointing Research Champions working with their school to gain 'Institutional Member Status'. Others are becoming part of a network of schools seeking Research Mark accreditation. Intellectual curiosity about not only 'what works' but also 'what might work' leads a drive towards engagement with impactful classroom practice. Within the ethical domain, we also consider the importance of paying attention to teachers' wellbeing and mental health. Failure to do this risks losing colleagues from the profession either through ill health or through disillusionment. If the teacher is not on form, then children working with them will not be on form either. The term 'altruism' is one that was debated before its inclusion as a facet of professionalism. Some union commentary was that it should not be a requirement of professionals to exhibit this quality. However, it is the power of the collective that is at play here – collectively, we would always wish the teaching profession to take an altruistic, compassionate stance.

To be a professional is to be trusted with expectations of high performance. The intersection between the ethical domain with the legal and social domain includes accountability. Society expects teachers to operate as individuals monitored through parameters of performance. Later in this chapter, we consider what happens to our profession at scale when accountability measures become too restrictive or stringent, but there is a necessity that teachers are responsible and accountable. As professionals, there is an expectation that teachers can and should be trusted. Ethical codes that support altruistic cultures are a feature recently embodied through the work of the Ethical Leadership Alliance, established in 2023, and the Framework for Ethical Leadership in Education.[2] The latter framework seeks to enable leaders to 'navigate the moral maze' through embodying the personal characteristics of trust, wisdom, kindness, justice, service, courage and optimism.

Legal and social domain

The third domain within the diagram encompasses the legal and social requirements of joining a profession. Within this domain, we recognise the importance of professionals being able to act autonomously, able to self-regulate and as part of a profession that has requirements of entry and career-long standards. Through the intersection of all these domains, we see the importance of high-quality CPD to establish professional identity, embracing accountability through an ethical approach that also builds trust. The notion of 'practice-informed theory' is of particular interest to our work at the Chartered College as we focus on supporting teaching colleagues to build repertoires of tacit and overt knowledge. Building on the work of Mezza,[3] we believe that enabling status, esteem, prestige and authority across our profession comes from a focus on each of the factors within the three domains. Ignoring any part of the three domains risks undermining notions of professionalism both within the profession and across society.

The importance of education and schooling cannot be overstated. It is within school that we learn about how to function within society, how to understand social norms and how to benefit from the power of the collective. School should be a safe place where each individual feels seen and valued, where every parent or carer is welcomed and where every member of staff knows that they are celebrated as part of a professional team doing their very best to enable every pupil to flourish intellectually, socially, emotionally and physically. This is easy to aspire to but much more difficult to achieve. For decades, the English education system has been failing to recruit sufficient teachers and struggling to retain them. This crisis has become far more acute recently. The macro-education culture in England has become increasingly performative. Budget cuts to central and extended services, lack of essential building maintenance and declining mental health and well-being amongst staff and students have all taken a toll. Against this backdrop, The Professional Teaching Institute (The PTI) convened an influential commission, 'Towards a Royal College of Teaching',[4] drawing parallels between the public service of education, compared with the Royal College of Surgeons, a prestigious College serving and informing the medical profession. The case was made that government funding should be provided to seed-fund a new professional body for teachers, and thus, in 2016, the Chartered College of Teaching was established. The Chartered College has its origins in the College of Preceptors, which was granted a Royal Charter in 1879. The latest iteration of the College, with supplemental Charter, opened as a not-for-profit charitable professional body and began building membership in January 2017. As membership across schools and colleges continues to grow, the core mission of the Chartered College is encapsulated thus:

> *Empowering a knowledgeable and respected teaching profession through membership and accreditation.*

This is not only a laudable aim, but also an essential one, if we are to maintain, sustain and grow a profession that colleagues are proud to belong to and that fulfils the requirements of professionalism as discussed above.

Pride in our profession is important, but public perceptions of teachers matter too. Parents and carers have traditionally placed trust in their local schools. However, when schools closed for the majority in March 2020, it was as if the societal habit of attending school was shattered. During the pandemic, English society at large appeared to have become disillusioned with the notion of schooling as a discipline. Attendance post-COVID has declined dramatically, and in many communities, relationships between schools and parents have become confrontational and fraught. A combination of factors has led to what former Her Majesty's Chief Inspector (HMCI) Amanda Spielman described in her final annual report as the 'unwritten agreement' becoming fractured between home and school, with families no longer routinely taking their children to school and respecting school policies, in return for a good education.[5]

Teachers and school leaders have been thrust into the role of a support service, often dealing with societal issues much bigger than those associated with teaching and learning. When communities endure the hardship of poor housing, lack of employment and poverty, the work of our schools becomes much more challenging. The best of our schools have responded with compassion and empathy, but the problems are not equal – the school system is expected to rise above poverty, being judged against an inspection framework that often judges schools more favourably in more affluent areas.[6] The issue is one of a lack of equity. Combine these challenges with the woeful inadequacy of funding and support for children with additional needs. At scale, teachers are finding that their training and available resources leave them unable to cope with the diversity of needs presented by their pupils.

It is our contention at the Chartered College that through respect for a plurality of views, we can illustrate that although colleagues relish a debate about aspects of practice, in reality, that which unites us is far more powerful than that which divides us. We are closely aligned as a profession, and although professional debate will always rage, the truth is that, as teachers, we are united in wanting optimal ways of helping our students to succeed. We need to rediscover the joy of scholarship as part of our national discourse, recognising the positive contribution that every teacher can make to children and their families. Establishing a climate of recognition and appreciation of the impact of teachers feels like an important next step.

When I returned to teaching, having had our two daughters, I moved from the secondary sector into primary and took up a job in a very small church school where I taught a class of 3 to 7-year-olds. Amongst the children in that delightful class was a little boy called 'Harry'. He showed himself to be an exceptional child from the very first days in school, with a deep love of nature, animals and stories from history. When I subsequently moved schools to teach Key Stage 2 in the next town, Harry came with me. I taught a mixed-aged class, and effectively, I became Harry's teacher throughout most of his primary years. When he left school at 11, his family moved away, and we lost touch. Roll forward 20 years, and I began to receive a Christmas card from Harry each year until he wrote that he would like to come and visit me, and could he bring his mum? So, this Spring, I found myself welcoming a grown-up Harry and his mum to my home for lunch. It was lovely to see him, and once I had accustomed myself to the fact that he was now almost bald, I could reconnect with his cheeky grin and see the lad whom I had spent so many years teaching. He proceeded to tell me that secondary school had not been a success for him and that, ultimately, he had left school without any exams. His parents had separated, and for a while, he went to live with his dad, but ultimately, his father died, and he had to return south to be with his mum. He found a job in a factory and saved so that he could buy his own flat. He began to feel that something was missing and realised that he was 'born to be a writer' and that he wanted to prove that this was something he could achieve, in spite of his negative secondary school experience. He read a great deal and began practising his writing; he took on a tutor who was a Royal Academy of Dramatic Art (RADA) student, and she encouraged him to enter competitions. Harry looked me in the eye and shyly told me that he had waited until now to come and visit because he wanted to show me that he had been successful. He had taken part in writing and speaking competitions and had initially been placed second but eventually won. He had performed a soliloquy from Shakespeare and won first prize, and had contributed an essay that similarly achieved first prize. He told me that he had been promoted from the factory floor to the office and that, every evening, he sat down to write before meeting his friends to socialise. This is a powerful example of why education matters, but it is also a humbling example of the influence that teachers can have on our lives. I share that story to illustrate the way in which education and learning are of such importance throughout our lives. As a teacher, hearing of the progress made by one of our students after formal education can bring great satisfaction.

The Early Career Framework was introduced by the Department for Education (DfE) in 2019 as a policy designed to provide further advice and support through school-based mentoring for all teachers new to the profession.[7] Additionally, increased non-contact time was provided. This is linked to what has been described as 'the golden thread' of career-based National Professional Qualifications (NPQs) offered free of charge until 2024. This suite of qualifications, in addition to the opportunity to become a Chartered teacher, leader or mentor, means that for the first time, the government has taken seriously the need to offer a nationally recognised pathway of career development. The Chartered College offers a vision for the future flourishing of our profession. We have Chartered accountants and engineers, why not teachers? Research by Fletcher-Wood and Zuccollo[8] found that the most impactful resource in any school is a highly effective teacher. It is no longer sufficient to fall back on graduate training as the basis for a future career in the classroom. We need colleagues to engage with practice-informed theory to enhance their efficacy. The Chartered College has established rigorous accreditation standards against three core areas of defined professionalism:

1. Professional Knowledge
2. Professional Practice
3. Professional Principles

Working with recognised Continuing Professional Development (CPD) partners, Chartered scholars study a suite of modules, each offering individual certification. Recognition of prior learning is given through courses such as NPQs, Masters and Doctoral programmes. Study can take up to three years and is best engaged with after a minimum of three years of core practice in the classroom. Three strands of accreditation are offered for teachers, leaders and mentors. Upon graduation, Chartered colleagues are required to maintain evidence of their exemplary practice throughout their career. This route is increasingly understood as being highly prestigious, giving successful candidates post-nominals 'CTeach'. Our vision is that, over time, schools universally will be proud to promote Chartered colleagues as teachers and leaders of the highest calibre.

If we are to enhance teachers' status, we need authentic champions. In July 2024, after the General Election, a new Secretary of State for Education, Bridget Philipson, bowled over the English teaching profession with her apparent commitment to listen and to act on behalf of teachers. Her positivity, informed by knowledge of the sector gained during her period as Shadow Secretary of State, was impressive to witness. We need political support and positive stories of impact within the media to sustain a narrative of continuous effort and improvement across education.

I recently joined a Facebook group for Hadham Hall, the secondary school that I attended. As I scrolled through the posts, with photographs of the school site and recollections about events, I was particularly struck by the many messages and fond memories of one of our teachers, whom I also remember clearly and with affection. More than 50 years have passed since I was first taught by Mr Doyle, but the impact of his teaching remains with me. He was a good teacher. He introduced his subject with clear passion and extensive knowledge. His use of mnemonics was way ahead of his day, but what an effective tool that was to remind us of key facts. He used humour, he knew us well, and he was kind. Years later, I met him in a supermarket and he immediately recognised me, recalled my name and was keen to hear about what I was up to and who I had heard from amongst the school community. Again, the power of a good teacher is immeasurable.

As society changes, so should schools. The impact of the pandemic on recent life has been dramatic. Prior to this, a strong case for adopting more flexible working options was already building. Workforce development was already illustrating that too many young women were leaving the classroom due to what has become known as the 'motherhood penalty' of rigid working hours. There is an urgent need to review how much time in the school day is spent actually teaching as opposed to everything else that fills the day, and to utilise teaching expertise accordingly. A part-time physics teacher, inspired and dedicated to her subject, is likely to be far more impactful on her students than a full-time generalist being asked to teach a specialism. If the timetable needs to be adapted to encompass the flexibility needed, then this is something that should routinely be considered. It has been inspiring to see the work of WomenEd[9] and leaders such as Emma Turner and the Maternity Teacher/Paternity Teacher (MTPT) project campaigning for fairer opportunities.[10] Statistics about the workforce[11] illustrate how underrepresented colleagues from the global majority are within the teaching profession. This is particularly stark when considering promotion into leadership roles. In 2021, of the 20,786 headteachers in England, only 1% were Black.[12] Reinstatement of DfE programmes designed to support leadership development for specific sectors of our profession is much needed, alongside greater recognition of the importance of equality and diversity across our workforce and within our school curricula.

Accountability and the role of Ofsted are another area for reform. I was pleased to be part of the National Education Union (NEU) Commission 'Beyond Ofsted', chaired by Lord Jim Knight, that made recommendations to the incoming Labour Party.[13] Chief amongst the reforms suggested was that single-word judgements labelling schools should be abolished. The Labour government has listened and has replaced single-word grades with a broader range of measures. The new His Majesty's Chief Inspector, Sir Martyn Oliver, has committed to ensuring that mutually respectful professional dialogue is at the heart of inspection. If we were to harness the energy that currently goes into inspection preparation into a collective endeavour that aims for excellence in curriculum design, pedagogy and assessment practice, our profession could justifiably be proud of its transformation. Imagine the power and promise of enhanced collaboration through engaged communities of practice at scale. It is my contention that the Chartered College of Teaching, ultimately becoming a Royal College, could be the engine that enables this.

As a Professional Body, the College will always advocate for teachers and leaders to have access to the highest quality professional learning. We are not a union, and although we work alongside our union colleagues, it is not our role to advocate for improved pay and conditions. We are confident, however, that the most effective education system will always require deep, sustained and generous investment if all our children are to thrive. The most important resource any child has access to is an empowered, knowledgeable, respected teacher. As a charity, the Chartered College is run by its members and is governed by a Council elected from the membership. We seek to respect a plurality of voices; presenting articles, research summaries and opinion pieces that enable teachers as professionals to determine what they believe will work best for their children, their schools and their community. The Chartered College is apolitical – rising above the political fray whilst nevertheless brokering opportunities for consultation and informed debate. We are building a trusted group of professionals who are interested in the development of evidence-informed practice inspired by ethical leadership.

Teaching is a public service. Recognition that the work of professionals is to be valued and recognised at the highest level through our professional body becoming a Royal College would be a source of great pride. It would mean that with one fell stroke, we would be represented by a Royal College alongside other prestigious organisations, such as the medical Royal Colleges. The Royal Charter enables qualified teacher Members to use the post-nominals MCCT. Fellows with a minimum of ten years of teaching experience are eligible to apply for Fellowship thereafter, using FCCT in recognition of their contribution. The collective sense of belonging and pride that a Royal College would contribute both within and beyond the profession has the potential to make a huge difference to the perception of what it means to become and remain a teacher.

In conclusion, for many teachers, our profession feels joyful and wise. Our best schools are led by ethical colleagues who recognise that the culture they create has a positive ripple effect across the community. In my view, becoming a school leader is a huge privilege. I look back on my career as a teacher and headteacher with pride because of what we were able to create together as a team. Now leading the Chartered College of Teaching, I am privileged to see so much exemplary, dedicated practice. I visit schools and colleges where teachers, support staff and pupils are keen to impress, proud of their education and their own agency as future members of society. There is much for us to celebrate within our profession and even more to feel proud of as we do all that we can to support local communities and to work with others in pursuit of childhood flourishing. As I write, I am fuelled by optimism for our collective future as educational professionals. I believe that more than ever before, professionals recognise the difference that they make and seek to illustrate this beyond seeking Ofsted banners that 'prove' their worth. Our best schools strive day in, day out on behalf of our children and seek to build the most productive partnerships they can in pursuit of this. Collaboration and collegiality make our schools stronger, more productive places. If we can join up the strands of subject expertise nationally, so much the better. I am particularly proud to contribute to this book as a PTI initiative and hope that the celebration of subject knowledge and expertise continues to grow, inspired by their great work.

With due attention to the cognitive, ethical and social and legal domains, we are well placed to grow our professional authority and status, building prestige and esteem for all those tasked with teaching the children of our future.

Notes

1 Müller L-M and Cook V, *Revisiting the notion of teacher professionalism: A working paper*, Chartered College of Teaching, 2024.
2 *Navigating the Educational Moral Maze: The Final Report of the Ethical Leadership Commission*, Association of School and College Leaders, 2019. *Leading in Practice: A review by the Committee on Standards in Public Life*, The Committee on Standards in Public Life, 2023.
3 Mezza A, '*Reinforcing and innovating teacher professionalism: Learning from other professions*', OECD Education Working Papers 276, OECD, 2022.

4 Leslie C (ed), *Towards a Royal College of Teaching: Raising the status of the profession*, Teacher Development Trust, 2013.
5 *The Annual Report of His Majesty's Chief Inspector of Education, Children's Services and Skills 2022/23*, Ofsted, 2023.
6 Elliot Major L and Briant E, *Equity in Education: Levelling the playing field of learning – a practical guide for teachers*, John Catt, 2023.
7 *Early career framework*, Department for Education, 2019.
8 Fletcher-Wood H and Zuccollo J, *The effects of high-quality professional development on teachers and students: A rapid review and meta-analysis*, Education Policy Institute, 2020.
9 Marsh H and Derbyshire C, 'Flexing our schools' in Porritt V and Featherstone K (eds), *10% Braver: Inspiring women to lead education*, Sage, 2019, pp 115–124.
10 Turner E, *Let's Talk about Flex: Flipping the flexible working narrative for education*, John Catt, 2020.
11 Worth J and Faulkner-Ellis H, *Teacher Labour Market in England – Annual Report 2022*, National Foundation for Educational Research 2022.
12 Wilson A, *Letters to a young generation: Aspiring school leaders*, 9:10 Publishing, 2023.
13 Perryman J, Bradbury A, Calvert G and Kilian K, *Beyond Ofsted an inquiry into the future of school inspection*, UCL, 2024.

Afterword

Michael Young

In one of her first public statements, in an interview with *The Observer*, Bridget Phillipson, the Secretary of State for Education, made the focus of her priorities very clear. In her interview, she stressed that:

1. Much of her focus will be on 'working-class children, as they are the ones who ….most need ladders of opportunity out of poverty, and whose chances have been reduced so greatly by 14 years of Tory government'.

2. 'Too many working-class kids are being shut out of opportunities to play sport, to get involved in music and drama and creative subjects. That is what parents want and I want'.

3. 'We need to cultivate a sense of a joint mission between government and the teaching profession that resets the relationship between government and schools'.

There are signs in the aims of the Review of the School Curriculum that she launched that the first two of these priorities will be addressed. Furthermore, in Carolyn Roberts's Introduction and a number of the essays in this book, this broader vision of the future of schooling is supported by headteachers.

However, she gave little attention to how she will focus on the continuing educational inequality that affects so many working-class pupils. The report by the Children's Commissioner, Dame Rachel de Souza, on the riots that followed the murders of three children in Stockport emphasised that many of the young rioters, some as young as 11, showed a lack of trust in the police and the absence of opportunities in their community, including schools, although her report does not explicitly mention schools.

The overall message of the headteachers' essays in this book is, in the prevailing context of a shortage of specialist teachers in all subjects, encouraging and optimistic, and a sign that the professional morale of, at least, headteachers associated with the Professional Teaching Institute (PTI) remains high. They do not focus explicitly on the Secretary of State's priority of improving opportunities for working-class pupils. This would, of course, involve not only schools and further and higher education, but also the attitudes of employers to recruiting young people. However, there are signs in what some of the headteachers write that they are aware that teachers in a democracy such as ours can have a role beyond their school.

Ken Jones, a senior officer in the NEU, reviewed *Knowledge and the Future School*, the book that David Lambert and I wrote, and Carolyn Roberts contributed to. It was, initially, widely praised. However, Ken Jones commented that while our curriculum theory, arguing that subjects should be the basis of a curriculum for all pupils, had much to recommend it, this was not so for our analysis of the external pressures that teachers face. He points out that without the engagement of specialist teachers (with the support of parents for some), subject knowledge can become little more than memorisation of facts rather than an opportunity for new thinking on the part of pupils. Some pupils, with strong support at home, make this change on their own, but many do not.

We, and I include policymakers, researchers like me, and headteachers and their staff, need to ask why this transformation is so rare. Carolyn Roberts, in her essay, sees discovering new knowledge by pupils as an example of 'wonder, joy and wisdom'. The problem all teachers face, and many come to accept as inevitable in order to go on teaching, is that this transformation is rare among pupils from working-class families, not because they are an example, as some thought of working-class 'cultural deficit', but because the cultures of school and home are so different as to be experienced as almost incompatible.

For Aristotle, and no doubt others in different cultures, learning and the search for knowledge are something we are born with. However, our competence is not innate, as some psychologists such as Cyril Burt originally thought; it is a competence that is only activated in our first interaction with our parents (or carers) when we cry because we are hungry. However, such social competence remains at best an unrealised resource in the development of all children, despite becoming increasingly urgent with the expansion of schooling. I do not claim any originality for proposing this form of social competence; it builds on the ideas of the most famous sociologist of education, Basil Bernstein, who was a Professor of the University of London and died in 2001.

The idea is that 'social competence' is universal for all human beings – we would not survive long without it. I start by recognising that there are two quite distinct ways in which human beings learn and acquire knowledge that are unique to them, and that for a pupil to develop in becoming an adult, the second type of learning has to bridge these differences. The first way that we are born with is that we learn from our experience as we interact with the world and others – in our everyday life – the names of our family, the plants and animals that are food and the trees of forests and fields of grass and wheat, and other features of our environment, such as the weather. For many people, prior to recent centuries, this was adequate.

This process of incidental and informal learning, often known as socialisation, continues throughout our lives when, as we grow up, we learn to play games and become members of families and other social groups. When we first go to school or some attend a church, we face a new kind of complex and specialised knowledge which is sometimes quite separate from our experience. It is organised quite separately, and not being directly related to our experience, has to be acquired voluntarily – in other words, young children (and, of course, older children and adults) have to be motivated to acquire it.

Hence, the crucial role of teachers and what we refer to as their pedagogic knowledge and skills of this knowledge and their pupils. This means that as children grow up and move from primary to secondary school, teachers need a deeper understanding of different subject knowledge and why it matters, as well as the knowledge involved in convincing pupils why such knowledge is worth acquiring. The key difficulty for teachers is that this knowledge – whether history or physics – is part of a specialised subject culture which is quite at odds in its structure and purposes with the values of culture that many children bring to school. It is this cultural differentiation that dominates the relationships between home and school for significant proportions of each cohort of pupils and so often leads to disaffection and even dropout. Overcoming these negative consequences involves one of two strategies. One is to bring the two cultures closer together – an approach adopted by Finland and, to some extent, other Nordic countries, so that the differentiation only operates for older children and the majority now all continue to free higher education. The alternative has been our anglophone approach, in which pupils were divided, initially, into types of school and increasingly between different types of curricula that aim to be more consistent with the abilities of pupils who are treated as still having differentiated social competence. The latter strategy, however well-intentioned, is always inclined to perpetuate inequalities. Unless it is seen as a strategy of small steps that are part of a longer-term vision, it inevitably raises political questions beyond the scope of this book and, more explicitly, this Afterword.

Index

Note: Page numbers in *italic* refers to Figures. Endnotes are indicated by the page number followed by "n" and the note number e.g., 111n5 refers to note 5 on page 111.

A levels: assessment burden 141; declining uptake of arts subjects 63; declining uptake of English language 168; large range of choice 49; long-term rise in grades 133, 137; tension between supporting academic progression and informing employers 165–166
academies *see* free schools and academies
Adonis, Andrew 47
Adorno, Theodor 234–235
Anderson, Elizabeth 191–192, 193, 197, 198, 199, 200
Apprenticeships, Skills, Children and Learning Act (2009) 135–136
Arendt, Hannah 48
Aristotle 173, 174, 176, 177, 264
Arnold, Matthew 60, 183, 245, 246
artificial intelligence (AI) 141, 145, 167, 169, 207, 227, 230
Arts in Schools: Foundation for the Future 65, 66, 67
arts subjects: arts practice, importance of 66; assessment of 66; Capabilities Framework for 67, 69; clearly defined curriculum, importance of 68; collaborative learning 67; declining uptake of 63, 168; social and emotional health promoted by 69; societal value of 62–63, 68–69; systemic downgrading of 63; *see also* creativity

Ashbee, Ruth 106
assessment: accountability, pressures of 128, 129, 130, 131; accuracy 130; assessment burden 141; attainment gap exacerbated by traditional methods 128; balanced unity of assessment and curriculum, importance of 140; digital revolution in strengths-based assessment 150; formal assessment of young children 127–128; general dissatisfaction with current system 128; mental health impacts of high-stakes assessment 127, 128; personalised digital assessment 129; play in learning, allowing for 130–131; potential to distort teaching priorities 128, 129–130, 145, 163, 165, 180; reflecting breadth of curriculum 131; summative vs. formative 128, 131, 150; teacher-assessed grades 166–167; trade-offs in assessment practices, inevitability of 141–142; *see also* examinations; qualifications
Association for Science Education 62
attendance crisis 28, 32
Australia 155, 156, 158
autodidacticism 22

Bacon, Francis 232, 233
Bacon, Sally 62–63

Barton, Geoff 128
Beadle, Phil 249
Beal, Jonathan 39
Bernstein, Basil 264
Biesta, Gert 59, 61, 147
Bishop Vesey's Grammar School 225–227, 228
Blair, Euan 215, 216
Blair, Tony 230, 233
Bleiman, Barbara 61
Bourdieu, Pierre 62, 206, 245, 246
Bowles, Samuel 206
Bowman, Carl 32
Boyle, Edward 193, 194, 198
Bradshaw, Ted 38
Brighton, variety of school provision in 48
British Cohort Study 49
broad and balanced curriculum: addressing unconscious teacher biases 250, 251; balance as politically contested 249; breadth as indeterminate concept 249; essential for nurturing individual talents 248–249, 251; undermined by ethnically unbalanced teaching workforce 249–251
Bryce Report 240
Butler, Richard Austen 45

Callaghan, James 243
Cambridge Assessment 128
Cambridge Primary Review 48
Canada 155
Caplan, Brian 17, 18
Carmichael, Neil 162–163
character education 23–24, 122, 239
Chartered College of Teaching 253, 255, 256, 257, 258–259, 260–261
Chartered Institute of Personnel and Development 218
Christodoulou, Daisy 106
Churchill, Winston 241
citizenship education 59, 63, 75–76, 78, 79, 99, 173, 176, 225, 240
Clarke, Fred 241
climate change: addressing through long-term educational thinking 207; as central educational issue; concept of good education in light of 54; failure of education to change public consciousness 231
Coe, Rob 133–134
'Code' of Public Elementary Schools 238–239
Cognitive Load Theory 120
common features of good schools: articulating a vision of education 26–27; community engagement 33, 34; cultivation of human capacity 29, 147; definition of 38; evidence base for 27; positive and safe environment 28–29; prioritising the most vulnerable 27; professional development, prioritising of 30; relational trust between schools and families 32–33; relational trust between teachers and leaders 30–31; sense of belonging and inclusion, for children 28; social contract, fostering of 32; strong governance 33; working conditions, relational culture of 31
communication skills, decline in 23
community: 'cathedral-building' analogy 39–40; community stories 40–41; COVID-19 pandemic and 38–39, 41, 42; serving individuals and serving communities, as intrinsically linked 37, 38, 40; school engagement with communities 33, 34, 42
complex competences: importance of clearly articulated focus on 154; OECD framework 151, *152*, 154; prosocial vs. epistemic 150–151; reluctance of educators to embrace 149–150; Skillsbuilder framework *153*, 154; *see also* creative thinking
compliance mechanisms: agency of schools and teachers endangered by 2, 4; culture of compliance created by Ofsted 175; demoralising effect 1, 4; fearfulness created by 2; joy and wonder, unconducive to 2; legitimacy of 2; national emphasis on 2; outcomes focus, schools driven to 2, 3
Comprehensive schools 241–242, 243, 246

Condorcet, Nicolas de 232
conformity in the classroom 178–181
Counsell, Christine 108, 131, 249
COVID-19 pandemic: attainment gap widened by 127, 130, 167, 184; childcare provision function, interruption of 16; communities, served by schools during 38–39; conformity among students reinforced by 181; examinations disrupted by 136; fractured school–society social contract 3, 128, 257; Higher Education disrupted by 53; mental health crisis worsened by 39; ongoing impact in schools 41, 42, 49, 176, 208–209; reinventing ways of teaching and learning 38–39; suspension of national examinations 44
creative thinking: Centre for Real-World Learning model 155, 156; five dimensions of 154; formative assessment of 156; PISA test 150, 154, 156; progression frameworks for assessment of 156–159; split screen teaching 154–155; see also complex competences; creativity
creativity: assessment of 66; in Capabilities Framework for arts 67–68; conformity vs. 179–180; decline of arts subjects, as impoverishment of 62–63, 65, 168; fear of failure as obstacle to 66; highly valued by educators 67; highly valued by employers 66, 68; hostility to assessment of 156; not particular to the arts 65; societal benefits 68; Spens Report 240; tradition and the individual talent 251; see also arts subjects; creative thinking
Creativity Collaboratives 149, 156
Crick, Bernard 225
critical pedagogy 234
critical thinking: assessing in arts subjects 66; rote-style learning vs. 83; specific subject knowledge required for development of 82, 120, 121, 123; whole school focus on 101
cultural identity: challenging racist ideas 100; fostering community tolerance and understanding 99, 100–101; mixed and complex identities 100; validating cultural identity of students 98–99, 100
cultural learning 62
curriculum development: assessment-driven distortion of 109, 163; balanced unity of assessment and curriculum, importance of 140; as constant iterative process 119; curriculum leader as curator 110; curriculum pedagogy 107–109; ethos and culture of 116–117; intrinsic vs. extrinsic value 103; joy and wisdom 111; reflection of current social and political issues 104; subject knowledge fundamental to 110; temporal progression vs. subject-specific curriculum progression 105–107, 109; see also memory
Curriculum for Wales 68

de Souza, Rachel 22, 263
Dearing, Ron 44
Deng, Zongyi 26, 27, 29, 229
Dent, HC 241
Dewey, John 119, 121, 123, 210, 218
Diderot, Denis 232
digital education 169
disengaged students and families: active intervention by schools, need for 186; competing narratives on responsibility for 183–184, 187–188; equity, school commitment to 187; home learning, support needed for 186; identity incompatibility 185; incompatibility of home and school cultures 264, 265; listening to, importance of 186; separating powerful knowledge from knowledge of the powerful 187; social identity threat 185; teacher bias 185; visibility of working-class students' achievements 186
Durkheim, Émile 205, 208

Early Career Framework 258
Eastwood, Owen 28
Education Act (1918) 234

Education Act (1944) 45, 47, 229–230, 233, 234, 239, 242
Education Endowment Foundation (EEF) 23, 30, 31, 107, 114–115, 139, 255
Education Policy Institute 31, 127, 128, 130
Education Reform Act (1988) 98, 244
educational cognitive psychology 105, 107
Eliot, George 211
Eliot, TS 251
Encyclopedia (Diderot) 232
English Baccalaureate (EBacc) 23, 63, 100, 165, 168
Ericsson, K. Anders 120
examinations: 'backwash' effect of 138, 139–140; COVID-19 pandemic, disruption by 136; as developmental snapshot 164–165, 166; differentially compensating students for disadvantage 136, 166; favouring of students with advantageous backgrounds 165, 166; grade inflation 136–137, 138; limitations of 164, 166, 180; long-term rise in grades, scepticism towards 133–134, 135, 137; reducing extent of 167; schools gaming system to meet accountability pressures 135, 139; stability of value 136–137, 138; stressfulness of 141–142, 166; system-level performance measured by 165; trustworthiness, as basis of public confidence 136, 138; *see also* assessment; qualifications
Extended Project 168
Eysenck, Hans Jürgen 123

Fair Education Alliance 190
fairness in education: capability to write one's own life story 194–197; equal outcomes, as chimaera 190–191; just deserts, as chimaera 191–193; partial role of education in generating capability 199–200; pessimism about attaining 189; potential maximisation, as chimaera 193–194; variation as natural and inevitable 190–191; veil of ignorance 197–199
Farage, Nigel 214

Ficino, Marsilio 231
Finland 45, 46, 155, 265
Fordham, Michael 106
Foucault, Michel 119, 120
Framework for Ethical Leadership in Education 4, 255
France 45, 50, 225
Francis, Becky 24, 130, 168
free schools and academies 45, 46, 47, 48, 98, 114, 146
Freeman, Richard 214
Freire, Paulo 234, 236
Fukuyama, Francis 231
functionalist view of education: British values 16; childcare provision 16; dysfunctional initiatives and processes 16–17, 18; foundational skills for employment 15, 16; inadequacy of 41; inefficiency of post-primary education 17; inherent complexity and messiness of schools 16, 18, 19; mental health support 16; navigation skills for modern world 16; personal function of schools for teachers 18, 19; socialisation 15, 16, 22, 176–177; tackling socio-economic inequality 16

Gadamer, Hans-Georg 104
Gardner, Howard 122
Gatto, John Taylor 22
GCSEs: assessment burden 141; attainment gap 165; correlation of grades with earnings 164; declining uptake of arts subjects 63, 168; long-term rise in grades 133, 135, 137; origin as exit qualification 16; outcomes focus 2; reducing content burden 167–168; Secretary of State's control of content 47; subject content documents 138–139; tension between supporting academic progression and informing employers 165–166
Germany 51–52
Gintis, Herbert 206
Good Childhood Report 28, 144
Goodwin, Matthew 213
Gove, Michael 98, 180, 212, 255

grammar schools 193, 198
Gray, John 236
great subject teaching: essential to good schools 81, 84, 88; leadership capacity developed by 87–88; societal value of 83; standardised lessons and materials, detrimental to 85; professional development 85–86, 88, 98, 115–116; subject advocates, teachers as 85; teaching as technical skill, limitations of 84–85, 88, 144
Green, Andy 45
Greenleaf, Robert 146

Habermas, Jurgen 104
hidden curriculum 97, 206
Higher Education (HE): failure to redress skills shortages 53–54; as labour market bridge 52–53; overqualification 53
Hirsch, ED 83, 246
Hirst, Victoria 34
Hofstadter, Richard 212
homeschooling 48
Howorth, Verity 32
Human Capital Theory 215
human flourishing, as collective vision for education system 26–27, 34
Hunter, James 32
Huxley, Aldous 218–219

Illich, Ivan 235–236
incidental and informal learning 264–265
International Baccalaureate (IB) schools 23

Jones, Ken 264
joy and well-being in education: difficulty of measuring 177; joylessness of curricula 174; as responsibility of school leaders 177; valued highly by parents 174, 177
Jubilee Centre for Character and Virtues 23

Kant, Immanuel 234, 235, 236
Kennedy, Mary 17–18
Korea 155
'knowledge-rich' school: arts subjects, importance of 62–63; didactic lessons, risk of 179; memory, focus on 3; pedagogy and curriculum, interdependence of 61; as reaction to skills-based curriculum 2–3, 82–83; standardised texts and lesson content 3, 83, 85; student empowerment as guiding principle 61; Sutton Trust Report 115; value of individual subject disciplines 61–62, 63

Lacan, Jacques 250
leadership: emancipator, leader as 145, 147; New Managerial approach 144–145; servant leadership 146
'learnacy' 82–83
learning disabilities 18
Leeds City Academy 71–79; see also values-centred school
Leeds West Academy 116–119
Lemov, Doug 32
local curriculum development: connecting with local external agencies 94–95; cross-curricular integration of adjacent disciplines 90–91; engagement value of local curriculum content 90; fieldwork 94–95; as labour-intensive investment 90
Locke, John 191, 233
Longitudinal Educational Outcomes 164
Lucas, Bill 128–129

MacAskill, William 204, 207
Major, John 245
Mandela, Nelson 37, 223
Marx, Karl 205–206, 208, 233–234
Maternity Teacher/Paternity Teacher project 260
memory: Cognitive Load Theory 120; cognitive scaffolding 120; emotional engagement 121–122, 123; knowledge-rich curriculum and 3, 82, 113; retrieval practice 120, 122; spaced repetition 122; working memory and executive functions 120–121
mental health crisis among children: COVID-19 pandemic, effects of 39; demands on teachers 41; demoralising state of 1; inadequate resources 146; low

well-being scores 28, 144, 147; ongoing decline of well-being 49, 174; phone and social media addiction 23
Menzies, Loic 164
Millennium Cohort Study 49
More, Thomas 232
Morris, Estelle 173–174
Multiverse 215
Munby, Steve 135, 139
Myatt, Mary 131

National Child Development Study 49
National Curriculum: equity and attainment as enduring aims 45, 50; as instrument of state control 44–45, 176, 224–225; relative loading of 46; reviews and revisions of 23–24, 44, 46, 48–49, 51, 54, 98, 245; shifting balance of central and local government power 45–47, 48; subject choice 49; subject knowledge, return to emphasis on 83; values of 244–245
National Professional Qualifications 258
Neill, AS 234
New Public Management 144
Newmark, Ben 18, 191
Newton, Paul 140

Oak National Academy 84, 88n1
Oates, Tim 128, 129, 130, 208–209
Ofqual 134, 135–136, 137, 140, 166
Ofsted: cultural capital 187, 245–246; culture of compliance 175; curriculum assessment 3; curriculum research 113; Education Inspection Framework 119, 175; establishment of 245; inspection outcomes conditioned by published performance data 134–135; passing fashions promoted by 17; respectful professional dialogue, recent commitment to 260; setting-wide snapshots 163; as tool for systemic change 165
Oliver, Martyn 260
oracy 67, 101, 159
organisational clarity 117

overeducation: anti-intellectualism 212–213; as life-affirming excess 218; as counterintuitive notion 210; elite overproduction thesis 217–218; Human Capital Theory thesis 214–216, 218; in popular culture 211–212; resentment of graduate class 212–214

passion for subjects 2
personal agency, as a general good of education 49
Petrarch 231
Phillipson, Bridget 259, 263
physical education (PE) 72, 77, 173
Piaget, Jean 120, 251
Plato 210, 231
Popper, Karl 235
poverty: community engagement with 34
powerful knowledge: as core function of schools 16; curriculum content not determined by 60–61; development of human capacity 29; knowledge of the powerful vs. 187; limitations of concept 60; social justice promoted by 129; taking students beyond their experience 60, 62
Prevent Strategy 225
private tutoring 48
professional development: empirical evidence for good design of 139; establishing professional identity 256; great subject teaching enabled by 86, 88; retention benefits 30; sigmoid leaps enabled by 92–93; subject knowledge development, importance of 84, 86, 98, 115–116
Professional Teaching Institute (PTI): commission to establish a Royal College of Teaching 256; mission of 1; networking 87; pillars of curriculum development 95; professional development 84, 86; re-centring of subject knowledge 3, 82, 83
Programme for International Student Assessment (PISA) 28, 50, 133, 144, 150, 154, 156, 163
'Progress 8' 78, 130, 144

Progress in International Reading Literacy Study (PIRLS) 132, 163
Puetz, Kyle 32

qualifications: correlation with income 164–165; certificates of participation 163; Extended Project 168; social function of 137–138; *see also* assessment; examinations

Rawls, John 195, 197–198, 199, 201
Reach Foundation 32, 34
religious schools 48
Rees, Tom 18, 191
Research Champions 255
Richards, Colin 249
Ricoeur, Paul 104, 110
RISE project 115
Robinson, Ken 123
Roosevelt, Eleanor 42
Rosenshine, Barak 107

Sarojini Hart, Caroline 195, 199
Savage, Graham 241–242
schema theory 105–106
school choice, as supposed driver of improvement 48, 175–176
school funding crisis: arts subjects hit worse by 63; circular effect on education quality 3; demoralising effect 1; long-term approach to 208; readymade lessons, resort to 4; time squeeze for teachers 4
self-efficacy 29, 34
self-realisation, education as 23; *see also* character education
Sen, Amartya 195, 197, 198, 199, 249, 250
service, concept of 37
Sexton, Stuart 47
shared culture: citizenship education 225; cultural inclusivity in schools 226; Durkheim's collective conscience 205; National Curriculum as attempt to shape 224–225; negotiating political and religious tensions in schools 227; in past societies 224; schools as custodians of tradition 225–226; tradition and the individual talent 251

Shaw, George Bernard 37–38
Singapore 155
skills shortages in national economy 52, 53–54
Social Mobility Commission 194
societal benefits of education: addressing global challenges 207–208; arts subjects 62–63, 68–69; collective conscience 205; creativity 68; great teaching 83; long-term perspective, importance of 207, 208–209; *see also* shared culture
special educational needs (SEN): school's approach to, as indicator of values 99; sense of inclusion, importance of 28; teacher-assessed grades biased against SEN students 166; underfunding of 18–19, 257; Warnock Report 244
specialist schools 175–176
Spens Report 239–241, 242
Spielman, Amanda 257
Steiner schools 48
St Edward's College, Liverpool 89–95; *see also* local curriculum development
Stenhouse, Lawrence 46
Style, Emily 251
subject discipline orientation: authentic engagement 61–62; crucial to knowledge-rich schools 61; enthusiasm of teachers for 86–87; skills-based learning vs. 82–83; student engagement 87; *see also* great subject teaching; knowledge-rich schools
Sutherland, Stewart 245
Sutton Trust Report 115
Swaner, Lynn 29
Sweden 45, 48
Sweller, John 120

Tambling, Pauline 62–63
teacher supply and retention crisis: circular effect on education quality 3; demoralising effect 1, 128; performative culture 256; poor pay and working conditions 3; readymade lessons, resort to 3; reduced scope for autonomy and

professional judgement 84, 86; stress and burnout 30, 256; technological workarounds 3

teaching as profession: accountability 255; cognitive domain 254; Early Career Framework 258; ethical domain 255; ethnic diversity, need for 260; flexible working options, need for 259–260; legal and social domain 255–256; National Professional Qualifications 258; pride in 256, 261; professional development 256; professional excellence 117; social trust and respect for, eroded by social inequality and poverty 257; unity within professional debate 257

Thunberg, Greta 230–231

Trends in International Mathematics and Science Study (TIMSS) 132

tripartite of learning styles 114

tripartite post-war school system 193, 198, 242–243, 265

Turchin, Peter 216–218

United States 52, 218, 246

Universal Declaration of Human Rights 234

utopian educational visions: Condorcet's vision of learning without limits 232–233; education as last post-war refuge of optimism 234–236; education as liberation 234; embeddedness in Western culture 231, 233, 236; Enlightenment concern with historical advancement 231–233; future-oriented nature of education 229; Marxism 233–234; necessity of 236, 246; persistence of 230, 236; Renaissance humanism 231; Spens Report 239–241

values-centred school: authentic embrace of values 74, 78–79; citizenship-based curriculum 75–76; connectivity across institution 73–74; dynamic evolutionary approach 76; extra-curricular enrichment 77; integration of values into positive behaviour system 74; measurable and unmeasurable benefits of 78–79

vocational route 51–53

Vygotsky, Lev 120

Warnock Report 244

Wilson, Harold 230, 233

Winch, Christopher 106

Wolf, Andy 29

Wolf, Martin 54

Woolf, Leonard 211

Wright, Sammy 164, 165, 190, 201

Young, Michael 29, 60, 62, 129, 187, 191, 194

For Product Safety Concerns and Information please contact our EU representative GPSR@taylorandfrancis.com
Taylor & Francis Verlag GmbH, Kaufingerstraße 24, 80331 München, Germany

www.ingramcontent.com/pod-product-compliance
Lightning Source LLC
Chambersburg PA
CBHW081945230426
43669CB00019B/2928